CONFUCIUS AND PIAGET MEET ONCE AGAIN

Teaching Chinese and Korean Students in the Western Classroom

Jonathan Borden

Amazon

This book is dedicated to the thousands of children of Chinese and Korean background who are studying in Western-style schools . . . and to their teachers, who work each day to make the world a little smaller.

"Acquire new knowledge whilst thinking over the old, and you may become a teacher of others."

CONFUCIUS

CONTENTS

Title Page   1

Copyright   2

Dedication   3

Epigraph   4

introduction   9

CHAPTER 1: WHO ARE WE TALKING ABOUT, AND   23
WHERE ARE THEY COMING FROM?

CHAPTER   II: CULTURAL   STEREOTYPING   OR   31
ANTHROPOLOGY?

CHAPTER III: CONFUCIUS MEETS PIAGET   51

CHAPTER IV: CONFUCIANISM 101   54

CHAPTER V: HISTORICAL BACKGROUNDS of KOREA   60
AND CHINA

CHAPTER VI: CONFUCIAN HEIRARCHY and RESPECT   77

CHAPTER VII: CONFUCIAN COLLECTIVISM AND   92
CONFORMITY

CHAPTER VIII: CONFUCIAN RELATIONSHIPS   112

CHAPTER IX: CONFUCIAN RELATIONSHIPS - Home and   120
Family

CHAPTER X: CONFUCIAN RELATIONSHIPS -   135
Classmates and Peers

CHAPTER XI: CONFUCIAN RELATIONSHIPS - Within   139

Social Groups

CHAPTER XII: CONFUCIAN RELATIONSHIPS - Within 146
the Nation

Chapter XIII: CONFUCIAN BASED EDUCATION – The 163
One Right Answer

CHAPTER XIV: INDIVIDUAL EXPERIENCES 195

CHAPTER XV: SMASHING STEREOTYPES - Looking at 238
Individuals

CHAPTER XVI: Working with Korean and Chinese 246
Parents

CHAPTER XVII: WORKING WITH KOREAN AND 307
CHINESE STUDENTS

CHAPTER XVIII: Working with Local Staff 360

CHAPTER IX: CONCLUSION 368

APPENDIX 370

SUGGESTED READINGS 373

RESOURCES 377

About The Author 381

Books By This Author 383

INTRODUCTION

Thank you for choosing to read *Confucius and Piaget Meet Once Again!* In writing this book I assume that you, the reader, are or soon will be an international educator, and probably expect to have Korean or Chinese students in your classroom. You may have been enjoying this "international educator gig" for years, cruising the world in search of that perfect school filled with perfect kids. For you, hopefully this book will be a confirmation of much of what you have observed and learned on your own over the years while adding to it greater perspective and focus. Or maybe you are heading into international teaching for the first time, and simply want to learn more before you get on that plane. For you, this book should serve as an introduction to an exciting and rewarding chapter ahead in your career. You soon will have many stories to tell. Read this book before you go - and again after a few months. Use it as both a preparation for what is ahead, and a sounding board for your new experiences. Hopefully, you will find much that will resonate.

In either case, whether veteran expat or "newbie", I both congratulate and applaud you. My own career in international education began quite unintentionally in 1976, and I never looked back. Not only are there wonderful and exciting international jobs for educators overseas, but the daily opportunity to make the world a little smaller, to bring the next generation of world leaders a little closer, to help nurture young people from such varied backgrounds into a world where differences are understood but do not divide, is immensely rewarding and fun. Your students really are so comfortable with the cultural differences of their friends and their host country that they simply see them as the background to their own lives, not as anything unusual. Fortunately for today's international teachers, these opportunities are expanding at a rapidly increasing pace, in part due to the world hunger for Western-style education. International teachers are the vessels that are helping to satisfy that thirst.

The world of the 21st Century has become, and will continue to be, a world in which the cultures and nations of East Asia take ever-increasing roles. It is imperative that the next generation of leaders has an understanding of these cultures. Just as Asia has reached out to the West, the West needs to increasingly understand the East, and play by its rules at least some of the time. I hope that this book will help the reader to better understand the culture and people of East Asia, particularly as they relate to their educational systems. In this way you become increasingly part of the solution to the challenges of intercultural understanding, and are making your own contribution to world peace, however elusive that goal might seem to be. Go for it. Each day is your opportunity to make a real difference in both individual lives and in the search for global understanding.

* * *

The publishing of *Confucius Meets Piaget: An Educational Perspective on Ethnic Korean Children and Their Parents* in 2000 was somewhat of an experiment on my part. While my wife, Soon-ok and I had done some workshops around East Asian international schools on the topic of the cultural and educational backgrounds of Korean students; the widespread interest in both the topic and the book from across the world surprised us. After being rejected by a publisher specializing in books on cultural subjects I decided to self-publish, which while limiting the availability of the book also provided me with some very interesting email conversations with educators on every continent who wished to purchase a copy. From college and graduate students, to newly minted international school teachers, to missionaries in central Asia and Africa, I gained a deeper understanding and appreciation for the wide variety of experiences of those with an intercultural bent and those educators who either wanted to prepare themselves for the experience of teaching Korean children that lay ahead of them or were scratching their heads saying "What's going on here with these kids?" I grew to understand that Korean kids were attending international schools all around the world far beyond my own experience – whether at small missionary or company schools at remote outposts in the jungles of Borneo or in a dusty central Asian city, or at one of the hundreds of international school in cities such as London, New York, Shanghai, or Mumbai. In addition, an explosion of East Asian high school students attending government and independent schools in Western countries broadened my audience to include those teachers who were not moving to new countries and schools, but rather who never left home but woke up one morning to realize that East Asia had come to them, and that their school's student body had somehow undergone a fundamental change in terms of ethnicity and national origin, and much more important, in terms of human interaction and culture. Interestingly, I repeatedly heard from other international educators through email and at various conferences and that many of the characteristics so widely attributed to Korean students also applied to other East Asian ethnic groups as well – most obviously Japanese, but also ethnic Chinese from across a wide swath of geography, as well as Thai and Vietnamese students. However, with only minimal personal experience outside of Korea, I retreated from the temptation to put myself out there as any kind of authority on "East Asian" students, limiting my "expertise" to Koreans for the time being.

When I wrote that first edition of *Confucius Meets Piaget* in 2000, I had been working at Seoul Foreign School, an international school serving expatriate children living in Seoul, since 1976. After 29 years as a teacher and principal in Seoul, in 2005, however, my wife (a preschool teacher at the same school) and I moved to Shanghai to take jobs at Shanghai American School, which had a similar population to Seoul Foreign School except that the dominant background among our students was ethnic Chinese from North America, Taiwan, Hong Kong, Singapore, and mainland China. From a student body that was over 90% ethnic Korean in Seoul we encountered a student body of only about 15% Korean in Shanghai - which fundamentally impacted the interactions among the Korean students themselves and between them and students from other ethnic groups. More important to me personally was that I now had the challenge and opportunity to interact with a much wider number of student home cultures, predominantly Chinese, but quickly realized that "Chinese" in itself defies easy definition (more on that later). What I also soon learned, confirmed by conversations with educators with much longer histories in China, including local Chinese teachers, that many of the behaviors and attitudes seen in Korean students and parents also were common in many Chinese (or Japanese or Singaporean or Taiwanese or American-born Chinese) students. As time went on I was able to better understand what made these groups similar, what made them different, and then embarked on a quest to understand the "why's" behind these differences. This experience, followed by ongoing research and conversations with experts who are familiar with Korean, Chinese, and Western educational cultures has allowed me to include in this new book discussions and comparisons of an entirely new and much larger population than only Koreans. I hope that this inclusion of Chinese students and parents will make this book both helpful and valuable to a much wider readership while providing a richer and more multi-dimensional discussion of Confucian-based cultures and educational systems.

Readers who enjoyed and benefited from *Confucius Meets Piaget* will find much that is familiar in this expanded edition, but will also see obvious changes due to distances of both time and place. The international student worlds of 2000 and 2020 are very different, and the world itself has changed. Korea is certainly a different place than it was in 2000, as is any rapidly growing and developing East Asian country with the possible exception of Japan, having been both the first to "develop" economically after World War II while also being perhaps the most conservative and resistant to change culturally. Mainland China continues its explosive economic growth, with a parallel expansion in the number of true international schools and local schools hiring expatriate, Western teachers. Even as China jealously guards its educational heritage and culture, there is an immense thirst among educated Chinese parents and even in many offices of education across the various culturally "Chinese" nations for the application to Chinese education of Western pedagogy featuring "Twenty-First Century" teaching and learning.

The opinions and observations shared in this book are the result of impressions formed over more than forty years of experience working with East Asian students and parents in international school settings. Professional reading has also provided a good deal of background material, as have hundreds of intentional conversations on the topic with students, parents and educators from a wide variety of cultural backgrounds. Living in a bicultural family has given me both a close-up look at Korean values and educational priorities as well as a critical eye towards what might too often be a "foreigner's stereotype" of East Asians. This book admittedly presents my own American perspective, although many of the opinions expressed have received support from Korean, Chinese, and

Japanese educators and parents with varying degrees of Westernization. Of course, I take full responsibility for all that is contained on these pages.

* * *

There are many individuals to whom I owe great thanks for their guidance over the years, without whose comments, admonitions, and encouragement as I have navigated two great cultures – Korean and Chinese - this book would never happened. My wonderful secretaries and "distributors" in Seoul and Shanghai, Ms. Woo HyeSun and Ms. Sylvia Shen, numerous Shanghai American School Chinese language teachers (to whom I repeatedly have apologized for being such a poor language student): Liming Ma, Jane Sun, Isabella Sun, Stephanie Shao, and Ada Chen. A special thanks goes to former colleague and international educator Dr. Susan Zhang – a regional expert on Chinese language teaching and my cultural interpreter when I first arrived in Shanghai.

I especially wish to thank two people for my ongoing cultural education. My former colleague and friend Dr. Suyi Wang – native of Taiwan, long time resident of Korea, teacher in mainland China, school principal in Hong Kong, and a Chinese language and culture expert of some renown in international school circles – has been an invaluable and patient resource to me over the more recent years in my journey of cultural exploration, tirelessly giving me cultural perspectives and challenging my own preconceptions.

Finally, and most importantly, I owe a huge and continuous debt of thanks to my Korean-born wife, Soon-ok Pahk Borden. As an international school teacher who was educated primarily in the Korean system, she has been personally involved in both Western and Asian-style education, both as a student and a teacher. As we both visited and consulted at international schools around East Asia, we learned a great deal about our own cultures, as well as about international education. Without her constant support, invaluable cultural insights, constant encouragement, and frequent and necessary redirection this book would never have even been conceived, not to mention revised, now almost twenty years later. Her voice resonates very clearly in these pages.

With this introduction, I am pleased to publish *Confucius and Piaget Meet Again*, very much expanded younger sibling to *Confucius Meets Piaget*.

Jonathan F. Borden, Ph.D.

Savannah, Georgia, USA

November, 2020

The Story Of Charlie

Charlie Huang was a new 7th grader, coming to Seoul Foreign School from a local school in Taiwan. Charlie was one of those kids who you immediately liked – he smiled easily, his English good enough to be understood but heavily accented, he was accepted quickly by the other kids, he was athletic but very focused on his academics. He was in a new country, a new type of school, making new friends, and he was ready to take on this exciting challenge. As his middle school principal, I could have had a whole school of Charlie's. He was just a great kid.

Charlie gotten to a great start. He eagerly attacked his new language and his new books. Every 7th grade boy wanted to hang out with Charlie. He was on the fast track to language proficiency and social integration to his new school culture. About a month after he began school, I happened to be meeting with his Humanities teacher about another student, and as she was getting up to leave I asked "Say, how's our little guy Charlie doing these days? What a great kid!" She gave me one of those "You really don't have a clue, do you?" looks that teachers who know you well enough feel free to send your way from time to time. "Our little Charlie is heading for trouble," she said firmly. "He's on a collision course with 'crash and burn.'" She went on to tell me that after a two-week honeymoon, Charlie stopped doing his work. Homework was turned in barely begun, and his classwork was hardly better. He had bombed his first unit test. His quick smile had disappeared, and he was starting to lash out at other kids, especially when he couldn't quite find the English words necessary to negotiate some minor conflict. Sweet Charlie was apparently quickly becoming the kid who couldn't seem to sit next to anyone without causing some kind of disturbance. I was floored by her comments.

"Do you mind if I talk to him to see what's going on?" I asked. It seemed that my "good kid radar" hadn't worked very well. A quick check with Charlie's science and math teachers confirmed what his Humanities teacher had told me. Charlie was in trouble. I wondered what had happened. Something to do with his transition? Was he being bullied? Was his pretty good verbal English covering up major weaknesses in his academic English? Was something going on at home?

The next morning I checked his schedule and asked to borrow him from his Humanities class for a few minutes. She very readily agreed to send him to me at the beginning of class with the comment, "And keep him as long as you need him." Ouch!

Charlie came in, a little warily at being called into his new principal's office. Our conversation went something like this:

"Sit down, Charlie," I greeted him. "I just want to check up on how things are going now that you've been here a few weeks."

"OK . . ." he managed to squeak warily through his old grin.

"So Charlie, how is school going?"

"Great! I really like it here."

"Are you making friends?"

"Yes, everyone is really nice."

"Do you like your teachers?"

"Yeah, they are really helpful and nice."

"How about the work, Charlie? It's quite different from what you experienced in Taiwanese school, isn't it?"

"Hmmm. I guess so. But I really like it."

"Are you getting all your homework done?"

"Of course! No problem!"

"No problems at all with school?"

"No sir!" he smiled.

I realized I was getting nowhere. Charlie obviously knew

what principals wanted to hear. I had to try a different tact.

"Uh, Charlie. Look at me. (Eyes on the carpet) Charlie, that isn't what I'm hearing from your teachers. In fact, I was just talking to your Humanities teacher yesterday, and she said that you aren't doing your homework. And I'm not sure that you've been getting along with the other kids. I understand that your recent science test wasn't too good. I want to help you, but you need to be honest with me about this. What's going on?"

Silence.

"Charlie, look at me." He tried again, but failed. He blankly stared at the floor between his feet. I let the silence do its work. Finally, his chin started to quiver. The drips started to run down his cheeks without a sound, but quickly became a torrent of gagged sobs. I gave him some space to get it all out and use up a good week's worth of tissues. The flood eventually subsided into occasional seventh grade snuffles.

"Ok, Charlie. Let's try this again. I really want to help you. Forget I'm the principal if you can. I know it's hard to start in a new school, especially one so different from your last one. What's the problem?"

"I'm so scared! In my old school in Taiwan I was Number 1 in my class. Here, I can't seem to be Number 1!"

"But Charlie, there is no way you'll be Number 1 here for a

while, anyway. Your English needs to improve before that can happen. It's OK. In fact, we don't even have a Number 1 student. No one expects you to be Number 1."

"My dad does!" he nearly shouted. "He is really mad at me because I am still in ESL class, and said he's going to take me out of this school if I don't become Number 1 in my class right away!" The sobs started up again.

"Charlie, I'm afraid I disagree with your dad. I'll talk to him about how much you are trying, and that even if your grades were the best in the class; we wouldn't name you "Number 1."

"Are you working hard, Charlie? Are you studying for your tests?"

"Yes, I'm studying until at least 11:30 every night. You can ask my mom! I really am!"

I held off on my "get enough sleep" sermon until another time. "So, Charlie, if you are studying so hard, why do you think you didn't do well on your tests?" How are you studying?"

"I don't know. Are there more than one ways to study?"

"Uh, Charlie, are you trying to memorize the entire chapter?"

"Yes, I promise I am! Look at my book!"

He opened his social studies book, and sure enough, between the lines of Times New Roman he had meticulously printed tiny Chinese characters. He had translated the entire chapter and then memorized it in Chinese.

I played along for a moment. "So Charlie, if you are memorizing the chapter, why do you think you did so poorly on the test?"

"Well, the test didn't have any of the stuff I memorized. I know all the names and dates, and all the new vocabulary. I know all the facts in that chapter. But the teacher asked weird stuff on the test. We had to compare and contrast two different people and their beliefs. But she didn't even ask us the year they were born! Another section of the test was something to read, and we had to tell why we agreed or disagreed, and WHY! But the teacher never told us what to think about that! It isn't fair!"

I should have known. Here I was, future author of Confucius Meets Piaget, and I had missed it. There was so much to do for Charlie. Parent education. Charlie education. Teacher education. And we had to do it quickly, before the teachers got any more frustrated and Charlie burned out in a flame of late nights and tiny Chinese characters.

It was quickly obvious what was going on. Charlie (and his dad) was simply applying the rules and measures of success, and the means to success, from his school in Taiwan onto Seoul Foreign School. However, very little of what worked so well in Taiwan was working for him in Korea. Over time, and with a good deal of help from his teachers, counselor, and ESL teacher, Charlie began to "get it." We made sure he was getting enough sleep. We checked to be sure he wasn't translating his chapters into Chinese. We discouraged him from memorizing pages of facts. I had a frank chat with his dad about reasonable expectations. And we slowly helped him how to "learn to do school" in a new, western-style environment. I'm not sure we ever completely convinced his dad, but over time Charlie became a successful student, with appropriate goals and study habits that ensured success at Seoul Foreign School.

There are thousands of Charlie's in our schools, whether they are international students attending schools in North America or Europe, or attending international schools scattered across the globe. Charlie could just as easily have been Vietnamese, or Japanese, or Korean, or from Mainland China. It's your job as his teacher to anticipate his challenges and avoid the disaster that Charlie almost became. It's the goal of this book to help you do that.

At any gathering of international teachers, when the subject of ethnic East Asian students comes up, a litany of stories like Charlie's emerge. It is hoped that this book, an expanded sequel to the 2000 version of Confucius Meets Piaget, will help separate fact from fiction, and in doing so add some clarity and professional perspective to this ongoing and fascinating discussion. Let's do it for all the Charlie's in our classrooms.

CHAPTER 1: WHO ARE WE TALKING ABOUT, AND WHERE ARE THEY COMING FROM?

Before we go any further it would be valuable to define some ethnic terms. Specifically, we need to have a common understanding of the terms "Korean", "Chinese", and "Japanese."

These terms mean different things to different people, depending on their own past experiences. In their most basic definition they mean any person whose forebears came originally from Korea, China, or Japan. For the purposes of this book, which is directed at teachers working with such students at schools within and outside of East Asia, there are four main groups of ethnic East Asian children with whom Western teachers come into contact:

1. "hyphenated Asians" such as Korean-British, Chinese-Canadians, or Japanese-Americans — children brought up outside of Asia and who may "look" Asian on the outside but who have been totally acculturated into the Western culture in which they live and are citizens;

2. ethnic Korean/Chinese/Japanese children who are "sojourning" in other countries and cultures and who are attending international schools outside of their home country. This is usually due to their parents' work or assignment; normally such children's "core culture" is Korean/Chinese/Japanese and they are planning to return to their home country for higher education and for adult life (these children are frequently referred to in the literature as Third Culture Kids, or TCKs). This group of Asian "sojourners" has been growing very rapidly in the past thirty years in large part due to a) the explosion of Asian-based international businesses constantly seeking newly expanding markets (primarily mainland China and southeast Asia as of this writing) and cheap labor pools (primarily in south Asia and Africa), b) to a lesser extent Korean Christian missionaries who now number in the tens of thousands in both large cities and some remote corners of the world, and c) children who are attending international schools outside their home countries by choice, and who are living abroad in either western or other East Asian nations solely in order to avoid their own national educational system and experience western style education. The extent of this outward flow from all sources fluctuates somewhat with exchange rates and political climates, but in general the flow continues from East to West – or more accurately, from Confucian based educational systems to more Piagetian, Western type educational systems;

3. ethnic Korean/Chinese/Japanese children who have spent a significant part of their childhood **outside** of their home country in some kind of international environment, but are now living in their "home" countries that "match" their ethnicity and who attend either national or international schools, but whose futures most likely lie outside of their "ethnic-matching" country; and finally,

4. students who have always lived in their "home country" in East Asia, but have been able to gain entrance to western-style

international schools and thus share many cultural and educational characteristics with Western children.

JONATHAN BORDEN

Who Are The Koreans?

The term "Korean" in our context refers primarily to children of South Korean heritage. While certainly there are strong cultural similarities between The Republic of Korea (capitalist South) and the Democratic Peoples' Republic of Korea (communist North), the impact of seventy years of Kim Dynasty/ communist rule have changed Koreans north of the DMZ to the core, just as developing democratic institutions and raging capitalism, coupled with the resultant social revolution have changed the minds and hearts of those in the South during the same period. We won't know how different the children of these two nations will be when they someday sit side by side in international schools in the future; perhaps in a brighter day when the North finally opens itself to the world and more than a trickle of diplomats loyal to the Kim regime begin to travel around the world will we find out. Many in both Koreas eagerly look forward to that day. (I wrote similar words in 1999, hardly expecting that they would (sadly) be even more applicable twenty years later.) Despite the fact that the current North Korean leader, Kim Jung Un, attended international and local schools in Switzerland for a while during his high school years, he was the notable exception rather than the rule. While he seemed to fall in love with American sports culture during those years, it appears now that few Western values rubbed off on him, a tragic failure on the part of his liberal western education. The eventual fall of the North Korean regime, whether catastrophically or via a more evolutionary path, will be a fascinating story, as will the impact of a new breed of thousands of North Korean students on the international world educational system. Hopefully we don't have to wait yet another twenty years for that to occur.

I mentioned earlier that this new book has been written in an attempt to help teachers and others who work with ethnic Korean and Chinese children to better understand them by understanding their backgrounds - their values, their histories, their families, and their goals for the future. One might fairly ask, "Why would we single out children of Korean or Chinese descent any more than we would children of German or Lebanese descent? What would make them different from any American or British or Canadian or German child? Aren't distinctions such as this openly racist?" The answers to these fair questions depend on who is asking them, and which type of ethnic Korean child described above is being discussed. Teachers in North America or Europe, for example, (or in international schools in Korea) who have ethnic Asian children in their classes who seem "Western" in culture may be the first to ask. For them, my response would be that these children are the products of their parents' upbringing as well as of their own Western style life experiences. As Koreans are among the very newest of ethnic groups to emigrate in large numbers to the United States, they are still affected much more strongly by their native culture than, say, German or Scottish Americans, or even most Chinese-Americans, who as a cultural group have been in America much longer. Koreans as an American immigrant group have had a much shorter time to acculturate, most having emigrated since the late 1970's. U.S. Census data from 1980 showed that only 16% of those who classified themselves as ethnically Korean were born in the U.S. (Handbook for Teaching Korean-American Students). Therefore, even by the time of this publication in 2020, any second-generation children born since 1980 and brought up in North America would most likely have children only in elementary or middle school, and would themselves be children of immigrants. Thus, all except 16% of adult ethnic Koreans in the United States today would necessarily be immigrants themselves or the children of immigrants, and would therefore be strongly influenced by their own or their parents' Korean cultural background. Of course, ethnic Chinese have a history in North America more than a century longer than that of Koreans, and so in most cases are fully acculturated. However, many still hold on to some cultural values matching their non-European ethnicity. Generally, the more recently their family immigrated, or the more their family self-segregated into ethnic communities, the greater the impact of traditional Asian values on their upbringing.

The answer to the question of why we might focus on ethnic Korean and Chinese students is simpler for teachers of these students in international schools: These students are different from other students for the same reasons that students of other backgrounds are different from them - they have parents from very different cultures and in many cases have attended school in yet a third culture, and thus have different academic and social habits, cultural characteristics, and unique attributes. That is only natural; differences such as these make teaching in international schools as rewarding and enjoyable as it is.

Who Are The Chinese?

This question begs a much more complicated answer, because we are talking about a much more diverse group than the more homogeneous Koreans. Certainly, children whose parents grew up in Mainland China and were raised within Chinese culture regardless what particular ethnic group their ancestors came from, we would consider Chinese. Children from the island of Taiwan are most certainly culturally Chinese, although, as we will see later, somewhat different than Mainland Chinese. Hong Kong citizens are usually culturally Chinese, but are often much more westernized than their cousins whose parents never left Mainland China. Singaporeans can be Malay, Indian, or Chinese, although the dominant culture in Singapore is Chinese. Finally, we have hyphenated Chinese – American Born Chinese, for example. So while someone claiming to be Korean is almost certainly ethnic Korean, Chinese come from much more varied cultural backgrounds due to the diaspora of Chinese that goes back hundreds of years. Emigration from Korea, on the other hand, is by comparison a very new phenomenon, beginning primarily after World War II, increasing greatly since the 1980's.

It should be emphasized that whenever any group is described in general terms, there are of course many individuals who do not conform to all, or even to some, generalities. One challenge that faces the reader is to sort out what information and insights shared in this book are applicable to students in his or her classroom, and which are not. Some information may fit perfectly and be of immediate help. Other thoughts may seem totally out of synch with the reader's experience. Such is the nature of the wide range of backgrounds of these children: each has a unique family history and personality that has deeply affected the development of their cultural identity.

Thus, accepting the inevitability of being "proven" wrong by those who can provide legitimate exceptions to the characteristics described in this book, I'll forge ahead hoping that many readers will be able to better understand in some small or significant way the wide variety of ethnic Korean and Chinese students found in their classrooms on Monday morning.

CHAPTER II: CULTURAL STEREOTYPING OR ANTHROPOLOGY?

Occasionally when I have given presentations to groups of teachers I am challenged by someone with the legitimate question of whether or not even discussing the cultural characteristics of Koreans or Chinese or Japanese (or Americans) smacks of cultural stereotyping: "Certainly each child is an individual; how can you lump them all together with generalizations and broad brush assertions?" I would agree – each child is unique, each family is unique. Each is who he or she is due to a set of unique "nature and nurture" experiences, which can and do mold the child in unique ways over time. However, it is also true that much of what determines who we are as humans are the cultures in which we live, both our external culture and our family's culture. Thus, those who share the same culture with others also share many of the same cultural bases and biases, although individuals can of course alter these biases through education, thought, and maturity. However, we all have to start somewhere in our life's journey of "becoming," and that "somewhere" is our culture and family. To put this question on a more intellectual level, we would ask, "What is the difference between baseless stereotyping and intellectual anthropology?" Fundamentally, these two approaches of looking at cultures are worlds apart. One paints all individuals assigned (either by self or by society) to a particular group with the same brush regardless of individual differences; the other acknowledges cultural similarities and characteristics that makes people tick, while also asserting that everyone is an individual in as many ways as there are individuals. One is imposed from above, the other is an acceptance that while we are all children of some culture that defines who we are to some degree, the degree to which our assigned culture determines who we are as individuals is in fact an personal choice, that choice increasing in degree as we mature throughout our lifetimes. New experiences and knowledge (such as suddenly moving to a new country and attending school with kids from other cultures) challenge the cultural norms that we import to this new culture. It is always fascinating to watch a new student, fresh from his or her national school system, evolve both academically and socially over the course of the first months in an international school. That kid from Detroit (or Seoul or Shanghai) steps into a new international "kid world" and is forever changed by it. Before long the shock of jumping into the frigid waters of an international school environment wears off, and after a while even feels warm and comfortable. Getting back out of the water into the "normal" world after a few years of living internationally more often leaves us alone and shivering and wanting to get back into the water, much to the amazement of our dry friends "back home" who never took the plunge. Reverse culture shock is often worse than original culture shock.

I often had the opportunity to meet prospective teens as their parents "checked out" a new international school. Particularly if the family was new to living internationally, the students were often resistant and uncommunicative when asked how they felt about the move. When they were sitting in my office with their parents, they would often say that it was OK,

32

that they were looking forward to learning about a new culture, etc., etc. Then I would ask the parents if I could talk with their child alone. When I asked the student again how they really felt about the impending move, they would often say, "It sucks!" Three or four months later I would remind them of this conversation, and they would often (not always) be embarrassed, and talk about how they now liked the school, that they realize that every kid who "looks Chinese" isn't really Chinese on the inside, that they would like to stay beyond the inevitable initial two years. And how many spouses agreed to go along with an international assignment, after getting an agreement that it would be at MOST two years – and then two years later asking for an extension? We all fear change to some extent, and a change in culture is perhaps the scariest change of all, particularly for an adolescent.

As we near the first quarter mark of the Twenty-first Century, millennia-old issues of ethnicity, racism, prejudice, and discrimination are clashing head to head with large and rapid migrations of varied peoples brought on by war, famine, and economic or political hardship. Our world is rapidly being contracted in time, if not in space, by high-speed transportation and instant communication. It is being torn apart by the conflicting movements of "one-world-ism" on one hand and those of nationalism, xenophobia, ethnic pride, religious fundamentalism and regionalism on the other, forces that we have seen played out on the political stage in recent years as nations struggle to marry national security concerns and national identity with compassion and moral responsibility for refugees others moving to new nations for economic and political reasons. The BREXIT movement and the anti-immigration moves during the Trump administration in Washington, countered by angry and anguished responses, are stark examples of this worldwide societal stress. Indeed, international school teachers are actually part of that worldwide migration in search of new opportunities – while not exactly refugees (although some might consider themselves to be, depending on the state of education in their home countries), we are all in a very real sense simply well paid and highly educated migrant workers – sometimes welcomed, sometimes not, by our host countries. The biggest difference between us and the migrant worker picking apples in Oregon is that we have so many more opportunities open to us – and we are immensely better compensated for our efforts.

Forces such as international commerce, multinational corporations, the Internet, CNN and BBC, increasing numbers of multi-national military operations, and the lower cost of travel are all making the world more homogeneous. Each of these forces brings cultures and individuals into closer contact than ever before in history. As people of various cultures and backgrounds have interacted and inevitable clashes have occurred, the natural tendency towards conflict has thankfully been most often balanced by an equally strong impulse to understand one another and to get along, if only for reasons of economic profit and human survival. Despite the newspaper headlines reporting horrific evidence otherwise, overall this mixing of cultures has brought out the better nature in most individuals, and has led to increased understanding of the customs, religions, beliefs, and value systems of others. It has also led to the politically correct but somewhat misleading belief, at least in the United States, that "deep down inside, we're all the same" and that seeming differences are really only a veneer of fascinating variations in skin color, language, clothing, food, and music. Like the iceberg that is only one-tenth out of the water, however, language, clothing, food, and music are only the very visible (and usually most enjoyable) aspects of any culture. As anyone knows who has lived in a culture other than his or her own for any more than a quick tourist visit, however, unfortunately the other nine-tenths of the cultural iceberg are hidden, and are a culture's real life and soul. When we live in a culture other than our own, we soon come to the realization that despite what we might have been taught as children, everybody isn't "just the same under the skin." While we are all intrinsically of equal value to each other and to our Creator, there are deep, serious, and critical differences in areas of values and identity that vary greatly from one culture to another. The fact that these are hidden makes them dangerous and unexpected, and can send us into culture shock and onto the next flight out if they hit us too hard! These hidden values and critical beliefs are the parts of a cultural iceberg that can catch us in unexpectedly cold and rough water, slam into our cultural hulls of security and propriety, and send us to the bottom before we know what hit us.

This Cultural Iceberg Model of cultures is helpful in imagining and understanding the structures and values of various cultures. This model was developed during the 1970's by sociologists and anthropologists in the United States; a quick on-line search will provide plenty of articles and visuals describing and illustrating this model. (For more on the iceberg analogy, see L. Robert Kohl's *Survival Kit for Overseas Living, Third edition*.)

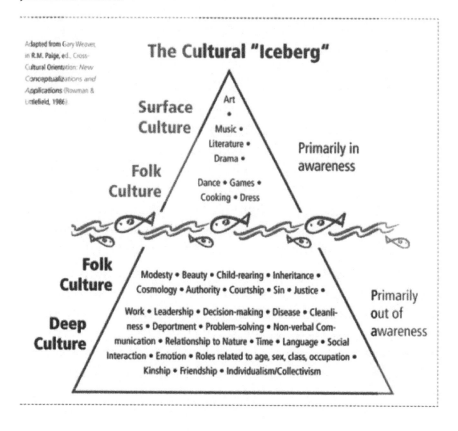

The Cultural "Iceberg"

Adapted from Gary Weaver, in R.M. Paige, ed., Cross-Cultural Orientation: New Conceptualizations and Applications (Rowman & Littlefield, 1986)

Surface Culture

Art
•
Music •
Literature •
Drama •

Primarily in awareness

Folk Culture

Dance • Games •
Cooking • Dress

Folk Culture

Modesty • Beauty • Child-rearing • Inheritance •
Cosmology • Authority • Courtship • Sin • Justice •

Deep Culture

Work • Leadership • Decision-making • Disease • Cleanliness • Deportment • Problem-solving • Non-verbal Communication • Relationship to Nature • Time • Language • Social
Interaction • Emotion • Roles related to age, sex, class, occupation •
Kinship • Friendship • Individualism/Collectivism

Primarily out of awareness

Quite simply, the model helps us conceptualize the experience of anyone who has moved into a new culture – or is suddenly surrounded by individuals from another culture. We quickly realize that there is much that we don't know, and in fact usually we don't know that we don't know it. Just as the beautiful white part of an iceberg, floating on the sea, is only about ten percent of the iceberg, what we see on the surface of the culture as an outsider is only about ten percent of the whole. The other ninety percent of the culture is hidden under the cultural surface. Which part of the iceberg is the more dangerous to us? Of course, the hidden, much larger part that lurks under the surface is more dangerous – some of it briefly appearing from time to time, but most of it deep under water, ready to rip the bottom of our self-confidence and sense of control, making us vulnerable to the cold cultural unknown that may quickly envelop us in uncertainty and fear.

Roots Of Culture And Culture Shock

We've all heard of Culture Shock, and probably also denied that we can get caught in its trap. However, very few of us actually do. There are four distinct stages, each of which may be longer or shorter for each individual. These are the Honeymoon Stage, the Frustration Stage, the Adjustment Stage, and the Acceptance Stage. A look at these stages will pull us into a larger discussion of cultural differences in general.

Honeymoon stage:

A visit to a new culture normally begins with the sparkling visible top of the iceberg. This is the "honeymoon" or "tourist" stage of cultural adjustment. These are the first few days when everything about the newly encountered culture is fascinating and almost always pleasant to experience. We marvel at how cheap everything is, how polite everyone is, how beautiful the scenery is, how wonderful the food is, and how fascinating the dances and clothing and language are. This visible part of the cultural iceberg convinces us that this must be paradise on earth, and we wonder why we never visited before. Maybe we should even move here! Life is good in this paradise!

Frustration phase:

However, after a week or so, having experienced a few disappointments and frustrations that are difficult to just brush off, we begin to realize that there is more to this culture than pretty scenery and delicious food. Maybe even the weather doesn't cooperate with our sense of wellbeing or we enjoyed just a little too much street food with predictable results. Maybe a taxi driver took us on a "scenic route" or someone (we think) was rude to us, or the tourist map wasn't to scale like we thought it should be or the map on the back of a business card was only an artistic suggestion of reality. At that point we may begin to realize that the children don't seem too well disciplined, and we hear from our young tour guide that yes, hers is an arranged marriage. Further, she tells us that she and her husband are working as tour guides, sending their only child to live with grandmother in the country, because her older brother inherited all that her father left when he died from forced work in the coal mines. We read in the local paper about the foreigner who ended up in jail for an offence that we would consider trivial. Slowly we begin to understand that this new, beautiful culture has some characteristics we don't completely agree with lying just under its sparkling surface. We often complain and push back against these uncomfortable realities, but have no choice but to smile and go along. After all, we don't want to be ugly foreigners or worse, get in trouble with the local authorities. At this point, we are at cultural sea level where it is becoming increasingly evident that the beautiful top of the iceberg has a less inviting, even menacing underside.

If we are tourists we can get on the plane and leave at the end of our two weeks in paradise. However, if we are "sojourners" who will be staying longer to work or live, we continue to learn more and more about the hidden culture. Some of it we like, some we are just okay with, and other parts we find truly offensive to our core values. Why should Mr. Kim get promoted to "Chairman" of our governing school body just because he is the owner's son when there are other much more capable candidates? Why are problems solved behind closed doors, and why do we seem to always want more "transparency?" Why is it that people seem inevitably relaxed about arriving at meetings on time – or so up tight about what people in certain positions should be wearing or who sits where at a lunch meeting? Why is it so hard get candid opinions from a group of local students/parents/employees in an open meeting? Why don't the kids ask questions in class? Why did Susie burst into tears when she saw the B+ on her report card? And why are these students falling asleep in class all the time? All these questions are legitimate, and they challenge some of our deepest beliefs that possibly we didn't even realize we held until they are challenged. These are questions that involve the deepest depths of our cultural iceberg – hidden from casual sight, but catching us unawares and sometimes sending us into a cultural tailspin that can prove to be personally challenging and even publically embarrassing. This deep culture includes normally unarticulated issues such as concepts of who and how people lead, attitudes towards the expression of emotions, problem-solving strategies, or roles related to social class or occupation or age or gender. It involves the deep cross-cultural, sociological dimensions of national culture identified by Finnish researcher Geert Hofstede: power/distance, individualism/collectivism, masculinity/femininity (task/relationship), uncertainty avoidance, long term/short term orientation, and indulgence/restraint (see Geert Hofstede, *Culture's Consequences: Comparing Values, Behaviors, Institutions, and Organizations Across Nations, 2nd Edition*, Thousand Oaks CA: Sage Publications, 2001). Hofstede's work is fascinating; I invite you to take a look and compare your own culture to your host culture along his various dimensions of culture. It will help to develop a much less judgmental, and more balanced, view of one's own and other cultures.

Adjustment Stage:

The third stage, one of adjustment, is crucial. If we are not able to move into this stage, we either become very unhappy and negative, counting the days until our overseas sojourn is over, or we opt out by simply getting on a plane and going home. However, if we do continue into this stage we begin to come to terms and adjust to the sometimes frustrating differences we have experienced in our new culture. We begin to understand that no matter what we do, some parents will send their kids to seemingly endless hours of after school lessons to the detriment of what we consider healthy sleep patterns and completing our assigned homework. We understand that no matter how frustrated we get, people on the subway will still push against us without apologizing. We adjust to the loud and unruly children running past our table in the restaurant. We accept that people will be staring at us wherever we go. If we cannot successfully negotiate the adjustment stage, we either decide (or are forced to) stay in the new culture, constantly frustrated and generally unhappy, or we leave and go home.

Acceptance Stage:

In this final stage, while we may not totally understand or even agree to the cultural differences that have frustrated us, we understand that, in fact, it works in this culture. The after school hours spent at academy are really crucial for a student to get into that prestigious university that her grandfather demanded she attend. We accept that, in her family, her graduation from that particular university is a matter of great pride for the family. We accept that, regardless of the student's individual desire, the wants of the family are more important. We stop being quite as frustrated by the pushing on the subway when we realize that there really isn't enough room and people need to squeeze. We accept the fact that the grandma's will fight over being first in line at a supermarket egg sale when we remember that they have personally experienced famine and watched family members die. When we return "home" we might even miss not standing out in a crowd, and no longer being somehow "special." We decide that we'll stay, enjoy those things we enjoy, and not let those other less attractive parts of the culture ruin every day.

41

Moving through the stages of culture shock can be made a little less emotionally demanding if we understand the larger picture of cultures, often researching our new culture, and applying some of the models such as the cultural iceberg and Hofstede's cultural dimensions. Why are such models helpful and important to understand as we work cross-culturally? Because when we can put our frustrations and questions and challenges in some kind of theoretical framework, while it doesn't make these issues go away it does help to explain them as part of a larger understanding of what it means to be human and citizens of this polyglot world we live in. It helps us to understand that in fact we are frustrated because this "new" culture is truly different from ours (which seems so normal to us) - but at the same time we realize that our own culture can be measured with the same theoretical yardsticks, and thus it may well seem just as strange to our new friends as their culture seems to us. With that understanding, we can learn to be a lot less judgmental and find that taking a deep breath and giving our students (or their parents) just a little cultural benefit of the doubt is a little easier. Finally, if as Western teachers of Eastern kids we can use these same tools to explain our culture to our students and local co-workers, they too can be asked to give us a little slack at times when we serve them yet another or our cultural mess-ups. Hopefully theoretical tools like these will help Confucius and Piaget to get along with each other a little bit better.

To focus this theory somewhat, examine the chart below that takes a look at some of the values found in all cultures (either obvious, above the surface or hidden below), but in this case specifically to Eastern/Confucian and Western/Judeo-Christian based cultures – not yet specifically narrowed to different ethnic/cultural groups. By looking at how these two types of cultures exhibit the same values in decidedly different ways, we can begin to focus more on some of the behaviors and attitudes we see in our classrooms each day. Three that have a direct impact on teachers, classrooms, and kids are Hofstede's areas of Relationships, Authority, and Social Orientation. As much as it is somewhat politically incorrect to say that "deep down, we really are different", as mentioned earlier reality requires us to admit that at some level – above the primal level needs of food, shelter, love, and procreation – for a variety of reasons the ways in which individuals in various cultures approach life's challenges are truly different. The sooner we can honestly admit this to ourselves and others, and without applying value judgments to these differences (a real challenge for most of us), the sooner we can get on with the daily business of working to understand each other. In the case of teachers, we must have some degree of cultural understanding of the children sitting in our classrooms before we can hope to connect in any meaningful way. Before we whisper in frustration "Where are these kids COMING from?" it's a good idea to ask ourselves, "WHERE, literally, ARE they coming from?" Geography does influence behavior. A good discussion of where Eastern and Western societies "come from" philosophically is found in the short but dense book *The Geography of Thought: How Asians and Westerners Think Differently...and Why* by social psychologist Richard Nisbett (2003). I recommend it highly. It provides some historical and philosophical explanation as to why we do think, act, and meet our very human needs in such different ways, depending on whether our societal ancestors were from Greece and Rome, or from Xian and Nanjing.

Let's look at some of these "under the surface" differences between East Asian and Western cultures. The purpose of the chart below is to simply illustrate how two of the world's major populations have organized their societies, and how this often plays out in individual and cultural behaviors. Some of these characteristics shine brightly in the 10% of the cultural iceberg rising above the ocean; many explain why the 90% hidden under water cause us so much frustration and catch us so unawares.

A Quick Comparison Of Traditional Of Ideal Western And East Asian Values

Values	Western (Judeo/Christian)	East Asian (Confucian)
Politics	Democratic	Authoritarian
Gender	Male dominated/deference to females	Male dominated/deference to males
Relationships	Strong values outweigh relationships when brought into conflict	Strong relationships outweigh values when brought into conflict
Political History	Colonization of others	Dominated or victimized
Geopolitical stance	Internationalism	Isolationism
Status and authority	Achieved; Based on merit	Inherited/age based/assigned
Social orientation	Individualistic	Collective

Consider the social characteristics listed in the left-hand column above not as absolutes, but general cultural tendencies that exist along a continuum. For example, we certainly find examples of both democracies and totalitarian regimes in both the East and the West. However, we find more of a political tradition (at least in the last two hundred years) towards democratic institutions in the West, while in South Korea, for example, moves towards democracy have only been seriously attempted since the early 1990's. Mainland China openly struggles with adapting to a capitalist economic system while maintaining a one-Party system of government, while Japan's democracy was imposed on it after World War II. More important for us, however, is the realization that cultural variations in the concepts of democracy and individual rights exist not only in politics, but in the family, as well. For example, the idea that children have opinions and life options that are ultimately that child's responsibility is not given much credence in most Korean or Chinese families where the family is the basic social unit, and the needs and wants of the individual are secondary to those of the extended family. Looking at another characteristic, that of the sensitive area of Value Priorities (about which a good deal more will be discussed later), it is important to emphasize that honesty is certainly important in Korea and China, just as relationships are important to Westerners. However, when the two values come into conflict in the West, there is a strong cultural bias towards putting honesty above relationships, even if that isn't always played out in action. When that does not happen, it results in some level of social disapproval. Famous fables of the greatest American heroes speak to this. Most Americans, for example, would name George Washington and Abe Lincoln as among the greatest U. S. presidents. It is no coincidence that a commonly known quote (however mythical) of young George Washington, when asked about the felled cherry tree, is "I cannot tell a lie." And what is Lincoln's nickname but "Honest Abe?" Richard Nixon's fall from America's grace was not so much a result of his involvement in a criminal act; it was his lack of honesty to the American people in responding to it that sealed his political fate. As I write in 2020, during the administration of U.S. President Donald Trump, allegations and ongoing evidence of dishonesty and the publication of obvious "alternative facts" and claims of being attacked by "fake news" by those in the highest levels of the Trump administration threaten to permanently damage this presidency as much as does public opposition to President Trump's policies. Honesty is at the core of American values, even if it is sometimes ignored or abused. On the other hand, contemporary Korean news is rife with stories of dishonesty resulting from giving in to the urge maintain a relationship. For example, in the spring of 2017 the presidency of Park Geun-hye of Korea was destroyed, with her being first impeached and then indicted for corruption and misuse of power involving her close personal friends of many decades – the issue was her relationships as much as any particular illegal action. Korean heroes such as Admiral Yi Sun- shin or patriot Yoo Kwan-soon are famous for their intense loyalty to the nation, that is, to their relationship to the ethnic and national group, rather than to any particular personal honesty. (More on this later.) Readers are encouraged to examine each of the general characteristics and tendencies found on the chart and consider to what degree their own experiences with East Asians are congruent. The point is that cultures differ in some very fundamental ways that affect thoughts, values, and behaviors. When we question or wonder about the behaviors of some of our students who come from a very different cultural background, especially when they conflict with more Western school values and practices, we should not be surprised. We are, quite literally, worlds apart in the way we view and approach the world. Perhaps we should be more surprised that we get along as well as we do than we are when we have differences.

Because of an understandable reluctance to risk being labeled prejudiced or even racist, we often opt not to consider differences between peoples (beyond the fun food, clothing, language, and music level) at all. This is particularly true in the United States where many still believe in the dream of the happy melting pot "with liberty and justice for all" and where political correctness is a strong cultural value among many, if not most, Americans. On the other hand, each culture, including that of the United States, is quite comfortable stereotyping itself. For example, citizens of the United States will tell the visitor that they pride themselves on their "independent American spirit" and "strong egalitarian tradition." Stating such generalities begs such questions then, as "Do all U.S. citizens exercise the same degree of personal independence?" "Do all desire the same amount of independence?" "Do the words of the Declaration of Independence ring true for all?" Of course not, we answer. However, someone attempting to answer the question "What makes U.S. Americans tick?" would be ill-prepared without 1) taking a solid look at the historical, cultural, and geographic background of the nation, and 2) developing some understanding of the independent and self-reliant spirit that guides much public and private decision-making in the nation. Similarly, the British might consider themselves to be, within their historical and geographic context, "formal," or Australians "informal," or Japanese "polite." We are often very content to stereotype our own cultures while being equally resistant to stereotyping other cultures. In this context, and with the understood danger of being labeled racist or even bigoted, a look at the historical, cultural, and educational backgrounds of ethnic East Asian children and their parents (or those of any other cultural group) is appropriate in an honest attempt to better understand, quite literally and geographically "where they are coming from." As long as we are willing and able to distinguish between the general characteristics of a cultural group and those of its individual members (personal history, heredity, etc.), we are on safe intellectual ground, I believe.

In order to understand any culture and learn what makes its individuals "tick," then, we have to look below the surface of the iceberg to see how the value systems that underpin the society operate. When this is done in a positive, neutral, and non- judgmental way, it is called anthropology. When it is done from a myopic, judgmental, or nationalistic perspective, however, it is accurately called stereotyping. The anthropological comment that "Korean culture places a higher degree of importance on education than do some other cultures," for example, can be extrapolated to a stereotypical (and often heard) "All Koreans care about is whether their child goes to Harvard!" This type of narrow stereotyping is of course what we want to avoid.

To understand children from East Asian backgrounds,

whether they are children of immigrants to the West, children who happen to hold a foreign passport and find themselves in international schools, or "overseas Koreans/Chinese/Japanese" living temporarily outside their home countries, we must first understand the parents who hold the values, habits, and world views that mold their children. Specifically, we must examine the historical, cultural, educational backgrounds that many of these parents share with one another. We will also look at individual life experiences that create exceptions to these generalities. The children of these parents are sitting in our classrooms, and they bring the influences of their parents' background with them to school each morning. Some of these characteristics make them top students, friendly and positive kids who make up a teacher's idea of a dream class. On the other hand, some characteristics (often the same ones) can threaten to make us question the core values of our schools, institute draconian rules in an effort to control or better educate students, or just leave us disappointed and jaded.

Time To Write . . .

Perhaps a good way to begin reflection is for the reader to take a few minutes and jots down his or her own impressions of ethnic East Asian students he or she has taught. What are their general characteristics? Be totally honest with yourself — no one is going to check! Make two lists. In the "+" column, write down those endearing characteristics of ethnic (and culturally) East Asian children you have taught that seem to distinguish them from Western students. Then (be honest, now!) in a "-" column, write down those characteristics which are frustrating, troubling, or that you feel are simply wrong. Try to depend on your own experience rather than on what "everybody knows" is true. You may find the same characteristics listed in both columns! Then make note of any questions you have about these students - ask why they are the way they are. You might not find the specific answers to your questions in this book, but you might gain some insight into what makes them "tick" as well as some insight into what makes you find them so endearing – or not. Jot down your lists and questions in the back of this book, and take a look at them from time to time. As you read, hopefully connections will begin to appear and you will enjoy some "Aha Moments." Although you will most likely still have some questions when you finish reading, hopefully it all may at least begin to make sense and you will have gained a foundation on which to build greater understanding as your experiences and understanding continue.

CHAPTER III: CONFUCIUS MEETS PIAGET

The title for the original version of this book was somewhat of an accident, although it has become quite well known in educational and missionary circles. I struggled initially to come up with a title that didn't scare people away with educational jargon, yet I wanted to capture the essence of what the book was all about. As time has gone on the title wore well, and I think that is because it did capture the essential dilemma facing Western educators of Eastern children. The teachings of Confucius provide the basic structure for the moral, societal, and thus educational systems (which always reflect their cultures) of Korea, the various "China's," Japan, and to a lesser degree much of the rest of East Asia. By extension, it also provides the cultural basis and educational framework for understanding millions of immigrants to Western nations and to a lesser degree their children, grandchildren, and even (in the case of many ethnic Japanese and Chinese) great grandchildren. One need only read Amy Tan's *The Joy Luck Club* or Amy Chua's more recent *Battle Hymn of the Tiger Mom* (2011) to see how this Confucian influence has become an integral part of what it means (at least stereotypically) to be "Asian" in America.

These stereotypes are useful, but equally dangerous. As noted earlier, there isn't much space between stereotyping and anthropology. Stereotyping is what happens in our minds when a valid generalization about a culture is applied to all who might be perceived as coming from that culture: "Susie Kim is Korean, so she must study hard and be good at math," for example. The fact is that there is a Confucian based work ethic, particularly in education, that is a prominent characteristic of many young people (and their parents) in Korea, China, and Japan. Additionally, math as a subject is held in particularly high esteem in those nations, and students with a background from those educational systems are expected to "crunch the numbers" at an early age. There are many fascinating theories about why this might be true; for a really interesting discussion of this phenomenon, read *Outliers: The Story of Success* (2008) by Malcolm Gladwell, particularly the chapter entitled "Rice Paddies and Math Tests." Fair enough; experience and tests show that generally, kids from East Asian countries do study more hours than their counterparts in many Western countries, and generally, many tend to have a strong aptitude for math computation. From an anthropological perspective, after empirical research, supporting data that can be replicated, and experience of those "on the ground" (including myself, after 40 years of working with kids from Korean and Chinese families), we can honestly say that many, if not most, do practice longer hours of study than many of their Western counterparts, and are often skilled in math computation. However, while this might be true generally, Susie Kim in particular might be quite lazy, or not be particularly talented at math. Before we paint her with the broad brush of stereotypical bias, we need to know a little bit more about Susie's individual characteristics. Let's not place her in Advanced Math just because her name is Kim! Most of us know plenty of Kim's and Zhang's who struggle with math, and some Smiths and Gonzales's who don't.

With this disclaimer now firmly established, in subsequent

chapters I will be making many general statements about "Korean moms" or "Chinese boys." Understand that this is shorthand for "it is a general characteristic of many Korean mothers . . . " etc. My opinions and general statements are from a perspective that an anthropologist might take. My own experience has taught me that many generalizations are valid, but my better self also brings to mind individual kids I have known who shattered the stereotypes, for good or for ill.

One word of caution: This book will most likely not answer all of your questions about your East Asian kids. If it could, I would join Amy Chua as an author on the New York Times bestseller list and I could comfortably retire to a tropical island. However, I do hope that as you read this book you will develop a much more nuanced understanding of yourself in relation to your students, of the deeper reasons for some of the behaviors and characteristics that you find both endearing and not so endearing, and are able to more effectively and with a lower level of frustration engage them culturally where you find them. Hopefully, you can help them enjoy the many positive things that Confucius had to teach, while opening their minds to the wider world that Piaget and other Western educational philosophers and practitioners have to offer them. If you can, it will not only change them as students, but it will equip them to succeed in a much more open, creative, understanding, and accepting inner world than the one imposed on their parents, and which is still being imposed, to a large extent, on their cousins going to local schools back in Seoul or Shanghai or Singapore.

CHAPTER IV: CONFUCIANISM 101

I do not pretend to be a Confucian scholar; that would be a lifelong endeavor. However, for our purposes I'll include here a little bit about the man and his very basic teachings, as these underlie the cultures and educational systems that are the subjects of this book.

Kong Qui, or Kong Fu-Tzu, was most likely born in China's Shandong Province in 551 B.C., during the Chou Dynasty. This was a period of considerable social and intellectual turmoil, as well as moral decline in China. Confucius determined to remedy this situation through education; in his mind the job of an educator was to instill character and integrity in students through his philosophy of education and "curriculum" focusing on the "Six Arts": computation, archery, music, calligraphy, chariot-driving, and ritual. Though such an educational philosophy he hoped to instill stability and values into the unstable Chinese society of his times. http://www.biography.com/people/confucius-9254926

We won't spend a lot of time discussing archery and music and chariot driving here (although some drivers' ed might be welcome in China for another few years), but the inclusion of computation probably won't surprise you, and we'll be taking a look at the impact of calligraphy on modern education. We'll also examine the conservative nature of Confucian societies implied by a focus on ritual, the purpose of which, at least in part, is to connect the present to the past through routinely doing the same things that have always been done, often long after the initial significance has been forgotten. All cultures employ varying amounts of ritual which become so much a part of the way the culture operates that they aren't even recognized as "cultural" – at least not on their own home turf.

Confucius taught that society would be stable if only everyone just treated each other with kindness and decency. To accomplish this, he taught that everyone had to be very aware of his or her rank and status within society, and act according to an assigned role within a relationship driven social hierarchy. If everyone knew their place, and played their assigned role, then there would be peace, stability, and harmony in the home and in the nation. To accomplish this he identified four basic relationships: King/subject, Father/son, Husband/wife, Older brother/Younger brother, and Friend/Friend. Four of these relationships are vertical (hierarchical). The last is lateral. All are meant to be reciprocal. For our visual learners, I've included the diagram below.

Confucian Heirarchy

Superior/ Dominant role	KING	FATHER	HUSBAND	OLDER BROTHER	EQUAL FRIENDS
Inferior/ Submissive role	Subject	Son	Wife	Younger Brother	

Confucianism's first vertical relationship is King/Subject. As long as the subject obeyed the edicts of the king without question, AND the King took care of his subjects and didn't abuse them, then there would be peace in the land. China has a long history of totalitarian governments of one kind or another, from ancient times to the present. Concepts of Western style democracy are very, very young in East Asia and are still developing. Chinese history is rife with records of peasant revolts; Confucius meant to put a stop to that. The second vertical relationship was Father/Son. The son owes unquestioning respect and obedience to his father; the father should not abuse his son, but care for him always. By extension and in light of modern values of equality, we can now include mothers and daughters here as well, but they didn't have much social standing in Chou Dynasty China and weren't of much concern, apparently, to Confucius.) The third vertical relationship is Husband/Wife. The wife owed obedience and respect to the husband, and the husband was required to take care of and protect his wife. As long as both followed their assigned roles, Confucius said, there would be peace in the home. As much as this grates on modern sensitivities, this is what Confucius espoused. Although the Peoples' Republic of China has done a great deal to level the playing field between men and women, throughout the rest of East Asia men definitely still have the upper hand. The fourth vertical relationship is Older Brother/Younger Brother. This tradition is still very strong today (and enforced by older brothers) in Asia. Of course, in today's world the same would apply to older and younger sisters. Even in the circumstance of twins, the one born just seconds before the other is forever the "older brother" and is addressed as such by his younger sibling as "older brother" for life; having two "equal" brothers in a family would be a recipe for decades of discord and disharmony. Interestingly, even today in some more traditional families in Korea a younger brother maintains a superior status in the family hierarchy to an older sister; the dominance of males in Confucius' system still affects many families today, although this emphasis on male-ness is waning in younger generations. In Mainland China, while there is still generally a preference for male offspring, the Chinese "one-child policy" put an end to both birth order issues and male/female sibling issues. Finally, the fifth relationship of Friend/Friend is lateral. Here the relationship is not based on obedience, but on mutual loyalty and support, often lasting a lifetime.

Three of these relationships still can very much affect our school climates. Firstly, teachers enjoy the benefit of the Father/Son relationship, which can be extrapolated into Teacher/Student relationships. We'll take a look at that later, but in the meantime, enjoy the status and respect you probably would never get as a teacher in a Western country! Secondly, the Older Brother/Younger Brother relationship is played out in our school corridors, lunchrooms, and busses every day, often without naïve Westerners noticing it at all. Usually, it is quite benign, and consists of a quick nod of the head by the younger to the older – acknowledgement of an upperclassman or of a friend's older brother or sister. However, it can also become quite ugly, as I'll relate below. Thirdly, we'll see later why the Confucian style Friend/Friend relationships are so much more important, intense, and long-lasting than most Western friendship relationships, and can impact issues of academic integrity or solidarity in cases where the importance of relationships competes with that of honesty in a hierarchy of values.

Confucius, I am convinced, would have been quite comfortable in a contemporary but traditional-style East Asian classroom. He would find things to be orderly, he would be comfortable memorizing his text, he'd be happy about being tested on a very predictable body of knowledge, and he would be satisfied knowing that the teacher would lecture each day and would be the primary source of information to be learned. Classroom life would be socially harmonious, academically predictable, and intellectually safe. His parents would be happy as well; the classroom would be nearly identical to that which they experienced as children, and that their own parents and grandparents had experienced. Confucius would not be at ease in some of our more progressive western classrooms, however. He might find unsettling a more Piagetian instructional and learning environment featuring student choice, independent research on and off-line, learning and activity centers, and collaboration among students. Were he to observe students preparing presentations, the teacher moving around the room helping students stay on task and providing resources in the form of questions or suggestions, he might find chaotic. He would be very uncomfortable with a student questioning or challenging his or her teacher. The question we always need to ask ourselves is this: Who would be more comfortable in the classrooms in our school – Confucius or Piaget? Why does it matter to us? More important, why does it matter to our students and their futures?

The conflict between Confucius and Piaget is played out in classrooms of renowned colleges of education across Asia, and in classrooms and counseling offices of international schools around the world. During my years as principal in both Seoul and Shanghai I had the opportunity to talk with many school visitors from local educational systems – mostly education students from nearby universities. I made it a point to ask their impressions of what they observed as they visited classrooms. Very often, and frequently with some degree of embarrassment, a young teacher-to-be would be so brave as to comment that while the students seemed to be having fun, "the teachers don't teach." Digging further into this, I realize that they were looking for (and defined teaching as) the traditional "sage on the stage" style of instruction, with little interaction or student input save teacher questions aimed at the class as a whole followed by group response, with little checking for individual understanding. This same comment/complaint is common from some parents of students who have recently moved from local schools. The parents miss the very predictable text and lecture-based instruction, and interpret the lack of daily text assignments or teacher lectures as "not teaching." I have had parents approach me about a teacher, indignant that "When my child asks Mr. Smith a question, he suggests that Joon Mee research the answer for herself! Why is he so lazy as to not tell my child the answer? Why does he refuse to teach her?" We need to remember that just because parents chose to send their child to a Western style school doesn't mean that they understand the full educational implications of their choice. Often, we find ourselves educating parents so that we can get their cooperation in educating their children. Too often, we find out too late that we are working against each other, unaware that the child is caught in the middle.

CHAPTER V:
HISTORICAL
BACKGROUNDS OF
KOREA AND CHINA

From SUBJUGATION TO SKYSCRAPERS

Most of us would agree that the histories of our native countries – the trials, the victories, the wars, the heroes, and the triumphs – have had a great impact on our current state of affairs. Korea and China are no exceptions. Both have very long and proud histories. Chinese history is better known and acknowledged in the West; Korean history less so. However, artifacts of Paleolithic age have been found in Korea, dating habitation of the Korean peninsula back more than 30,000 years. History in the form of artwork reaches at least as far back as 4000 B. C. A highly developed, artistic society evolved over the next five millennia. A specifically Korean culture, with its own language, literature, social structure, government, religion, music, and cuisine developed, related to yet distinct from neighboring Chinese, Mongol, and Japanese cultures. Koreans are justly very proud of this culture and heritage, as Chinese and Japanese are of theirs.

Korea: A Shrimp Among Whales

Korea is a victim of its geography – a tempting peninsula dangling down from northeastern Asia, centered on a map between the plains of northern Asia, the coasts of China, and the islands of Japan. While its central location is today a huge benefit to its economy and commerce, its location historically has been an immense liability. Its history has been inextricably connected to that of China, which like a giant beating heart has been constantly expanding and contracting over the past millennia, if not through its actual borders (although it has done that), at least through its social and cultural influence on neighbors. Later we'll see an example of this in the expanding, then contracting influence of Ming China on Korea. Today's world finds China in a period of expanding influence, even claiming sovereignty over its neighbors and surrounding waters. The inhabitants of the plains of Central Asia, such as the Mongols, similarly have experienced the expansion and contraction of their power and influence over the centuries – often at the expense of China, as well as Korea and to a lesser extent Japan. Small Korea, at times a virtual vassal state of China, was the victim of periodic expansionist tendencies by the changing rulers both China and central Asian powers. Japan was a particularly tempting bait for them, and the easiest way for non-seafaring Asians to get to Japan was to march down through the Korean Peninsula and then be ferried across the Straits of Tsushima to attack Japanese Kyushu, using Korean seamen and ships as their vehicle of conquest. Similarly, when Japan counterattacked, or later during the late 19th and first half of the 20th Centuries when Japan decided to embark on colonial conquest to satisfy her own need for resources and create the "Greater East Asia Co-Prosperity Sphere", Korea again became a convenient bridge to northeast Asia, this time originating in Japan. Following the defeat of Japan following World War II, Japanese-controlled Korea was "temporarily" split in two by the victorious powers, namely the United States and the Soviet Union. That split still stands in the form of North and South Korea. Korea says of itself with a good deal of justification, "We are like a shrimp among whales!" This history of victimization has become part of the Korean national character, a once-valid complaint but today, in the context of today's economic powerhouse we call South Korea, somewhat anachronistic. However, vestiges of it remain in a contradictory identity of an amazingly successful nation that Koreans are justly proud of, and a crippling consciousness that the world out there is somehow once again going to consume it and it will be washed away by forces beyond its control. The fact that North Korea exists today as a remnant of such past indignities and national tragedy gives ongoing credence to that negative identity. There is ample evidence to support this victim identity; in just the past 120 years Korea has suffered the following tragedies inflicted by outside forces:

1904-1905 Russo-Japanese War (after which Japan was given the OK by the international community to take increasing control over Korean affairs).

1910-1945 Japanese Occupation/Colonialism (35 years of domination during which Koreans were forced to take Japanese names, suffer very restricted educational opportunities, endure their Korean language being suppressed in public, and experience Korean culture was obliterated in favor of Japanese.

1939-1945 Forced Labor/ "Comfort Women" during the late colonial period and during World War II, when colonial Korea was used as a staging area and "behind the lines" storehouse of the Japanese. During this era Korea was forced to provide both male laborers for the Japanese war machine (particularly in mining) and female "Comfort Women" who were often girls just out of middle school, promised factory jobs but ending up being forced to service the sexual demands of Japanese armies in the field under brutal conditions. These issues continue to erupt today, more then 75 years after they occurred, due to a lack of an outright apology by Japan and insufficient or non-existent restitution. They continue to sour both national and sometimes interpersonal relations between older Koreans and Japanese.

1930's -1945 Natural Resources Stripped. The stripping of sparse natural resources from Korea to support the Japanese war effort in China and elsewhere in East Asia was horrific. Scars can still be seen on older pine trees on the grounds of Buddhist temples in Korea that were caused by tapping the trees for sap – to be distilled into aviation fuel for the Japanese air force late in World War II. The northern part of the occupied peninsula provided much needed coal and other mineral wealth; the southern part provided lumber and rice.

1950-1952 Korean War Between June 1950 and July 1952, the great powers of China and the United States (and allied U. N. forces) fought the first flare-up of the Cold War on the barren hills of Korea. The capital of Seoul was won and lost no less then four times between June 1950 and March 1951, each time with terribly destructive consequences. Visitors to the sky-scrapers and subways of Seoul today with its eleven million people can hardly imagine the Seoul of 1953, when the city was virtually flattened and its population reduced to about 100,000. North Korean cities saw similar destruction due to massive Allied airstrikes.

1948- ??? Division of Nation The last time the Korean peninsula was a sovereign, united national was in 1897, before the Japanese moved in. Since that time it has been a colony of Japan, ruled by a short time by the Soviet Union and the United States, and then split into two nation states since the declaration of the Democratic Peoples' Republic (DPRK) and the Republic of Korea (ROK) in 1948.)

1952- ??? Korean Cold War This constant and continuing struggle of arms, nerves, threats, and rhetoric has been going on with only slight periods of detente since the end of the Korean War, with the South being backed primarily by the United States and some token allied United Nations forces, and the North backed alternately by China, the Soviet Union (today Russia).

The combined catastrophes of 1) forty years of Japanese occupation, during which time the national culture and identity were nearly destroyed systematically and often brutally, 2) a brief and rocky period of military occupation by the United States in the South (1945-1948), 3) an even rockier period of struggling political forces during which the nation was sliced in half by outside forces (1948-1950), and 4) the culminating mass destruction and nearly total social chaos of the Korean War (1950-1952), together shook a society and culture of thousands of years to its very core culturally, physically, geographically, economically, and socially. Even eight years after the end of hostilities, the South Korean society and economy were still in shambles. In 1961 social disorder was rampant. There were thousands upon thousands of war widows, over 100,000 orphans, and about 279,000 unemployed, of whom 72,000 were university graduates and 51,000 were discharged soldiers (A Handbook of Korea, 1978). The country was ripe for the coup that occurred in April 1961, when President Rhee Sung-man (Syngman Rhee) was forced to step down. Rhee had been the handpicked and strong-armed leader of the US-backed government (1948-1960). The coup quickly led to the military dictatorship of President Park Chung-Hee (1962-1979), which ended in his assassination at the hands of his CIA chief. Power was soon wrested by General Doo-hwan (1980-1988), who although his administration tolerated little opposition and amassed a good deal of wealth during his tenure, actually stepped down after his term of seven years was complete, which President Park had not done. It was then that democracy began to take root in South Korea, under the leadership of former General (and friend of Chun Doo-hwan)

Roh Tae-woo (1988-1993). He was followed by former democratic activist Kim Young-sam (1993-1998), who further advanced the cause of democracy and government reformation. His successor was left-wing Kim Dae-jung (1998-2003), a political dissident who was once sentenced to death under Park Chung-hee, survived multiple assassination attempts, saved at sea from drowning at the hands of the Korean CIA by the intervention of the U.S. CIA in 1971, elected President in 1998 and visited North Korea, and was Korea's first Nobel Laureate. Liberal lawyer Roh Moo-hyun (2004-2008) replaced Kim Dae Jung (and later committed suicide after leaving office as scandal developed around his family). Former Seoul mayor Lee Myung-bak (2008-2013) replaced him, followed by the first woman President, and daughter of President Park Chung-hee, Park Geun-hye (2013-2017) who was impeached and driven from office in 2017 due to ongoing scandals involving a lifelong family friend and confidant. As of this writing (2020) former poltician Moon Jae-In is President, and former President Lee Myung-bak is serving a 17-year jail sentence for corruption. Although there have been some setbacks, there has been a steady march from brutal police-state dictators to ardent democrats. The near constant street demonstrations accompanied by tear gas during the Park and Chun administrations, the ugly 1980 Kwang-ju uprising and subsequent massacre under President Chun, the always-present knowledge that politics was something better only discussed behind closed doors and in selected company (experienced by this author in the late 1970's and early 1980's) gradually gave way to tremendous political freedom, to the degree that in late 2016 citizens felt free enough to engage in ongoing street demonstrations in Seoul and across the country (and not met by teargas) that eventually drove President Park Geun-hye from office. In the winter and spring of 2018 charges of corruption (again related to relationships) resulted in her impeachment, ouster and eventual jailing for a 24-year term.

The fact that Korea remains divided, and that in order for South Korea to defend itself it must endure the shame of hosting 35,000 foreign (American) troops throughout the country, even until recently in its capital city, is an ongoing issue and an insult to national pride that lives in the consciousness of every Korean.

Another residual reality of the division of Korea lives on in our international schools. Every Korean boy knows that within two years of his high school graduation he must shave his head and put on a uniform to possibly guard the snowy mountainous border with the North, accepting the very real possibility that he is literally putting his life on the line. The Republic of Korea (ROK) army is not to be trifled with; training is tough and brutal, and beatings of recruits by older soldiers and officers are not unknown (Confucius is still alive and well). This is both a right of passage for any proud Korean male, and an unwelcome, unpleasant, and often-dangerous intrusion into their life for at least two years. I don't worry too much about some of our softer and more spoiled Korean boys; the Korean military is sure to "make men out of them" even if the methods can be sometimes brutal, and sometimes what we may consider abusive. Only the fact that all males must do it makes the experience bearable; in fact a Korean man who has not been in the military is missing an important and expected part of acculturation to Korean adulthood that would hound him through his lifetime.

The Peoples' Republic Of China – A Historical Perspective

The history of the Peoples' Republic of China contrasts greatly from that of South Korea, with radically different effects on its people. China, too, went through a period of humiliating foreign domination to both Western, and later, Japanese colonial forces, just as the centuries-old Qing Dynasty was crumbling, and the once-proud and powerful nation of China fell to outside forces. Just as warfare ravaged the Korean peninsula throughout much of its history, both civil warfare and invasion from without ravaged China for much of the history of the Peoples' Republic of China.

We know from history that China's recorded past goes back nearly 5000 years, with kingdom following kingdom and dynasty following dynasty. Frequent civil wars punctuate Chinese history. In more recent times, the Manchu Qing Dynasty (we'll hear from them again later) was growing weaker and weaker during the first half of the 19th Century, just as the tentacles of Western colonialism were finally making their way around the bottom of Asia and up the Chinese coast. First the British, who were unhappy with an unequal trade balance that was rapidly developing as it paid for Chinese goods (tea and porcelain, to name two) with silver, decided that Indian opium could both boost their colonial economy in India while also providing something to exchange with the Chinese in place of valuable silver. By flooding the Chinese opium market with cheap opium, the use of the drug became widespread to the point that addiction was becoming rampant among all social classes.

China of the 1840's and 1860's was marked by wars fought first against the British, and then against other European powers, primarily over the right of the foreigners to sell opium to the Chinese people. First resisted by the disintegrating Chinese government, the importation of opium from British India expanded greatly due to China's defeat in what is known as the "Opium Wars," lost due to the overwhelming modern military forces of the West, coupled with the weakness of the already crumbling Manchu (Qing) dynasty. As a result of China's loss in these wars, coastal "treaty ports" or "concessions" were carved out of China and control given to foreign powers, particularly after 1864. Shanghai, Tianjin, Qingdao, Darien, Hong Kong are but a few of these foreign enclaves wrested from the Chinese government. Tourists today will marvel at the beautiful, if often rundown, foreign buildings in these cities, dating from the late 1800's through the 1930's. The Shanghai Bund, a strip of Western style hotel, office and bank buildings that is spectacularly lit up at night, was built on the wealth of opium money. A wide range of fiction and non-fiction books tells the fascinating story of old Shanghai. It is not a story of Western Civilization at its finest.

A weakening China lost territory during the 1894-94 Sino-Japanese War and the 1904-05 Russo-Japanese War, while the 1900 Boxer Rebellion resulted in the capital of Peking (today's Beijing) being overrun by foreign troops "protecting" their foreign citizens. Although the Republic of China was declared in 1912, warlords continued to roam the country. Between 1931 and 1945 the Japanese took larger and larger chunks of Chinese territory, first slowly and later much more aggressively as they moved from occupied Korea into Chinese Manchuria. All the while the Communist and Nationalist forces struggled against each other while also trying to maintain sovereignty against Japanese aggression. With the Japanese threat gone after their 1945 defeat at the end of World War II, the Communist and Nationalists fell into a bloody civil war, ending with the Nationalists fleeing to the island of Taiwan in 1949 and the declaration of the Peoples' Republic of China later that year.

Within the living memory of many of the grandparents of

our Chinese students was Mao Tse-tung's 1958-1959 "Great Leap Forward," which resulted in a famine that left over 30 million Chinese dead. Mao's next experiment of the Great Proletarian Cultural Revolution (1966-1976) shook the very foundations of Chinese culture and society, as intended. Many of the somewhat older parents of our students remember this period as children, characterized by distrust of neighbors and family members, destruction of anything Western or old-fashioned, forced exile of young city dwellers and students to the countryside for nearly a decade (and for some much longer), the loss of family wealth and status, the tearing down of traditional values and institutions, and the closing of schools and universities for a decade. The Cultural Revolution turned Chinese society upside down and created rifts and scars in Chinese families, and in individual psyches, that are still evident today, although few who experienced this period will openly talk about it. While we see little direct evidence of this in our students, many parents who lived though it still carry its scars. An entire genre of literature has grown up around the subject of the Cultural Revolution. One excellent example is *Life and Death in Shanghai,* by a westernized Chinese woman who lived through it, Cheng Nien.

I would invite the reader to do his or her own research on the political changes, and political climate, of China under the leadership of the Chinese Communist Party. Any writing done here in much detail would both quickly be out of date, and may be unwise to include here in any event. There are many Western sources that can do it in much greater detail than can this author.

Despite its recent awakening, China has not forgotten its bitter past of humiliation by Western powers and Japan, and has waited patiently and worked mightily to finally be counted among world powers to be respected and even admired. Recent political developments confirm this nationalistic trend.

South Korea And The Peoples' Republic Of China: Economic Miracles

Since the watershed changes of 1949 in China and 1952 in Korea, both nations have made amazing progress on the social and economic fronts. Both countries had been devastated by terribly destructive wars and social upheaval. In the case of Korea, massive foreign aide, much from the United States, along with a determined populace led by strongman and former General Park Chung Hee, moved their country ahead slowly at first, then at an increasingly rapid rate to the economic powerhouse it is today. As democracy gradually took hold, given the educated populace and increasingly democratically minded leaders, so did economic advancement. Apart from the economic crisis of 1997 that ravaged most East Asian economies, Korea has been on a steady upward trail since 1952 economically, socially, and politically. This chart of the South Korean Gross Domestic Product (USD) from 1961 to 2018 illustrates this fact:

Korean Economic Recovery – 1961-2018

1961	$94
1965	$109
1970	$279
1975	$615
1980	$1704
1985	$2457
1990	$6516
1995	$12,333
2000	$11,948
2005	$18,640
2010	$22,087
2015	$27,105
2018	$31,363
Data Source: World Bank	

It is shocking to note that in 1961 – nine years after the end of the Korean War – the per-capita GNP of South Korea was approximately USD$94. Korea was the economic basket case of Asia, falling well behind Japan (which got an economic shot in the arm due to the Korean War five years after its defeat in 1945) and even the Philippines. North Korea, as late as the mid-1970's, was ahead of South Korea economically. By the mid-1980's, the South Korean per-capita GDP was still only about $2500. However, it had more than doubled by 1990 (just after Seoul hosted the 1988 Olympics) and then nearly doubled again in the next five years, with figures over $12,300 in 1995, $18,600 in the mid-2000's, and over $31,000 in 2018.

Other social and economic indicators are similarly impressive. During the Fifties and Sixties, and into the early Seventies, commodities were very scarce. U.S. government surplus food is still remembered by many older Koreans today as a regular part of their school lunches in the 1960s (the steamed cornbread was particularly enjoyed; the American rice, not so much). Let's take a look at some economic and social indicators of Korea during the years when the parents of the children in our classrooms were growing up and how they have changed:

From 1955 to 2017 the South Korean population grew over 240% from roughly 21 million to 51 million. (www.populationpyramid.net/republic-of-korea/1960/)

In today's dollars, the Gross Domestic Product grew from $3.9 billion to $51 trillion between 1960 and 2016 (https://data.worldbank.org/country/korea-rep)

Between 1960 and 2003 the number of elementary school children per teacher dropped from 58.8 to 34.5 At the middle school level, it dropped from 42.3 to 19.0 in the same period. (www.korea.net/Korea)

In 1949 the number of people per doctor was 4615; by 2012 this had dropped to 467. (Statistical Handbook of Korea, 2002 and www.tradingeconomics.com "Physicians (per 1000 people) in South Korea")

Life expectancy at birth increased from 53 in 1960 to 82 in 2016 (https://data.worldbank.org/country/korea-rep)

As is obvious, the Korea of the last fifty years has experienced sustained economic growth at a rate that is the envy of many more "developed" nations. Those familiar with the vibrant, exciting, technologically advanced, and economically aggressive Korea of today can hardly imagine that Korea was very much an underdeveloped country well into the 1960's, and a developing nation into the 1980's. During those difficult decades hard work, "connections," a competitive spirit, and a good deal of luck were about the only ways to succeed or get ahead; of those who did succeed many sent their children overseas for an education as Korean higher education was still limited in both quantity and quality. Many of our older students' parents were such "education immigrants" who managed somehow to leave Korea during this era.

Traditional South Korean society has changed deeply in the last fifty years as the economy has boomed. Since 1960 there has been a tremendous migration from the countryside to the city, with former peasants (or their children) now working in urban factories and office skyscrapers. The Seoul metropolitan area, with a population of 25.6 million, includes more than one-half of the nation's inhabitants. http://worldpopulationreview.com/world-cities/seoul-population/

As the farmers, fishermen, and factory workers of the Seventies sent their children to college, cities boomed as the countryside emptied of workers. As aging grandparents began to be left behind in the countryside, many moved to the cities to be with children and grandchildren. Traditionally-minded, retired farmers living with their urbanized and much more Westernized children and grandchildren in small high-rise apartments in the city, and a rapid improvement in the standard of living, has created family and societal stress. Signs of this stress can be seen in some of the ethnic Korean children attending our schools.

The importance of this data for us as educators as we approach the year 2020 is this: the parents of our current South Korean students, assuming they are between 35 and 50 years of age, were teenagers sometime during the period from 1980 – 2000. Growing up in the Korea of those years was vastly different than growing up in Korea today.

It is important to understand this post-war history because this was the Korea in which the grandparents and parents of our students grew up, and it has shaped the way in which they look at themselves, at their children and grandchildren, and at the outside world. They are the products of a formerly devastated nation, poor in natural resources and overcrowded in population. They were raised at a time of such scarcity that those who did not fight to get ahead were left behind, whether in the economic race, in the education race, or in the race to catch the bus to work. Competition for education, for jobs, for housing, for transportation, and for places in the ranks of the successful was incessant. Thus, while they were children and young adults, today's middle class (our current Korean parents) developed a sense of fierce competition both with outsiders and among themselves, and many grew up considering themselves to be the victims of discrimination by larger or more powerful neighbors. Their early years were spent in a dictatorial police state in which individuals in power, and the rule of law in general, were obeyed but not highly respected.

* * *

In the Peoples' Republic of China, the disparity between generations is even starker, due to a much more recent economic development inconceivable twenty years ago. As late as the mid-1990's the per-capita GDP was under $500; by 2015 it was closer to $8000. There is still today a huge economic disparity between the super rich in the cities such as Shanghai and Beijing and the poorer rural and migrant populations. Some parents and all grandparents of our Chinese students whose families are from the mainland experienced decades of war, famine, revolution, and the Cultural Revolution. Many of our students' Mainland Chinese parents are the first generation in their families to have gone to college, many of them not having a normal high school education due to the Cultural Revolution. Many of these families who can afford to send their children to international schools, of course, are the first and second generation "wealthy" who have had some oppor-

74

tunity for education outside of China. In contrast, ethnic Chinese families from Singapore or Taiwan would not have experienced this generational economic disparity to this extent.

The recent and amazing economic growth of Mainland China since about 1990, and most obviously since 2000, has been nothing short of miraculous. Chinese education, hard work, and masses of people have created a second "cultural revolution." This is most obvious in the larger cities.

Similarly to Korea, Chinese cities have grown exponentially to the point that a "small" city may have 5 million people. A great migration from the countryside and smaller cities where economic opportunity is limited to the larger cities has changed the face of the country. Landscapes brown with drought in the 1960's are now green with crops and crisscrossed by superhighways and high-speed trains. Cities are clogged with cars instead of carts and bicycles, and in cities like Shanghai parking lots are full of Teslas, BMWs, Audis, and Mercedes; even Bentleys and Maserati's are common. Twenty-year olds in new Ferraris speed past old men and women sweeping streets with bamboo brooms. While bikes and scooters are still very common, those who can afford to quickly buy a car.

Note that I have provided a much richer story about Korean economic and social development than I have for China. This is unfortunate, but is caused by a number of factors, notably the fact that getting reliable economic figures regarding China is challenging. For up to date figures on the rapidly moving target of Chinese economic development the reader should do independent research; one place to start might be www.tradingeconomics.com and information from the World Bank.

Why is understanding the economic histories of China and Korea important to our understanding of our students? Because this disparity of formative year experience between grandparents, parents, and current students, particularly among mainland Chinese and Korean students, helps to explain some of the apparent desperation and focus on "success" that we see in the eyes of many of our parents. They remember what it used to be like, and know that today's amazing economic success (which has allowed them to send their children to our international schools) is both recent, hard won, and fragile. Their children have educational opportunities that they never could have imagined, and for their grandparents would have been simply impossible. Thus, we often observe a "If you have a chance at Harvard, GO FOR IT!" attitude that is sometimes frustrating to hear and difficult to understand. We need to remember that most of us come from Western nations where there has been a history (at least since the end of World War II) of relative wealth and plenty for most people, where if you worked hard you could survive quite well without a college education if you learned some skills, and where, at the end of the day, most people were most likely not going to end up in poverty if they took advantage of the opportunities offered. Of course there are tragic exceptions to this even in the richest of countries, but generally, even the poorest of the poor in the United States, for example, were nowhere near as destitute as the poorest poor in South Korea of the 1960's (or North Korea today). Thus, different attitudes towards wealth and opportunity directly affect the attitudes of our Korean and Chinese parents towards educational and economic opportunity. If we understand and accept this reality, we can perhaps be a little more forgiving to Ms. Kim and Mr. Zhang when they insist that their child get straight A's, perfect SAT scores, and a full ride at an Ivy. This stereotype is well supported and understandable, given the historical perspective.

CHAPTER VI: CONFUCIAN HEIRARCHY AND RESPECT

William Yoon arrived at in international school in Seoul fresh from rural Indiana, where his dad had been a professor at a university. William was Korean in ethnicity only; he didn't speak Korean and had never lived in Korea. He was a 100% American teenager. In Indiana, there had been few ethnic Korean kids his age. His parents enrolled him in this top international school because it was the right place for him – a school with Western teachers, Western students, and Western expectations. He was a friendly, quiet tenth grader trying to find his niche in a new school.

One day after school soon after his enrollment, William was walking down the hill outside the school entrance when some older boys of Korean background surrounded him from his school. They didn't exactly attack him, but by the time they got done with him, he was pretty bruised up physically and emotionally.

The next morning William and his father appeared in my office to complain. William had not done any of these boys any harm; in fact he didn't even know any of them except by sight. He was able to identify their pictures, however.

The investigation revealed that in fact William had only spoken very briefly to any of these boys. However, they felt that as a new, younger student, he had not shown them the respect due to them. Passing them in the hallway, he hadn't given them the slight nod that they thought was both appropriate and expected. When one of them had spoken to him earlier, he didn't reply using the honorific "elder brother" title "hyung". In their eyes, he was Korean, and as a Korean he was being rude to them. Therefore, in the spirit of "educating" him, they decided to teach him how to show proper respect to his elders. Did these otherwise decent kids know better? Yes, when they were thinking like Westerners. But on that day they decided to be Korean – and force William to be Korean as well. His Western behavior was an affront to their own fragile cultural identities. This type of "enforced" acculturation by older Koreans, both boys and girls, is not uncommon towards younger ethnic Korean students.

Strict social hierarchy is inherent in a system of vertical Confucian relationships. In Confucian cultures, all organizations, whether the ROK Army or the Grade 6 Advanced Math Korean moms' group, inherently have hierarchies. Governments, school staffs, universities, international schools, clubs, churches, companies, alumni groups all have hierarchies that are much more vertical, and much more rigid than would normally be found in the West. This strong sense of hierarchy defines superior/inferior relationships; in Korea even the verb endings used when addressing someone of higher "rank" are different than those used with friends or "equals." Positional titles are important and normally used instead of names, so that a Korean would not normally address someone as "Mr. Kim" but as "Vice Director Kim" or "Head Section Chief Park" usually with an honorific suffix "nim," and often without the surname). Often, in Western and less traditional organizations in Korea people are more relaxed and may use the English titles of "Mister" or "Miss." Don't worry; foreigners are not expected to know all the nuances of addressing those above or below them in the organizational strata. Just be respectful and use the title along with a family name "Ms. Chung," for example. Only if you are invited to and you are very close to a person would you use a given name; traditionally given names were very private and only used at home, and sometimes not even then. I have Korean friends who were co-workers whom I have known for over 40 years whom I still address as "Mr. ____." This attention to hierarchy is much less evident in China, sometimes startlingly so. When I was moving from Seoul Foreign to Shanghai American School, on a pre-move visit I was introduced to the school secretaries with whom I'd be working. Immediately one of them said, "Welcome to SAS, Jon!" I was shocked – after decades of being called "Dr. Borden" or in Korean "Honorable Principal", I actually felt offended by the informality. I quickly got over it and grew to appreciate this, but it initially was really shocking and unexpected. Neither did I get the automatic bows from school guards that I always got in Korea, and I learned that this level of overt respect and politeness had apparently been a casualty of the Cultural Revolution. Later on, the only bows or head nods at Shanghai American School I got were from Korean (and Japanese) high school boys who know that I know something about their cultures! Of course, their parents were also traditionally respectful to their children's principal.

When two Korean adults meet, they immediately exchange business cards (NOTE: learn business card etiquette early on) and quickly calculate what their two-person hierarchy looks like. Normally, without other clues, age is the deciding factor. Because it is rare to find a young person in a higher position, age normally corresponds with rank. Rank within a social hierarchy such as a parent group at school can also be attained through marriage – the wife of the Vice President of Company X is usually higher in the pecking order of Korean 7th grade moms than the wife of the Sales Manager of Company Y. There is usually an Alpha Mom in every group – if you can identify her you have gained an important tool in both communication and forming public opinion. Don't assume, however, that a person coming to school to represent "all the other moms" is the Alpha. It could be that she just has the strongest English and is being sent by those higher up the ladder. This hidden structure can be somewhat bewildering to any Westerner, and is behind many an unexplainable cultural misunderstanding. To a lesser extent, all else being equal, students' social rank among others in the same grade will be based on age, or may reflect their dad or mom's professional status. Normally, in a school setting you would not run into hierarchical situations involving dads, mostly because dads don't have much of a role to play in school life, as we'll see in a later chapter. However, watching dads interact when they meet each other at a parent night or on conference day can tell you a lot about who is of higher "rank" among the dads. In the end, age is most often the determining factor among Koreans.

The importance of rank and status can be quite bewildering to Westerners, particularly those from Anglo cultures such as the United States, Canada, Australia and New Zealand. Our social structures are normally much more fluid and flatter, except in the most blueblood of communities. Our language structure does not demand immediate recognition of social status, and status is often situational. Quite often, those in positions of authority in business are more than happy to shed their high rank out of the office in the context of another organization or activity. The president of the local bank is content to help serve sandwiches at the Lions' Club soup kitchen, a lowering of status that would be unthinkable in Korean society. Mainland Chinese society is much flatter than Korean, both as a result of the original communist theory of class struggle, and the Cultural Revolution of the 1960's and 1970's that turned the social structure upside down. Gone are generations-old gentry; today the defining quality is money and other outward signs of wealth. Complicating this is the fact that many educated people are Communist Party members, something not openly talked about, but which offers a certain level of privilege and opportunity, especially if coupled with wealth. While there is certainly some hierarchy among Chinese moms, as there is with Western moms, it is much less evident and structured than among Korean moms.

Normally, this respect for those up the social or organizational ladder simply greases the wheels of social and business discourse. Individuals know their place and play their role, understanding that if they stay around or live long enough, they will automatically rise up the ladder and someday be the revered elder. This strong deference to authority and superiors is the root of Korea's impressive social stability as well as many of its frequent tragedies and ills. Sometimes it can turn ugly, even tragic. I refer to Gladwell's *Outliers,* this time the chapter entitled "The Ethnic Theory of Plane Crashes." Gladwell makes the point that even something as regulated and seemingly straightforward as flying an airplane can fall victim to cultural hierarchy, with tragic results. All too often, those in positions of inferior status don't speak up when they need to, fearing reprisal or risking insult to a superior on whom they later may have to depend. A tragic example of this is suggested by the March 28, 1998 Korea Herald story found below, regarding the crash of a Korean Air Flight 801 while approaching the airport in Guam on the night of August 6, 1997. Although this happened over 20 years ago, similar situations in which hierarchy trumps common sense continue to occur.

JONATHAN BORDEN

(Bold sections not emphasized in the original)

Cultural Factors on Trial at Korean Air crash inquiry

HONOLULU, Hawaii (AFP) — Indications that cultural factors may have played a role in the Korean Air crash in Guam last year are emerging from the investigation of the disaster which left 228 people dead.

Evidence of confusion in the cockpit of the Boeing 747 and the crew's failure to react to warning signs has confounded investigators after two days of hearing into the disaster here.

The jumbo jet plowed into a hillside some five km (three miles) short of the runway after the plane had descended below minimum altitudes. By the time the captain reacted, the plane was going too fast toward the ground to be saved, investigators say.

They have noted concern that traditional respect for age and seniority in South Korea may prevent junior officers from speaking up in the cockpit.

Captain Lee Jung-taek, chief of flight crew operations for the airline, testifying Wednesday, denied this was so. But he said that in the months after the crash, Korean Air has strengthened its training to give junior officers more authority in the cockpit.

*On the first day of the hearing called by the National Trans-
portation Safety Board Tuesday, the cockpit voice recorder
was played, covering the last 30 minutes of the plane's flight
on August 6, 1997.*

This particular story always stuck with me because I knew
an upcoming Grade 7 Korean boy and his dad who lost their
lives in this crash. I share it because it illustrates so well how
any philosophy can become either a force for great stability,
or conversely cause extreme harm. I also share it to honor
the memory of this young boy, working hard to learn English
and establish himself in Western education. He would now be
in his mid Thirties, and I grieve to think of how his life was
wasted in the cause of Confucianism in the KAL cockpit. We'll
encounter numerous issues related to hierarchy in school environments throughout this book.

Certainly the Guam crash was a particularly tragic example
of ancient Confucianism running headlong into modern technology. However, it is safe to say that business, politics, education, and any aspect of any Confucian society like that of
Korea is affected in both positive and negative ways by the
respect shown elders or those higher in rank. The much more
recent "nut incident" involving Korean Airlines, which, like
most large companies in Korea, was founded and still dominated by a single family. In this situation, the daughter of the
owner of Korean Airlines (himself the son of the founder), a
KAL executive herself, became incensed when on boarding a
Korean Air flight bound for Seoul at JFK in New York when the
pre-flight nuts served to her in First Class were served in a bag
rather than on a plate. The plane was already on the taxiway,
but she demanded that the Captain return the 747 to the gate
to eject the guilty flight attendant from the plane; she eventually required him to kneel before her in public apology. Despite the fact that the Captain was responsible for the plane, he

followed the directions of the owner's daughter and returned to the gate, resulting in delay for a planeload of people and a hefty added expense to KAL. Korean society was outraged at this abuse of power; the offender ended up in jail. Both the airline's owner and his errant daughter made abject public apologies, dressed in black, eyes downcast, replete with deep bows, in apology to the nation. There was little questioning, at least publically, as to why the Captain returned to the gate. It was generally accepted that he had no choice but to return to plane to the gate, even through the offending executive had no official authority over him. His job would have been in jeopardy if he had stood up to the owner's daughter. Korean society is slowly changing – 20 years ago this incident would not have gotten any attention. This time, modern Koreans were incensed over the overbearing authority of the rich and powerful. For an interesting discussion of the tug of war between relationships and hierarchy on one hand, and safety and common sense on the other, read Forbes Asia, December 14, 2014 *"Korean Air 'Nut Rage' Exposes Risk To Safety Of Hereditary Family Rule"* (Donald Kirk).

Within the home this superior/inferior relationship is taken even more seriously. Not only is great respect shown to parents, but to grandparents, older cousins, myriad aunts and uncles, and so on. On certain holidays and anniversaries of deaths special observances are held in the home or at gravesites to honor ancestors. Any older relative – even an older twin – is often addressed by their title, with appropriate honorific endings. In school, as we saw from the story of William above, both boys and girls fall into this environment of expected older/younger relationships, particularly among those of the same gender (and only within the Korean social group). Thus, a simple bow and the use of respectful language by younger students toward their "seniors" are often observed, and are probably harmless. Unfortunately, this is sometimes enjoyed a little too much by the older students who might not want to recognize that they also have a recip-rocal Confucian responsibility to take care of the younger students. If so, this may take the form of "teaching" the younger student(s) how to act respectfully towards them, as we read earlier in the story about William. Often, this is not a pretty scene, and frequently goes on un-noticed under unsuspecting Western eyes. Just as often, Korean parents wring their hands over incidents but just accept it as "the way things are."

This can get ugly. I personally know of situations where a younger high school student would go into BK or KFC far from school and on a weekend, and not recognize an "older brother" from his or her school sitting in back. The older student would get upset towards the younger because he or she did not show proper respect by coming to the table, bowing, and offering to buy lunch. Sometimes situations like this can deteriorate into physical violence. "Borrowing" lunch money is also a sign of inappropriate older/younger "respect" issues. It often takes a knowledgeable and discerning eye on the part of teachers to see this going on. I would recommend that an administrator or trusted counselor check in with Grade 9 Korean boys or girls privately from time to time to see if they are being intimidated by older kids. This is not something that should be tolerated. Older Korean students may argue that teachers are being culturally disrespectful by getting involved in time honored Korean "tradition." When "respect" is enforced by whatever means, we need to call it what it is: Bullying. We'll revisit this later.

On the positive side, respect for others in authority is what makes the city of Seoul, with its 26 million people, a place where one can walk the streets at night without fear. Only in recent years has there been talk of teenage delinquency, and one rape or murder by a single teen makes the front pages and evening news and causes Koreans to search their collective souls for what went wrong with their society. A similar crime in Los Angeles or New York would hardly make it past the police blotter. Thankfully, when a young boy or girl is harassed and bullied to the point of suicide, the country also wrings its collective hands and denounces the bullies and the high stress academic environment that contributes to these tragedies.

Korean And Chinese Names

While we are discussing hierarchy and rank, it is appropriate to discuss Korean and Chinese names, which are at the root of a person's sense of self and his or her place in the family.

Korean names are generally composed of three syllables: a family name followed by a two-syllable given name. (Remember, then, to always ask for "family" and "individual" names rather than "last" or "first" names on school forms!) Sometimes, one of the two syllables of the given name is a generational name shared by all children (particularly boys) of that generation in that extended family. These syllables are pre-determined for generations in the future. Thus, two Shin brothers may be named Shin Byong-kyu and Shin Wang-kyu, sharing the syllable "kyu." Their male cousins on their father's side would most likely also share the "kyu" syllable if the family were keeping with tradition (the second, rather than the final syllable could also be the shared generational syllable, for example Shin Ji-hun and Shin Ji-hu). A married woman keeps her own family name, only changing it informally to "Mrs. Soon-hee Park" (wife of Mr. Park, mother of Tommy and Susie Park) for the benefit of foreigners who may be confused if they are told that her real name is "Kwon, Soon-hee." Other women may choose not to be known by their husband's family name, particularly if they are professionals in their own right. Therefore, the fact that Mr. Park is married to Miss (or Ms. or Mrs.) Kwon does in no way indicate a blended family. Additionally confusing is that within the Korean community parents are often known simply as "Sung-ho's mom" or "Sue-hee's dad." A child's family name always follows the father's, as he or she is considered to be a member of that family. Further making Korean names difficult for Westerners (or maybe easier?) is the fact that there are very few family names, fewer than 250 altogether. The most com-

88

CONFUCIUS AND PIAGET MEET ONCE AGAIN

mon are "Kim" (Kimm, Ghim), "Park" (Pahk, Park, Bak, Bahk, etc.) and Yi (actually "Ee," but usually spelled and pronounced "Lee" outside of Korea). A few others such as "Choi" (Che, Cheh, Chae), "Chung" (Jung, Chong), "Cho," "Shin," "Yoo," and "Han" make up the lion's share of the remainder. All of these names are derived from Chinese characters, although increasingly Koreans are giving their children "pure" Korean names that are not so derived.

A Korean's given name is very personal property, and is not something to be thrown around carelessly. Only children are called by their given names; the author, after working closely with his secretary for more than 18 years, still calls her "Mrs. Woo" (Actually, "Woo" is her husband's family name that she uses only professionally. Outside of the Western school community, she still goes by her original family name of Hwang). Adults are never called by their given names except by older family members or close childhood friends, but even more often called and referred to as "so-and-so's mother."

In public, Koreans are most often called by their professional title or the catchall, "Son-saeng," which literally means "teacher," often with the honorific "nim" added at the end. Thus, a person may be called "Doctor," "Pastor," "Director," "Principal," "Pilot," etc., with or without a family name preceding it. Brothers or sisters (and even friends of the same generation) would call each other "brother" or "sister." Adult graduates of the same high school may call each other "son-bae" or "hubae" depending on whether they are older or younger (or in a class before or after) than the person addressed.

What's the safest thing for a Westerner to do? Simply call children by their given name, and call adults by the Western style "Mr." "Miss," or "Mrs." followed by their family name (When in doubt, use the family name of their children. Don't worry;

you'll be forgiven if you make a mistake!)

Normally, a Korean name can be written in Chinese characters as well as in Hangul (Korean alphabet), each character having a specific meaning. Additionally, when alphabetized, the same name can look much different. So what is the difference between Kim Jun-ho, Ghim Joonho, Kimm Joon Ho, or Gim Jun Hoh? There is none; when the person began to Romanize his name, his parents just arbitrarily chose a particular form and spelling. Written in the Korean script Hangul, it's all the same. The important thing for both the family and the school is to remain consistent so the school doesn't end up with multiple files, under different names, for the same student.

Chinese names follow the same format; Family name, followed by one or two syllable given names, written in Chinese characters, but like Korean, can be written in various spellings using Pinyin (Chinese words written in the Roman alphabet.) The generational name system, while used, is much less strict than in Korea. Chinese tend to be much less formal than Koreans in using titles or names, especially with foreigners.

Often younger Korean and Chinese professionals will assume Western names if they are working with foreigners or travel widely outside of their home country. While they might prefer to use their own names, Chinese names, when Romanized, sometimes end up being somewhat unpronounceable, at least correctly, for uninitiated Westerners. Korean names are much more phonetic, have fewer vowels, and are generally easier to pronounce somewhat accurately by Westerners. While Koreans tend to take names like Jennifer, Hannah, or Sue (or Jason, John, or David) that are often related to literary or Biblical characters, Chinese sometimes really reach out for something unique. I know young Chinese who have named themselves Snow, Ice, Rain, Ocean and Fish, as well as Carol, Vicky, Scott, and Kenneth. I recently heard of a young

Chinese professional who named himself "Sub-Conscious." Hong Kong Chinese tend to lean towards older out-of-date English or literary names, or things completely quirky – for example Magnum or Kinky. Names like Lancelot, Benedict, Wilfred, Watson, or Winston are common. In 2018 the most common "English" name for girls in Hong Kong was "Idrissa" with "Shreya" coming in second. Google "Hong Kong English names" for some interesting articles on the what's and why's of this phenomenon. Western language institute teachers are often tasked with anointing very young children with their first English name. They should resist the temptation to assign a questionable name (or an inside joke among fellow language institute instructors) that may be cute for a five year-old but will be less charming when she is 15 or 25, by which time it's hard to switch. Monikers such as "Mergatroid", "Gaga", "Elvis", and "Bucky" don't wear well over either time or distance.

NOTE: Be sure to emphasize to your high school students to be extremely consistent in spelling and form when registering for external exams or on their college applications. Boston College won't know that Hwang Sue-hee, Suhee Whang, and Susan Hwang are the same person, and more than one student has lost out on an acceptance because of Susan's SAT results didn't end up in Sue-hee's file.

CHAPTER VII: CONFUCIAN COLLECTIVISM AND CONFORMITY

Cultures that value hierarchical relationships often have highly developed characteristics of Collectivism and Conformity. Because in a hierarchy there are strong level-appropriate behavioral norms, people tend to conform to what is expected of them at their given level. Tradition, "appropriate behavior," and appearances are important, bringing to mind the Victorian Period when form and appearances were all-important. This creates an outwardly harmonious environment, although inwardly individuals may harbor resentment or resignation to their lot in life. Individuals also tend to become dependent on those above them in the hierarchy. This is the reciprocal responsibility in Confucianism – you must obey the people above you, but they will take care of you. You can depend on it – and on them. Someday you'll be in that higher position, but until then, you'll be taken care of. To the Western eye, this sometimes results in delayed maturity and a retarded acceptance of adult responsibility. Third, people tend to be obedient rule followers, at least outwardly. As we'll see later, making waves, bucking the system, or standing out is not a positive cultural value. Finally, there is a strong sense of respect for those in authority and for the past. Traditionally, those in positions of power and authority were older people. In Korea today the elderly are very well respected and treated, regardless of formal rank, to a much greater degree than is apparent in China. An elderly person getting on the subway in Seoul would immediately be given a seat, for example; this seldom happens in Shanghai. This respect for older relatives such as grandparents or deceased ancestors, for scholars of the past, for tradition and custom – these are all very highly valued in strong Confucian cultures. Whatever grandfather would have done (or instructed) is most likely the right way to proceed. The old, traditional way has an intrinsic value if it was practiced by ancestors or is espoused by someone in authority (such as a teacher), especially in school or in the family. This, of course, can work against innovation or risk-taking of any kind, whether in school, business, or industry. Similarly (and we will explore this in more detail later) we see that in schools the teacher, as a parent/ authority figure, is very highly respected; thus, the word of the teacher is taken very seriously and is not questioned, at least in front of the teacher. For teachers, this can lead to quiet and obedient students, but it can also lead students to be hesitant to ask questions, to challenge the teachers or any older students, or to think creatively. Students are much more comfortable with the safer "one right answer" than a creative response they developed themselves.

I learned this early in my Korea years through personal experience. It was the early Eighties, and I was moonlighting at a university in Seoul by teaching a TOEFL prep course to adults, most of whom were a good deal older than me, had already finished their graduate studies, and were preparing to go on to further education in the United States. My assigned TOEFL section involved grammar and usage – pulling apart sentences, examining vocabulary, identifying mistakes, and finally, choosing one of four possible answers. Normally

JONATHAN BORDEN

things went fine, and the students, whose knowledge of English grammar rules was much stronger than mine, agreed with my "correct answer." However, the text I was required to teach from was not particularly well written, and about once each lesson there was a question that in my opinion as a native speaker had either two possible answers or no correct answers. Usually, the students were polite and respectful enough to me to let it go and accept that the text (which had been written by the head of the department, and who was my supervisor) was flawed.

Sometimes, however, when there really did not appear to be only one "best" answer, students would still demand one. There were times that I gave in so we could continue and simply said, "Well, we know that A and C are incorrect, and B and D could both be correct. But let's go with B." Pencils quickly circled B. They were much more comfortable with one right answer, even if the teacher wasn't satisfied that it was the only one. On one occasion, I proposed that the word choice "shall" was just as acceptable in the sentence as "will" in a sentence. Susan shall go to the store, or Susan will go to the store? To me, in modern usage, it didn't matter, although I was convinced that at one dim point in English language history there might have been a difference. When I pushed the student as to how he was so sure that I was wrong, he insisted that it was because his middle school English teacher had taught him that there was a difference! I pointed out to him that by this point in his education he had much more English under his belt than his teacher had probably 15 years earlier, but he wasn't dissuaded. The fact that his middle school teacher had told him, even in the face of a native English speaker employed to teach English at the graduate school level, was what mattered. Obviously his respect for authority didn't include me! His, I believe, was an extreme case of respect for the revered teacher of the past, but it was a good lesson to me that I was sometimes up against teachers who may have long since retired, and who had limited facility in English themselves. This episode once again reminded me of the Confucian reliance on both 1) respect for the past and for elders (hierarchy), and 2) the desire for there to be one right answer that everyone can agree on (conformity). Obviously, by creating some waves and disharmony I was not being particularly Confucian.

A telling sequel to this story occurred a year or so after I had begun this moonlighting position. It was very common for foreigners to be employed in this way, even though our visa's stated that we could work only at our sponsoring school. Perhaps the reader can relate to this type of "off visa" work, common in Asia. Many of my co-workers did the same thing, and the hazy illegality of it never crossed our naïve minds. However, one day I was summoned to my school's legal office and was told that I needed to report downtown to the immigration office that afternoon. Thankfully, a school representative went with me. My name was called through the din of this crowded government office, and I went up to the desk where a rather elderly, rotund, and uniformed official sat ensconced, smoking his cigarette. He asked my name, and I told him, to which he replied "Get out of Korea in two days!" Rather shook, I still had the presence of mind (or foolishness) to ask him why. What had I done wrong? This gentleman then completely lost it, now quite believing that I was questioning him, and shouted at me, (now attracting a crowd because the young foreigner was obviously some type of criminal) "Because I say so!!!" Apparently, I had shown him disrespect by asking for a reason why I should leave my job and move my family out of the country in two days! I was much younger than he was, and in no position of authority. He was enjoying his Confucian advantage in both areas. Maybe he expected a carton of American cigarettes or a bottle of Seagrams? In the end, the school was able to somehow smooth things over, and I didn't leave Korea in two days later, but I stopped moonlighting soon after that. It took about twenty years before the demands of that incensed immigration official were finally realized, and I left Korea for Shanghai, without a government order to do so.

Counselors and administrators may run up against this respect for elders, although often it is invisible to the Western eye. Many are the times that I have sat down with parents, working to convince them that such and such a program or university was a better choice for their child than the "famous" one they had chosen. They would seemingly agree, and I thought we had made progress. However, the next day the student would come in and say that they had changed their minds after a phone call to Grandpa in Seoul. Grandpa may have known nothing about Western education, but he did know what conventional wisdom was in Korean education: The Name Brand of the university was much more important than the particular "fit" to the student's needs or talents. Grandpa's decision was final, and the family followed along. It was impossible to buck Grandpa, ill informed though he may have been.

On the other hand, while in Shanghai a Korean Senior whom I had gotten to know well bumped into me one spring morning, and I asked him (as we have a habit of doing to Seniors) what colleges he had been accepted at. He replied that he was accepted at Brandeis College, but that he couldn't go. His grandfather had vetoed the acceptance, because he had "never heard of it." I quickly realized what was going on, and asked him to call his grandfather that evening and tell him that the Honorable Principal would have been very pleased to send his own sons to Brandeis. The boy came back the next day with a smile. "Grandpa told me that if the Honorable Principal says that Brandeis is OK, then it must be!" He did go to Brandeis, and he had a rough four years, for a number of reasons, none of which had to do with its lack of name recognition in Korea. It was just a bad fit for this young man. Sometimes we should just listen to our grandpa instead of our principal.

The desire for Conformity and Harmony are related: if individuals conform to rules, traditions, and appropriate role/status behavior, then they won't make waves – and there will be harmony. Disharmony occurs when something doesn't match or fit as it should – think of musical disharmony caused by one wrong note in a chord which grates on our ears. Fix that one note so that it follows musical rules, and the disharmony disappears and the chord sounds fine. This works in societies and organizations as well – if everyone sticks to their assigned hierarchical role, then things will run smoothly. In order for this to happen, individuals need to subjugate their personal desires, opinions, and needs to those of the group. A well known Korean proverb states "The bamboo bends, the stick breaks." In a storm, bamboo will bend over in the wind, but it will seldom break and usually stand straight and tall the next morning. Its strength lies in its flexibility and strong root system. However, a rigid stick will be broken in the wind, and die. The moral of this proverb is obvious: Individuals, in order to survive in society, must "go along to get along." In any event, don't "Dare to be Different." This is a strong Confucian (and Taoist) value that is deeply ingrained in society. This is in stark contrast to Western values. From their earliest years Western children learn from their parents that following their individual conscience and values should take precedence over bending to the opinions or actions of a peer group. Across Western cultures, almost any adult can finish the sentence they heard so many times as children when asking for something " because everyone else has/does it." Finish this sentence: "Just because everyone else jumped off the bridge, _____?" I'll bet that 95% of readers completed this sentence in the same way. This Western emphasis on individual decision making and standing up against the grain for what one believes is deeply engrained in our psyche; simply following the crowd is not respected. Standing up for what you believe, running against the current, and otherwise making a "statement" however much it goes against the grain, is a positive societal value in the West. Someone who always "goes with the flow" or who "doesn't stand up for what she believes" is considered spineless, or even lacking in character. Conversely, not following along with what "everyone else is doing" is very much a societal negative in Confucian cultures. Of course, conforming is much easier in a homogeneous culture like Korea's, where nearly everyone shares a common language, culture, history, and general physical characteristics.

Conformity is played out in many ways, and the more Confucian a nation is, the higher the expectation there is to conform to societal rules. There is an understood "right way" to do things, and etiquette can be both formal and rigid. While this is loosening up a good deal among younger Korean parents (and in China), it is still very important "back in grandma's village." This raises a particular challenge for parents who have spent a number of years living in more permissive, informal Western societies. Re-entry to their home country can be a real challenge as they face enormous pressure to revert to narrower societal rules while also learning how those rules have changed during the time they have been away. Later we'll talk about how this affects returnee students, after they leave our classrooms and go on to their home country's universities or military.

Following along this Collective path, a proverb common in some form in more than one Asian culture states "The nail that sticks up gets hammered down." The message is that one should conform to societal norms and not stick out as an individual. Standing up for one's personal beliefs in the face of societal backlash, being the martyr for a cause, or simply being different all have negative connotations and values in a Confucian society. Individuality has a much lower cultural value than in the west. Those who "stick up" often get hammered down, either by their peers or by the government. The contemporary response of the Mainland Chinese government towards dissidents or those perceived to be too "different" is an example of this high value placed on conformity. From early childhood people are taught to contribute to a harmonious society. Don't "upset the social order" by being different.

This brings us to the application of Geert Hofstede's six dimensions of culture, one of which is Individualism/Collectivism, in turn associated with an emphasis on Conformity. According to Hofstede's model, every culture can be measured from high to low in this dimension, which indicates how an individual in a given culture views him or herself – as a distinct, unique, and independent individual (viewed primarily through the lens of "I") or more primarily as a member of one or more distinctive groups (viewed through the lens of "We"). Obviously, every person on the planet sees him or herself to some degree in both of these ways, but culture determines to what extent either of these perceptions is dominant, and moreover forms the basis for decision-making and behavior. While a Westerner would define him or herself in terms of personal characteristics (nationality, religion, physical characteristics, interests, talents) a person from an Eastern nation would more likely define his or her own identity in terms of what groups he or she belongs to (church, school, club, university attended, etc., as these can also help to define status within the society. Viewing nations comparatively, according to Hofstede European or European background nations (USA, Australia, UK, Canada, New Zealand, Italy, Belgium, Denmark, France, Sweden, Ireland and other European cultures) consistently rank at the extreme high end on the Individualism scale. In contrast, the Collective end of the scale is topped by (in order) Guatemala, Ecuador, Panama, Venezuela, Colombia, Pakistan, Indonesia, Costa Rica, China, Peru, Taiwan, South Korea, El Salvador, Thailand, and Singapore. I will leave it to those more familiar with northern South American/Central American cultures to explain their extreme level of collectivism, but in our context we quickly see that among the very top ranked countries in this dimension are China, Taiwan, South Korea, Thailand, and Singapore. (ref http://

americasdiversityleader.com/culture.php#national)

This phenomenon can be seen both "above the water" and "under the water" in our cultural iceberg. I was privileged to live in Seoul during the 2002 World Cup soccer matches. Korea was immensely proud to be chosen to co-host (along with Japan) the first World Cup held outside Europe and the Americas, yet another example of South Korea joining the ranks of advanced nations (following, most notably, South Korea's hosting of the 1988 Summer Olympics). The nation readied itself by building huge stadiums around the country, and huge video screens were put up in public areas across the nation, most notably in City Hall Plaza in downtown Seoul. It is estimated that 6.5 million people gathered in various outdoor spaces around the nation to watch a final game against Germany for 4th place. The most remarkable thing, however, was the emergence of the "Red Devil" phenomenon, where without any recognizable organization or plan everyone began wearing red T-shirts to these gatherings. Similarly, the slogan "Be the Reds" began to be on everyone's lips (and T-shirts). This sudden adoption of the color red to celebrate the home team as it advanced to the semi-finals was spontaneous – unannounced, unplanned, unsponsored by any group. Collectively, the nation turned red. There literally was not a red T-shirt to be found in any of the nation's immense markets that wasn't proudly covering someone's torso. It's what "everyone" was doing to support their team, and their nation. (http://www.korea.net/AboutKorea/Sports/2002-FIFA-World-Cup-Korea-Japan). Yes, this foreigner got caught up in the excitement, and somewhere has tucked away a bright red "Be the Reds" T-shirt, still in it's plastic package.

Korea also reacts collectively during times of trouble. During the international financial crisis in 1997 (called by Koreans "IMF" after the International Monetary Fund, which bailed the Korean economy out after years of financial risk-taking and resultant sudden collapse) lines of citizens were seen lining up at banks to donate their gold jewelry to the nation so that it could be used to pay off the nation's debts. It is said that so much gold was collected so quickly that it temporarily drove down the world gold price. Even more tragically was the national outcry of self-criticism and doubt when in 2014 a passenger and freight ferry, the Sewol, foundered and sank on the overnight run between the mainland and the tourist island of Jeju, drowning 294 passengers and crew, with ten missing. The majority of the victims were students on a school excursion on the way to Jeju Island. Although the captain of the ship and many of the crew were convicted and jailed (many left the ship without assisting those trying to escape, and passengers were repeatedly told by PA to remain in place below decks, even while the crew was abandoning ship) the real causes of the sinking were relationship based corruption and carelessness. Illegally issued design permits, lack of oversight during loading, malfeasance on the part of the ship operators in maintaining correct weight balance, poor maintenance even in light of a previous captain's warnings, lack of emergency training for crew members, and poor supervision on the bridge during the time of the accident all echoed of earlier times when Korea was advancing economically at an amazing pace and safety concerns took second rank to economic advancement or advantage, with corruption and profits being the repeated cause of disasters leading to horrific bridge and department store collapses – all traced to negligence and corruption resulting from tangles of relationships, greed, and hierarchy. When the Sewon sank, then, although individual responsibility was placed on the captain and crew, the nation cried out in anger and frustration that once again their nation and their society had failed to live up to its own standards and expectations. The fact that so many of the victims were high schoolers – the future of the nation – made the disaster all the more a matter of collective national grief and shame.

As noted above, people from collective cultures often identify themselves as members of various groups rather than by personal characteristics; most adults belong to a variety of formal and informal clubs or organizations. Whether it be a political party, a church, a men's club, a school, an alumni group, or even the inevitable "Seventh Grade Advanced Math Students Mothers' Club" people feel a much closer identification, sense of belonging, and mutual support to their chosen or assigned groups than most Westerners would. This is why a parent might show up alone insisting that he or she represents "all the other mothers." In fact, there may have been a pre-meeting to work out strategy and identify their representative, be it the Alpha mom or the mom with the best English or most experience in Western settings. You may often hear a parent talking about when their child "joined" the school. There is more here, I suspect, than just inaccurate word choice. Rather, they are thinking of their child becoming part of an organization. Where a Western parent may send their child to "attend" a school, they don't think of it as "joining" a group whose members share collective responsibility for each other. When one member commits some kind of misdeed, the entire group feels it – therefore peer pressure to not shame the group can be a positive force. When a crime is reported in the Korean press, almost always immediately after the name of the accused, is stated "who works for Company Y" or "who attends School Z." (Interestingly, and in a nod towards hierarchy, most often their age is also listed. Even the ages of game show contestants are sometimes noted beside their names on the television screen.) On the other hand, when the group is heading in the wrong direction, it is very difficult for an individual to resist; again, as noted above to stand up against the group is not a positive social value. On a much larger scale of collectivism, extreme nationalism, as we saw from the World Cup, is also a part of this collective view of society.

❋ ❋ ❋

Mainland China expresses collectivism in a slightly different way, and to a somewhat lesser degree. During the Cultural Revolution Mao used this collective spirit to great advantage, inciting perhaps the largest mass political movement in history bent on destruction of "The Four Olds": Old Customs, Old Culture, Old Habits, and Old Ideas. By enlisting millions of China's youth, releasing them from school to "practice revolution," as well as sending some 16 million educated young people from the cities to work on farms in the countryside, Mao brilliantly institutionalized what had been Confucian collective thought and bent it to his own political ends while ironically urging youth to tear down the remnants of Confucianism. Today's China still exhibits some of the same characteristics, although to a much lesser degree. Individual choice within the boundaries of the law is more acceptable. Nationalism is less tied to any ethnic or cultural pride, although certainly that is an important part of the Chinese psyche. However, government sponsored nationalism is very much apparent. Some of the more recent attempts at Chinese territorial expansion at sea is at least in part an attempt to raise a sense of Chinese greatness and nationalism, as China continues to work to shake off a sense of humiliation and shame from the century-long colonial period discussed earlier. Those living in Mainland China during the period that this book was written (circa 2020) were accustomed to hearing from Beijing about cleaning up corruption within the government and within the Communist Party. In addition, there were related calls for "party discipline." Decried by the Western press, the message from the government was to follow the rules and conform for the good of society. Don't dissent. Don't make waves. Don't be the nail that gets hammered down. This sounds suspiciously Confucian, although I doubt that Mao and his successors would label it such. As I write this in March of 2020, the coronavirus is sweeping the globe. China was the source of the virus, and was therefore the first to respond. Entire cities (notably Wuhan in Hubei Province) were put on lockdown. Hospitals were built in less than two weeks. The government issues orders to control the spread of the virus, and the people complied. How different the public response was in Western countries, with predictable consequences.

* * *

The differences between Individualistic/Independent and Collective/ Interdependent cultures go beyond a simple desire to be alone or be with a group, however. In Individualistic cultures there is a strong preference for freedom of individual actions vs. the preference for collective actions found in Collective cultures. There is a desire for individual distinctiveness and uniqueness vs. a preference for the individual blending harmoniously with whatever group he or she finds himself in. Additionally, Individualistic cultures put more emphasis on an individual's achieved status and rank, rather than on assigned or inherited rank. In a Western society a business owner automatically turning over the family business to one of his sons or daughters would usually be looked down upon and resented by non-family employees who have worked hard to advance within the organization. On the other hand, hereditary leadership of a company in a collective society is both expected and accepted. (Note the earlier discussion of the KAL "nut rage" incident.) Finally (and this shines light on major differences in criminal and civil justice systems) in Western legal systems there is a belief in the enforcement of universal rules (laws) in every situation: Equal Justice Under Law. However, in collective societies legal decisions are made much more on a situational basis. Who is involved? What were the circumstances? How might others be affected by the verdict? Where in a Western setting an accused may "get off on a technicality" because the legal procedures were not followed strictly, in an Eastern court the accused would most likely be found guilty, because despite any legal mistakes it was simply obvious that the person was guilty. The collective good of the society to rid the streets of crime outweighs the rights of the individual to a completely fair trial; the possibility that an innocent person might go to jail due to some mistake by the police or the judicial system is less important than being sure criminals are locked up. The interests of society take precedence over the interests of the individual.

A tragic example of how responsibility is assigned in Collective or Individualistic cultures is related in Nesbitt's The Geography of Thought: How Asians and Westerners Think Differently, referenced earlier. Nesbitt tell of how in 1991 in the earlier days of Asians populating U. S. college campuses, a Chinese student at the University of Iowa lost an academic award and also a subsequent appeal. In response he shot his advisor, the appeals official, and several students before finally killing himself. Note that this was in 1991, before this type of horrific incident was more common on U.S. college campuses. What is interesting to note in this case is the difference in how the University of Iowa (individualistic) press, and the Chinese (collective) press assigned responsibility to the student's actions. The U of I campus paper explained that the student had a "very bad temper," a "sinister edge to his character," had a "personal belief in guns being a way to redress grievances," was a "darkly disturbed man," and had "psychological problems." Despite the questionable assumptions about the student (really – a Chinese student in 1991 believing guns were the way to solve problems?), we note that all descriptions are centered on the individual. He had problems; it was his fault. Most Westerners would agree that while there may have been some negative external forces at work, the young man was the cause, or the victim, of his own personal problems. The Chinese press approached this tragedy from a much different perspective, as we might assume. It reported that the student "did not get along with his advisor," that he had a "rivalry with a slain student," that he felt "isolated from the

Chinese community," that he was a "victim of Chinese 'Top Student' educational policy. Finally, it stated that the crime was the fault of the "availability of guns in American society." Regardless of the validity of these claims, note that in each case, the Chinese explanation centered on the student's actions as a reaction to negative outside relationships or forces. Three of these explanations deal with poor relationships, and two with societal issues. None ascribe the responsibility to the individual. Taking a somewhat larger view, we should always be aware when facing a cultural issue that we may be approaching it with a completely different set of assumptions than our antagonist – the danger is in not recognizing that. We can quickly descend into assuming ill intent, when in fact our underlying assumptions are 180 degrees apart. We are sometimes flying blind into conflict and don't even realize it, with each side making assumptions of the motives of the other that are completely inaccurate.

In summary, we see that Confucianism is a much wider and deeper stream than simply a 2500-year-old political philosophy. Through its emphasis on the themes of hierarchy and collectivism, and harmony and conformity, it permeates the very bones of a number of East Asian societies, from the political system and legal systems to individual decision-making. As we have seen, the hierarchy also demands a society built on respect for those older, wiser, or who came before (remember the King/Subject, Father/Son relationships). We remember that one element of Confucius' ideal curriculum included ritual. The result of this is a tendency towards conservatism across society, and following the acceptable "right way" of doing things. In all these ways, we will soon see that it also impacts the structure and philosophy of educational systems, and thus many of the children and parents we see each day.

Before we go any further along this line, however, we need to again beware of painting with too broad a brush. We must differentiate between various modern nations that have been impacted by Confucianism, each of which interprets Confucian thought in slightly different ways, and to greatly different degrees. For a number of historical reasons, South Korea is today quite arguably the most orthodox Confucian nation on earth – certainly North Korean society, wrapped up as it is in the cult leadership of the Kim family as well as the very strict hierarchical party and government system, and complete lack of tolerance of dissent or anything less than wholehearted acceptance and enthusiastic worship of the current regime, is strongly influenced by Confucian thought, although one would wonder if the North Korean regime would agree with that label. However, as North Korea remains such an enigma to the outside, and as we have very few North Korean students in our Western international schools, I am going to leave the Democratic Peoples' Republic of Korea out of the discussion. Perhaps (hopefully) in some future years the North will be open enough so that the influence of Confucianism on North Korean society would make a fascinating study, as will the thoughts and actions of North Korean students in our Piagetian classrooms.

The influence of Confucianism on Asian cultures, and thus on their educational philosophies and systems. What historical explanations might there be for these differences from nation to nation?

As mentioned earlier, South Korea is arguably the most Confucian culture in the world presently. The diluting factor would be decades of Western influence, and a strong Christian element. Confucianism is not a religion in Korea, but a social structure. Few Koreans would identify themselves as Confucianists, but the influence permeates every aspect of the society.

Below South Korea in our "collectivism hierarchy" comes Japan and Taiwan. Japan's Confucianism is evident in the strong hierarchical social structure and on the pervasive conformity. Spiritually, it has been influenced by Shintoism and Buddhism. Taiwan is still quite strongly affected by Confucianism, but Taoism also has a strong influence in thinking and society.

Mainland China would come next, with Confucianism evident in social structures, but greatly diminished by decades of Maoism and Communism, especially after it was specifically attacked during the Cultural Revolution (roughly 1965 to 1975). China is very diverse culturally, so the influence of any ideology can vary greatly with location.

Hong Kong and Singapore fall below Mainland China. Hong Kong is culturally a Chinese city (and considered a part of mainland China by Beijing). However, more than 100 years of British colonialism made its mark. Taoism is also strong in these cities.

Finally, overseas Asian immigrant populations would still exhibit many Confucian characteristics, with each subsequent generation becoming less influenced by traditional Confucianism.

I owe much of my understanding of these differences to a former colleague and friend, Dr. Wang Suyi. Dr. Wang is a native of Taiwan, brought up in the Taiwanese educational system. As an adult, she moved to Korea, where she lived for ten years, married a Korean gentleman, and taught at the prestigious Ewha Women's University in Seoul. Fluent in Korean, she then taught and developed Chinese language programs in international schools in Beijing and Shanghai for over ten years, and as of this writing is leading a school in Hong Kong. Having lived in three of the major Confucian cultures, and been involved in the educational systems of each, Suyi is uniquely positioned as an expert in comparative East Asian education.

Suyi explained to me how and why South Korea is at the center of Confucianism today, and is undoubtedly the most conservative in the way in which it applies Confucian principles to its societal structures, from the government to the family, from the business world to education.

Confucius lived in China about 500BC. His influence was felt throughout China and greatly influenced Chinese thought and culture over the next 2100 years to various degrees. It achieved its height in China during the Ming Dynasty (1368-1644) which is often described by historians as "one of the greatest eras of orderly government and social stability in human history." (note the emphasis on stability and harmony). Due to Ming political and cultural domination of surrounding East Asian kingdoms, Confucianism spread eastward through the Korean peninsula and then into Japan. For 250 years this coincided with the era of the Korean Joseon (Chosun) Dynasty, which ruled from 1392 to 1897. Under Ming influence, Joseon readily accepted Ming/Confucian social structures and teachings. However, in 1644 the Chinese Mings were conquered by the non-Chinese (Manchu) Qing Dynasty (1644-1912), which had no such Confucian heritage and was generally quite liberal socially, in sharp contrast to Confucianism's conservatism. Thus, Confucianism fell from favor in China under the Qings. At the same time that the Manchus moved out of central Asia into China, they also threatened the Korean peninsula, resulting eventually in a period of 250 years of Korean isolationism, precipitating the proverbial Hermit Kingdom. Thus, while China liberalized and slowly moved away from orthodox Confucianism, Korea intensified its conservative Confucianism in a closed off, isolated country that put great importance on tradition and conservatism while rejecting more liberal foreign ideas. Today we see the result of that pressure-cooked Confucianism in Korea; even 120 years after the fall of the Joseon Dynasty, after 40 years of Japanese colonialism (with its own Confucian underpinnings), and now after nearly 70 years of Western cultural influence and exploding Christianity, Confucianism is still very much alive and well in Korea. While few Koreans today would describe themselves as Confucianists, the culture and society very much operates on Confucian beliefs and tradition. We can see evidence of that in our classrooms every day.

My thanks go to Dr. Wang for this explanation of why South Korea is still so influenced by Confucianism.

Time To Think . . .

What do you know about the backgrounds of the parents of your students? Try to imagine the Korea or China in which they grew up. How might those experiences influence the way in which they raise their children? How might they influence the educational expectations and dreams they have for their children?

To what degree are you influenced by the era during which your parents were growing up? How has their childhood and subsequent parenting molded who you have become?

Do you see evidence of hierarchy do you see in your classroom? If so, what does it look like? How does it influence your class in positive ways? Negative?

Do you see evidence of hierarchy among your students' parents? What does it look like? How might it be positive or negative?

How much do your ethnic Korean and Chinese students know about the history of their nations and cultures? How might you appropriately work this into your curriculum?

Learn more about the histories and cultures of these fascinating countries. Your students will appreciate it, and through it you will come to appreciate them more, as well. A reading list is provided at the end of this book.

CHAPTER VIII: CONFUCIAN RELATIONSHIPS

Maintaining Harmony and Balance

Inherent in maintaining harmony and stability in a collective society is the importance of building and maintaining harmonious, mutually beneficial relationships. Complementing this emphasis on harmony is the recognition that conflicting opposites balance each other and in themselves create a harmonious relationship. That these concepts are well represented by the flag of the Republic of Korea (above) is no accident. The circle in the center represents harmony and unity. Movement and fluidity are seen in the "um/yang" ("yin/yang" in Chinese) circle. Within this circle the two halves symbolize opposing but synergetic opposites (male/female, good/evil, life/death, etc.) Thus, the unity of life and the universe is complete and is created by balanced opposites. Each defines the other. The four sets of corner bars seen in the Korean flag, called kwae, further support this idea of opposites, representing heaven/south; earth/north; sun/east; and moon/west. Much of the philosophy behind these symbols comes originally from Chinese Taoist, although Korea otherwise is not at all what one would consider a Taoist culture.

Because Korean thought, and that of more traditional-thinking areas of Chinese influence (Taiwan, Hong Kong, and culturally Chinese Singapore) are so imbued with this basic idea of balancing opposites, situations that demand shades of gray, moderation, and relativity are difficult to understand and even communicate in the Korean language. Ideas like "biculturalism" or "mixed race" are anathema, either not understood or simply considered not "pure." Korean society has been mono-cultural and conservative for so long, with one traditional "right" way to do things that anything from outside or which may be different is seen as a threat. It is a testament to Korean practicality that despite these values, the nation has changed so dramatically in so many ways in the past seventy years, although not without tremendous social cost. As a result of the high value placed on doing things the "Korean way," diversity and differences are often considered to be negative. Homogeneity and conformity are valued; individuality and free thinking have negative value. The Korean emphasis on the past, on respect for authority and learning, on loyalty to the family or nation, and on conformity to the standards set by the group have worked against creativity and free thinking. These characteristics also place tremendous pressures on ethnic Koreans living outside of Korea. While conformity is important, they face the question of with whom they should conform — those of the nation in which they live? Those in the international community/ international school? Fellow Koreans? Unless they live in a Korean community overseas, they may find themselves non-conformists in their new environment. Conforming to the values of their new home, however, may imply disloyalty or dissatisfaction with the older Korean way and may make later re-entry to Korea very difficult, not to mention cause conflict with more traditional parents and grandparents. Conversely, many overseas Koreans express relief that they enjoy a meas-ure of social freedom (and release from domination from parents and in-laws) that they could never experience back home. Many are the expat Korean moms and wives who don't look forward to going back to Korea with its more rigid rules and extended family responsibilities. This "returning mom" phenomenon will be discussed further in later chapters.

This emphasis on cultural conformity is less evident in China, which is home to no less than 52 recognized ethnic minorities (including Korean).   Although the dominant Han culture is more or less the "official" ethnic group, and comprises roughly 90% of Mainland Chinese, there is much greater toleration of those who are different than one would find in Korea or Japan, which are basically monocultural. Most ethnic groups have their own dialects, in many cases unintelligible to others. Although Mandarin is the official and common national lan-guage, family and street language is often local. Even individ-ual cities may have their own dialects; Shanghainese is widely spoken alongside Mandarin in the Shanghai metropolitan area – but nowhere else in China. Therefore, the emphasis on con-formity looks different in China than in Korea – whereas in Korea is it cultural, with a nationalistic undertone, in China it is primarily generated by the government and the primacy and policies of the Communist Party. As millennia of Chinese leaders have feared, left to itself the immense geographic area currently called "China" could slowly fall apart. The government works hard to ensure that there are more advantages than disadvantages to remaining part of a united China for those 52 ethnic minorities on the fringes of the country. Those minorities large enough to resist national integration currently face "strong encouragement" to conform; the reader is invited to investigate groups centered around the cities of Urumqi and Lhasa. As the situation is fluid as I write, I'll leave it to the reader to do his or her own up to date research on non-Chinese government websites....

This emphasis on conformity is closely linked to the value placed on keeping harmony – in the family, in the workplace, in the society and nation. Once again, this is more pronounced in Korea than in China, but certainly it is valued in China as well. Let's look at how this ideal of maintaining harmony plays out in every day social interactions.

Certainly the primary expression of this societal emphasis on conformity is the real hesitancy among people to openly disagree with one another, especially within a social group, which would upset good feelings and harmony. A person who disagrees with someone he considers his "senior" quite often just says nothing (a phenomenon not unknown in the West!). Often the superior may express his or her opinion and everyone compliantly nods their heads, no individual being willing to speak up. One would also not say things that may make others feel bad, or refuse to go along with the group activity. As group drinking among men is very common, and getting drunk has been in the past an expected result of an evening out with co-workers, all too often a person who really doesn't want to join in goes along due to strong peer pressure. We are not talking about teenagers or college students, but about adult professionals. To say, "Just a coke, please" and not share the common and all too frequently filled cup as it is passed around is to upset the harmony and sense of "group-ness."

This tendency to keep things on an even keel also often results in people keeping bad news from one another until the last possible moment. This can wreak havoc with international Asian families, in which dad or mom might not be told by their employer until late in the game that they are being transferred to another country. The employee might in turn keep it from their spouse for a while. Together they may then keep the news from the children until the very last minute so that their sadness at leaving friends won't upset their studies. Many are the students who say "good-bye" to their friends before a short school break only to learn the next day that they are moving to another continent within the week, without benefit of important rites of closure and proper Good-bye's being said. Sadness, unaddressed, can quickly become anger – not a good way to begin in the new home and country. Research into life changes repeatedly indicates that for a good beginning to take place in a new environment, it is imperative that the ending goes well in the old one. Today, with students so connected digitally, this is not as bad as in the past, but it can still be wrenching. I know personally of children who were told at winter break that the family was going to Japan for skiing. After arriving in the airport outside Tokyo, however, the story changed. "Actually, we are going to the U.S., where dad had already accepted a job," the kids were told. In another case, heading to the cafeteria late for lunch one day I bumped into a lost-looking Chinese parent and asked if I could help her. It eventually came out that she had come to school to pick up her son, to take him to the Shanghai airport to meet his dad and fly out to the U.S., never to return. The boy had no idea of this plan, but his suitcase was all packed and in the car in the school driveway. Fortunately, I was able to convince the mom that such a sudden move would be bad for their son, bad for their relationship with their son, and bad for the school climate ("Where did Tommy go? He said he'd meet me after lunch.") The boy did not go to the U.S. with dad that afternoon, and in fact had another very successful four years of leadership and academics at our school. When I later asked the parents why the boy knew nothing of this plan, the mom indicated that the parents didn't want to upset him and thus affect his grades before he left. I can report that years later the mom was gracious enough to thank me for talking her out of her plan. But suppose I hadn't gone to lunch late that day? How much did that chance encounter with his mom change this boy's life? I was shocked at the entire scenario, but was glad I exercised enough cultural awareness in the moment to recognize what was going on and stop what could have been a really tragic situation for everyone.

The net result of this emphasis on harmony is cultures in which bad news is often covered up or ignored until too late; nations of people often wearing masks. Koreans often criticize foreigners for being too open with emotions, be it happiness or anger. Korean girls are taught to cover their mouths when they laugh. Loud laughter is frowned upon; similarly anger is held in check. Koreans are often known to show expressionless faces in public, this has caused cultural difficulties in places where they come into contact with more emotive cultures; it has been the source of conflict in Los Angeles between Korean neighborhood store owners and their African-American clientele, for example, when their blank faces can be perceived as haughty or superior. Once again, this hesitancy to show emotions or create disharmony is evident in China as well, but less so than in Korea, particularly in more cosmopolitan cities. The delay in reporting and outbreak of CV-19 in the Chinese city Wuhan early in January of 2020 (definitely in the category of "bad news") quite possibly contributed to it becoming a global pandemic, still raging as of this writing in September of 2020. Conversely, emotions are very evident at funerals, when wailing, crying, and moaning are expected. Traditionally, a rich family may even have hired paid "wailers" to cry in their place.

Related to this tendency to contain emotion is the necessity to maintain dignity and save "face," both one's own and that of others. Seldom does one want to make another look bad; even more important is the desire to never bring any kind of shame on one's family. Public apologies are rare; it is expected that everyone "understands" that one did something wrong and is of course sorry - that in itself is considered shame and apology enough. For the same reason, Koreans will not normally apologize for sneezing or coughing, or acknowledge that someone else did. Why bring attention to yourself after you sneeze by apologizing? And why shame someone else by acknowledging their sneeze with a "Bless you"? Just pretend it didn't happen and move on.

This reluctance to disagree/maintain harmony should be remembered when working with parents; seeming agreement by them does not necessarily mean compliance. You may never know what Mrs. Kim is really thinking, despite the fact that she smiles, nods, and says, "Yes, yes." This has caused countless occasions of cultural misunderstanding in business situations. A team comes from Detroit to Seoul or Shanghai to hammer out a new joint venture agreement with new partners. Three days of discussion go well; the Korean or Chinese side seems to agree easily to everything. Everyone enjoys a lavish restaurant dinner that goes into the wee hours to seal the deal. The western side flies back to Detroit, only to find in their in-boxes emails from their new "partners" requesting clarification on certain points, and re-opening the discussions on some others. "Foul!" cry the Americans! "These Koreans are reneging on our agreement! Can we really trust these Chinese?" In reality, the three days of smiles and nods from the Asians indicated "We hear you" much more than "We agree to your terms." Imagine this scenario on a nation-to-nation level – self-confident Western leaders who pride themselves on their business acumen in hammering out multi-national trade deals should listen carefully to their more culturally minded advisors. "Yes" does not always mean "Yes." This is not an example of any kind of double-talk, just a matter of a difference in communication styles. More on this later.

An important aspect of maintaining harmony is the recognition of the hierarchical system of social relationships discussed earlier. As long as each individual knows his or her place, stays in that place, and pays proper respect to those above, harmony results. When a person upsets the status quo by not recognizing proper etiquette, by humiliating another, or by causing unnecessary conflict, relationships become unbalanced and disharmony results. Individuals and cultures suffer as a result. A very important aspect of maintaining harmony is the appropriate use of names and titles, as discussed earlier.

CHAPTER IX: CONFUCIAN RELATIONSHIPS - HOME AND FAMILY

If you ask Westerners what they would consider the basic building block of society, most would respond "the individual." The response of many in Confucian societies, rather, is "the family." The importance of the family, both nuclear and extended, cannot be underestimated in Confucian societies such as Korea and China. One's allegiance is first to the family; it is no accident of language that in Confucian societies the family name comes before the given name. When a person gives his name, he or she is first identifying from what family he or she comes (traceable back to a particular village and a particular ancestor over many hundreds of years through genealogies still in print); the next two syllables of the name are the generational (in Korea) and individual names. Quite literally, family comes first.

It is important to remember that "family" very often means the extended family of grandparents, uncles and aunts, and cousins, particularly on the paternal side. It may seem harsh and cruel to a Westerner that Asian parents might leave a child behind with relatives in China or Korea during an overseas move; this seems perfectly logical and normal to them. The parting will of course hurt, but at least the child is with family. As is the case in many areas of life, this focus on the family, and on bloodlines, is more intense in Asia than elsewhere. In Korea, a childless brother often becomes the legal and practical parent of a child of another brother who has more than his share of sons. The child may never know that "father" is really a biological "uncle"; on the other hand, it is not that important — family is family. Although adoptions are traditionally uncommon among Koreans (except within a family), when they do happen they are occasions for sadness and pity. More often than not, the child is never told that he or she is adopted. To do so would make the child feel that he or she has no family, as they in fact are not part of the adoptive family's bloodline. Koreans have a very difficult time understanding, and are truly in awe of Western families, who can adopt a child as their own and love this child who looks so different and does not share a bloodline like "one of the family." This prejudice is slowly changing among younger families as governments encourage domestic adoptions from within Korea and China. However, since the end of the Korean War in 1953, more than 200,000 Korean orphans or abandoned children have been sent overseas for adoption, about four-fifths to the United States.

Chinese society has also traditionally spurned adoption, as evidenced by the fact that between 1999 and 2016 almost 270,000 Mainland Chinese children, most aged 1 and 2, were adopted internationally – about one-third of them to the United States.

https://internationaladoption.org/6-statistics-china-international-adoption/   The importance of having a biological son to carry on the family name, support parents in their old age, and perform ancestor veneration ceremonies, coupled with poverty and a rapidly rising standard of living, often caused girls or children with any kind of disability or mal-formation to be abandoned. As in Korea, boys may be adopted within a family to provide a son where needed. The Chinese one-child policy, instituted in 1979, only intensified the social need for a pregnancy to result in a son. Although sex identification before birth is against the law in China, ways are found among those who care and can afford it to ensure that a boy resulted from a pregnancy – or that a previously born girl disappeared. Although the policy is no longer in effect, its influence remains strong – two generations of Chinese have been only children, and it only seems natural that they should give birth to only one. In the past abandoned girls flooded the international adoption flow from China. However, in recent years this preference for boys has diminished to a great extent, although for many impoverished families the cost and responsibility of raising a child with special medical or developmental needs still leads to abandonment and absorption by the Chinese government social services or private group homes. Most adoptable Chinese children are now those with some kind of medical issue, sometimes minor (an extra toe, for example) or major (heart problems, blindness, major skeletal issues, or developmental challenges). Beth Smith, China Director of Adoption Services for Holt International, one of the oldest and most respected international adoption agencies states, "In truth, most of the children now living in China's social welfare system have special medical or developmental conditions, or are older. And as families are often surprised to learn, many of them are also boys." http://holtinternational.org/blog/wp-content/uploads/2012/06/Changing-Face-of-China-Adoption1.pdf. Once again, although we see a traditional preference for boys and reluctance to adopt, in China, it is nowhere near as pronounced as in more Confucian Korea.

The traditional emphasis on large families with lots of children (males) to do the farm work, contribute to the family's wealth, and carry on the family name (note the emphasis on ancestors) has been overcome by the response to population pressures at the national levels. In Korea, an aggressive family planning program in the 1970's and 1980's and constant admonitions to have only two children was very successful, and supported the economic development of Korea during this period. A country with limited land and even more limited natural resources needed people – but also needed to be able to feed itself. Large numbers of unemployed would not have been socially healthy. Today, almost two generations into this movement, the nation is seeing a graying population and an upside down demographic pyramid, with not enough young people to support a now healthy elder class. However, emphasis on family and bloodlines has remained strong. Japan and China also face graying populations with a much smaller bottom to the pyramid.

Western and Eastern cultures tend to approach the goals of parenthood and child rearing very differently. In Western societies, the assumed goals of parenthood is to eventually, over the course of 18 or so years raise a psychologically and financially independent child, who can, after a few years of adjustment, fly on their own. Western psychologists tell us that one of the goals of adolescence, in fact, is to break away from parents and family and become "one's own person" with an identity separate from that of the family. This is completely opposite to Confucian thinking, where the child never really psychologically or financially becomes independent, even after decades of reaching adulthood or a possible move half way around the world. Due to intense family bonds, family support and nurture extends far beyond childhood. Financially an adult child is still considered part of the family economic unit. Adult children are expected to continue to maintain close relationships with other family members and care in some way for aging parents. Older parents may buy an apartment and car for their adult son and family who are returning "home" from overseas; after all, the apartment really doesn't belong to the son, but to the extended family; it's a family investment, and the returning adult child and his or her children are part of the family, deserving the financial support of the family even as they are expected to contribute to it. Even when going off to another city to college in Korea, it is common for a young person to live with a relative, and it is not uncommon for the mother of an Asian college or boarding school student studying overseas to rent an apartment nearby so that the student can be taken care of – making food, washing clothes, providing spending money. Young women in particular are protected and are often expected to live at home during and after college until marriage. Today, choice of a mate is wider than ever, but still about half of all marriages in Korea are partly arranged by parents who set up "meetings" between their adult child and an eligible (and acceptable) partner from the family of a parental friend or co-worker. Normally young people are given "veto" over these attempts by parents to find a good mate, although the pressure can be high when there are younger siblings waiting for an older brother or sister (uncommon in "one child" China) to get married so they can marry in turn. Any unmarried woman in China over the age of 27 is known as a "sheng nu" or "leftover woman." However, men don't have it very easy, either. It is very difficult in Shanghai, for example, for a young man to find a wife unless he first owns his own apartment – a considerable financial burden. After marriage, things are much more equal in China than in Korea for both of the pair. It must be understood that a young person (a young woman, in more traditional Korea) is not just marrying a young man; she is marrying into a new family. She becomes a member of her husband's extended family, and the connection between her family and his family is now cemented and may have future financial or other benefits for both families (similar to European royal matches of the past). It is still very common to read in Korean newspapers that a rich young woman from family X with a tradition of service in government or politics has been married to an even richer young man whose family Y is deeply involved with business or high finance. Not only are the individuals married legally; the families are married socially, and everyone benefits, or may soon do so. For an interesting modern twist on this, visit the weekend afternoon Shanghai marriage market at Peoples' Square Park, where many hundreds of parents meet to compare their eligible sons' and daughters' bio's and resumes to see if there might be a match with another older couple doing the same. Young people – the object of their search – keep clear of this informal but weekly gathering, or hide elsewhere in the huge park (although able to be summoned by cell phone) as desperate parents and grandparents work to speed up the process of marrying off their sons and daughters. Google "Shanghai Marriage Market" or go to http://travel.cnn.com/shanghai/play/sausage-fest-2020-future-shanghai-marriage-market-086672/

After marriage, a young Korean woman joins her husband's family, possibly moving in with parents-in-law especially if the husband is an oldest son. Should the new couple need a car, or apartment, or money to start a business, the husband's parents would often expect to provide these if they could. Letting a new couple "suffer it out" for a year or two before they get on their feet is not considered responsible parenting. Even married, professional sons in their thirties and forties are often the recipients of an apartment from parents. While this may seem like a case of extended apron strings, as noted above the apartment does not really belong to the couple, it belongs to the extended family, and is an investment in the extended family's future. A young couple never really "sets out on their own" but rather becomes a new segment of the husband's extended family. Again, in Mainland China this phenomenon is less extreme. This dependent status can be particularly difficult for a couple that has spent the first few years of their marriage living overseas, enjoying their independence and making their own decisions. Should they move back "home" to China or Korea, they may suffer considerable culture shock for an extended period as their independent status abroad changes to being both dependent upon, and responsible for, their aging parents (note Confucianism's reciprocal Father/Son relationship at work here). The children of these returnees may well be in your classroom!

It is true that in the traditional Confucian family, the oldest male rules the roost. His word is law, and he is both revered and feared. However, the traditional Western image of the Asian wife dutifully following twelve steps behind her husband is only half the truth. While in public, a more traditional Korean wife will often take a very subservient, servant-like pose. In the home, however, the wife is both influential and powerful unless guests are present. It is no accident that in the Korean language, one of the words for "wife" literally means "inside person;" that for "husband" means "outside person." This does not refer to washing the dishes or planting the rice; rather, it indicates that the husband is the family's "front" to the world, and the one who goes out to bring home the income. Conversely, the wife is in control of much of what goes on within the home, and is not afraid to take responsibility and wield great influence there. Two areas in which women are particularly influential within the walls of the home are finances and the raising of children, including being responsible for their education.

Most often, when a Korean husband comes home on payday (in days past, with a wad of cash) he figuratively hands it over to his wife. She then gives him his spending money. She is both the chief financial officer and holder of the keys in the family. If the couple lives with parents-in-law, the son's salary may go into the common pot controlled by his mother (as female head of the house) instead of to his wife. It is still uncommon to find even a young Korean husband working in the kitchen or helping around the house; gender roles are still quite rigid although loosening with each generation.

This is quite different in Mainland China, where husband and wife are equal, and parents do not have quite as strong a hold over adult children. This separation from traditional Confucian behavior was one welcome casualty of the Cultural Revolution that has taken many decades to loosen up in Korea. Chinese men often do the cooking and share much more in household chores. Interestingly, the degree to which this occurs depends in part on the city or region in which the couple lives.

In line with her role as the CFO of a Korean family, the wife may make real estate decisions, invest money, or lend to or borrow money from friends or relatives, sometimes without the husband's agreement or even knowledge. More than one marriage has broken up (behind closed doors) when the wife lent money to a friend to whom she could not say "no" (because of their relationship), and the investment was lost. Husbands are often guilty of this, as well. Small groups of Korean women often pool their money in what are called "kye" so that one or another has enough cash on hand to marry off a daughter, buy a new apartment, or make an investment. Unfortunately for the wife in an overseas situation, she may find herself without any purse strings to control. She may not be able to speak the local language and may have no money in a local bank. She may be dependent upon her husband or a local national in the company office to help her in this area. This may rob her of a very important tool of real power in the family, and may cause her no small amount of insecurity.

The other area for which the Asian wife and mother has almost total control and responsibility is that of the raising of the children, particularly supervising their education. As we shall see later on, education is a harsh experience for Korean and Chinese children. From the moment they enter elementary school until the day they graduate from high school, they are in a rigid, unforgiving, highly competitive, and sometimes cruel system. They must study grueling hours and compete relentlessly against others who may be more talented.

Mothers, particularly in Korea, provide the discipline to make this happen. This emphasis on the mother's role is somewhat mitigated in China due to the long-standing "one child policy" as we shall see below, and the fact that mothers work outside the home much more often, with grandparents doing much of the child rearing.

Possibly to compensate for the rigor of school life ahead in middle and high school, small children are often indulged outside of school – in China, that fact that many children are raised primarily by grandparents also contributes to this spoiled child phenomenon. Discipline is often very lax by Western standards, whether in a restaurant or even at a wedding, where children are allowed to wander (run) around at will. Children seldom have a set bedtime; toys, candy, and money are often given out freely. Boys are especially spoiled in this way, particularly if they are oldest sons. They are waited on at home and may expect the same treatment in school. In Korea, it is a common opinion among young women that they should not marry an oldest son because they don't make very responsible husbands (and few want to live with an overbearing mother-in-law who will likely soon begin demanding a grandson!) Children seldom have chores or responsibilities at home; they are to devote themselves to their studies. This can have negative ramifications in later life if they go off to university overseas and have to take care of themselves; they may be very proficient students, but they often lack basic life skills. Well-meaning mothers and grandparents who focus primarily on providing a pristine academic environment for their offspring often create young adult children whose idea of cooking is holding a instant ramyon bowl under a hot water dispenser, and have no idea that sheets actually need to be changed more than once a semester. They face a steep learning curve. One of the top three reasons that roughly one-third of Chinese college students attending school in the U.S. drop out is that they simply don't have the skills take care of themselves. Their mother had so thoroughly organized their lives and responsibilities that they became professional students – but not very good at taking care of themselves. Again, childhood is extended for many of these children. If they remain within their own culture, the system works. However, if they decide to go overseas to study or work, their lack of life skills can be debilitating unless mom comes to the rescue and decides to split her time between husband and child, further extending dependency.

This practice of spoiling children is amplified in Mainland China due to the government's one-child policy, which was instituted in 1979 in an effort to counteract Mao's encouragement during the 1950's for families to have more children. In 2016 some families were given permission to have two children; so far, especially in cities, couples are not taking the government up on its offer. Evidence of a strong family planning impulse is seen on nearly every corner store and supermarket checkout counter in China, which offer a literal rainbow of condom selections. It is almost impossible to go to any grocery or convenience store and not be faced with a condom (and other various sex aides) display at the checkout counter (for an interesting video on the one-child policy, see http://time.com/4598999/china-one-child-policy-family-planning/ or read https://www.thoughtco.com/chinas-one-child-policy-1435466). Conservative Korea may consume plenty of family planning devices, but they are not quite as conspicuously displayed in every Family Mart for younger children to ask questions about.

From a child rearing perspective, over time China's one-child policy, as it entered its second generation, had a profound impact on the structure of the family. Let's suppose that a two couples in 1980 decided (under intense government pressure) to have only one child. We have four parents, each with one child (total of two children). Twenty-five years later, in 2005, those two children are 25 years old and marry, and soon have their own single child. We now have four grandparents and two parents – six adults - all focusing their combined energy and love (and hopes and dreams) on just one child. In cities, most adults work, so the parents of the child are out of the home most of the day, and leave the child at home for at least one set of grandparents to raise. In Shanghai, it is unusual to see a young married couple alone in public – they almost always have a child and one or two grandparents in tow. What is interesting is that almost never are the parents carrying or pushing the child – the grandparents are. The result is a single child spoiled by four permissive grandparents who understand that later on the school and teachers will straighten them out. When a grandparent is not available, a driver or ayi (maid) is on hand to carry books, close car doors, and escort the child to school. It is very common to see crowds of elderly grandparents waiting outside a school gate at dismissal time to meet their grandchildren; it is equally common to see middle and high school students walking home from school with grandparents – and with the elderly grandparents carrying the knapsack full of books. In international schools, this phenomenon of the "Little Emperor" or "Little Princess" is well known, as is the "ayi syndrome" – kids who are accustomed to literally be waited on hand and foot. This is not unknown in Korea, although the intensity of the influence of grandparents on the grandchildren is usually not nearly as strong. Very small children new to the school environment may sit down at lunch and open their mouths like little sparrows, waiting expectantly for food to be dropped into their mouths. Hunger normally takes care of that learned behavior within a day or two! See the article "Korean Mothers were Valiant" in the appendix for a take on the maternal role from a Korean man's perspective. Little Soldiers, by Lenora Chu, also provides insights into the involvement in Chinese mothers in their child's education.

On the other hand, discipline can be both terrible and swift, with a firm spanking being applied when a mother or grand-mother finally tires of a whining child. For older children, getting hit across the palm of the hands with a bamboo stick or ruler, being hit across the back of the calves with a good sized stick (even at school), being sent out of the house to sleep on the doorstep, or getting the "silent treatment" from parents for a few days is not unusual. In a society that puts great importance on inclusion and belonging, this type of forced isolation is a very effective psychological weapon. In the case of physical punishment, actual bruises are rare, but certainly not unknown. Asian discipline for both children and adults is based on shame rather than on guilt; therefore any-thing that makes the child feel ashamed, even publicly, meets its intended purpose. International educators are sometimes placed in difficult positions when a child has done something that must be reported to the parents, knowing full well that as a result the child may receive a form of discipline at home that is outside the Western range of acceptability. Later on we'll take a look at the necessity for international schools to develop and adopt a formal child-abuse policy to provide guidance and protection to teachers, counselors, and adminis-trators in these situations.

A Korean (and to a less extent, Chinese) mom bears responsi-bility in the eyes of her family and friends for her children's shortcomings and mistakes. If a child is not successful in school it is considered to be as much the mother's fault as it is the child's. If a child gets in trouble in school the mother will acknowledge that the child did wrong, but then in the child's presence may say that the child should not be punished because actually it was the mother's fault (sometimes the father will say this about the mother, too!) She is a bad parent, she was too lenient, she didn't teach the child properly, etc., etc., but now the child knows better, and needn't be discip-lined at school, especially if there is some kind of academic or recorded school response. Being faced with a parent who is pleading not to discipline a child can present a challenge for school authorities who are trying to maintain a consistent discipline policy. Parents are often particularly worried that the incident will be noted in the child's permanent file, as it would be in Korean or Chinese school, and fear that this may affect future educational plans. Telling parents that you must keep a record of this incident for future reference can send Korean or Chinese parents into a tailspin. This can cause a dilemma in situations in which a child is suspended from class for some reason in high school, as U.S. universities often request information on suspensions. Not trusting the university to take a look at the situation and make a reasonable judgment on its seriousness, parents will do nearly anything to prevent a record being made of the suspension. Schools need to develop a policy on what is reported to universities, and what is not, to relieve counselors and administrators the dilemma of making these decisions on their own.

As a middle school principal in Seoul, I was meeting one afternoon with a Korean dad, mom, and son in my office one time to discuss the boy's lack of effort regarding his schoolwork. I was trying to impress upon both the child and the parents the importance of consistency, focus, etc. – all the things we talk about when kids aren't succeeding very well. Suddenly the dad interjected, "I am ashamed!" he shouted. "He's (points at boy) no longer my son!" I was shocked, and asked the boy to leave the room. I then told the dad that he would never say that again to his son in my presence, and why. Thinking about it later, I realized that I was witnessing 1) dad's shame at the poor performance of his son, and 2) shaming by marginalizing and making his son feel like an outsider to the family. I also realized that this show of force by dad was a performance for my benefit to show me what a good father he was – because I must be thinking that he was a bad parent because of his son's bad grades. I felt badly that the son had suffered this in order to impress me, the principal. I also wondered about the conversation between the mom and dad after they got home. In the dad's eyes, most likely Mom's lack of effective parenting of her son had resulted in a humiliating visit by the dad to see the school principal; mom as well as her son had brought shame to the family (and by extension, grandparents, aunts and uncles, etc.)

Parents in most cultures want their children to "fit in" with the important peer group. In cultures in which "the nail that sticks up gets hammered down" that desire is even more evident. Children are not generally counseled to stand up against the peer pressure of the group, but to go along and not upset the harmony lest they run the risk of exclusion. The need to be part of the group, to not be seen as strange or different, is crucial. Asian children are not unlike children elsewhere in using this pressure as a way to get what they want from parents. Requests for the latest iPhone, a certain brand of jeans or backpack, etc., etc., do not fall of deaf ears at home. If "everyone else has one" and your child doesn't, your child may not fit in properly. The group solidarity may be disrupted, and certainly your child may end up as an outsider rather than as a safe group member. This would reflect poorly on both the child and the family. Apple or Nike sales go up as a result.

This behavior continues into the teen years. It is very common for a teenage child to ask a parent for money to treat friends to dinner at a decent restaurant. Granted, there are almost no opportunities for a teenager to earn money on their own (they should be studying), but the frequency and amount of money demanded would floor many Western parents. Carried on even further, it is not unusual for Chinese college students in the West to be driving around in a BMW convertible – needed to save or gain face in front of other Chinese friends. Many parents would accept this as an acceptable need for their child.

Children are at the bottom of the Confucian hierarchy, and are certainly to be seen and not heard. Alternately spoiled and disciplined, possibly it is only Confucian respect for parents that keeps the children from rebelling. They are usually really nice kids!

CHAPTER X: CONFUCIAN RELATIONSHIPS - CLASSMATES AND PEERS

After a child has learned the rudiments of Confucian relationships at home, he or she is ready to branch out into the world of peer relationships. It was mentioned earlier that vertical older/younger relationships within the family are learned early in life, developed for security here and now. Horizontal (lateral) friend/friend relationships, however, are also developed by young children, but with an eye both for present and future security. Korean (and to a lesser extent Chinese), children, particularly in high school and college, consciously build relationships to last a lifetime. The importance of building strong, quality relationships with the "right kind" of people from the "right" families is crucial to one's future. The importance of peers (and peer pressure) is much more than a passing adolescent need; it is the basis for adult relationships, as well. Friends address each other by the same relationship terms (older brother, younger brother; older sister, younger sister) as they would their biological brothers and sisters. Close relationships formed among high school or college classmates can be depended upon when they need to call on each other for social or economic favors or help decades into adulthood, whether it be getting a building permit, getting a niece into a college, getting a son out of trouble, or even asking for a private loan. In addition, a young person who attends a particular university may well spend much of his or her professional life working with fellow alumni, as many of the larger Korean companies hire graduates primarily from a particular university, which is often the alma mater of the founder of that company. Even in education this holds true. Today the overwhelming majority of Seoul National University professors are graduates of that school; this type of inbreeding is not uncommon. Many of those in positions of power and influence during the Park Chung-hee, Chun Doo-hwan, and Roh Tae-woo regimes during the 1960's, 70's, and 80's had been classmates of these leaders and of each other decades before at the Korea Military Academy, and built their military careers on those relationships. (In an interesting twist of fate, Park Chung-hee's classmate from the second postwar class of the ROK army officers' training course was a man named Kim Jae-kyu, who was not only Park's chief of the many-tentacled Korean CIA, but was also Park's eventual assassin. In this case apparently the old school tie wore too thin, and familiarity built contempt.) It is no coincidence that favors were passed out and money changed hands at such a rate during the presidencies of Chun and Roh that both men and many of their classmates spent time in jail following their leaving office as President. This web of personal relationships that go back for decades is also strong in China, particularly within the ruling Communist Party.

While the tangled web of personal, family, academic, political, military, and business relationships gives Korean society a good deal of its resiliency, it also is the root of many of its weaknesses. In a system in which the maintenance of relationships ranks near the top in social values, in which the rule of law has traditionally not been respected (at least behind closed doors), and in which any small advantage can make the difference between success and failure for one and one's family, graft and corruption can eat away at the core of society. Favors are cemented with gifts; good deeds are not forgotten by either party. "Winking" at the rules by government officials to help an old friend or even a friend of a friend, acknowledged by an envelope of cash or promise of future favors, has resulted in more than one bridge or building collapse, and once exposed has cut short the tenure of more than one cabinet minister, company president, or even, in the case of President Park Keun-hye (daughter of President Park Chung-hee), her term as President. Ongoing political scandal is a fact of life in South Korea today, even as the nation struggles to don new garments of democracy and open government. Democracy has taken firm root in South Korea, but graft and corruption are endemic in society, government, and business. This unfortunate phenomenon was summed up by a Korean political science professor at Sook Myung University amid widespread public cries for clean government even back in January 2000. "We understand that we can't survive or compete in international society as long as our system is based on corruption and bribery. But it's something like air for Koreans. It's very difficult to eradicate." (The Korea Herald, p. 11, January 25, 2000). This factionalism and lack of trust in politics is still very much alive and well in Korean politics today (2020) as we see each new Presidential administration digging up dirt on the previous administration with a certain degree of vindictiveness. Fortunately, most Korean individuals do not reflect this darker side of Confucianism. Korean culture is amazingly generous and gracious – but these qualities are seen primarily only among people who are friends, colleagues, former classmates, or fellow members of a particular group or organization. There is a distinct sense that for every individual, there are those who are outside the circle of trust, and those inside. The maintenance of lifelong relationships very often takes precedence over the law, or even common sense.

CHAPTER XI: CONFUCIAN RELATIONSHIPS - WITHIN SOCIAL GROUPS

As noted earlier, the importance of membership in a group rather than standing alone as an individual cannot be underestimated. Beyond the family and smaller peer group Koreans, and to a lesser extent Chinese, are closely identified by, and gain much of their identity from, the larger groups to which they belong. Once a relationship is established between an individual and other members of a group, it is very difficult and painful to break. Normally, when an individual is mentioned in the newspaper (whether it be complimentary or not) he or she is mentioned as a member of a particular company or a student at a particular school. If a young person gets in trouble, the police immediately call the school, rather than the home, and the newspaper will report that "Park, second year student at "X" High School, whose father is employed by "Y" Company . . .." If the student in question attends a "posh" international school, the news report can be particularly savory. Companies pride themselves on the "family" atmosphere they create among their employees, and work hard to develop relationships within the company, even within a strictly hierarchical corporate structure.

Traditionally, employment at a particular company lasted until retirement, and the Korean economic disaster of the late 1990's that resulted in forced closings and layoffs was much more emotionally traumatic than it would have been in the West. Men (predominantly) didn't just loose their jobs; they lost their identity and relationship within a particular company. In China, when ubiquitous state-owned businesses began to be privatized in the 1980's and the iron rice bowl was being phased out, the same thing happened, although for different reasons. In addition to the obvious loss of income for the laid-off employee, the idea of being expelled from the group that had been a source of both economic security and personal identity was sometimes fatal. During economic crises and resultant layoffs, more than one Korean father and husband has committed suicide or pretended to go to work for months rather than admit to his wife and children that he no longer has a job, so much is one's identity tied to the company. Until the economic crisis of 1997 in Korea, changing companies in mid-career was both unusual and suspect. Only since then, with large numbers of men who worked for very respectable companies out in the street after a corporate collapse, did this become more socially acceptable. This is true for smaller organizations, as well. After being away now from Seoul Foreign School since 2005, there are, from a foreign staff of well over 150, less than five foreigners still there whom I worked with. However, except for those who retired, the Korean staff is largely the same – some of the secretaries have worked for seven or more principals over the years. They simply stay from the time they were young college graduates until retirement at age 65 – and sometimes beyond. There are security guards working there who I knew when we were both young men, but who now have grandchildren. Loyalty to the school goes far beyond simply being a paid employee.

A strong, decades-long emotional attachment keeps them there.

One group that most international schools must acknowledge is the "Korean/Chinese moms' group." These informal groups exist for mutual support in an unfamiliar educational environment. Each has its own hierarchy (based on comparative ages, colleges of graduation, or husbands' positions). The groups usually work quite well in terms of mutual support, but they can sometimes become so exclusive that certain women are not allowed in, sometimes on the basis of their children's comparative school success (or rather, lack thereof). It would take a strong woman to disagree or act not in accordance with the feelings of the group or its leader.

One morning I met with an 8th grade Korean mom who was upset because we were moving her daughter out of the avanced math section into regular 8th grade math, which was already advanced for the age group. It had obviously been a poor placement on our part, and the girl's grades were crashing; she needed to be moved to the less advanced group (on grade level) in order to succeed. The mom and I went round and round, me trying to convince the mom that her daughter needed to be moved, and mom refusing to agree to the change. Finally the mother admitted that she knew that from an academic standpoint, her daughter would be better served be being in the correct math level. But still, she would not budge – her daughter must stay in the advanced group! I pushed back – and suddenly she began to tear up. "What's the matter?" I asked. Through her tears she admitted that the real problem was not her daughter's, but hers. "Don't you realize what this would do to me?" she gagged through her tears. I had to admit that I didn't. "If my daughter moves out of the advanced math group, I will be expelled from the advanced math class mom's group that meets every Tuesday morning at the Hyatt. I will be shamed if I have to leave! My friends will desert me!" Eventually the girl was moved (to avoid flunking) and I am not sure what happened to the mom, but I'm pretty sure she had to find something else to do on Tuesday mornings. Once again, expulsion from the group took on an importance that would seem ridiculous to most Westerners. It was a good lesson to me that there are often hidden forces at work when things don't quite make sense. Often in such cases our cultural ignorance is blinding us to an important part of the story. Once we more fully understand the cultural context, while we may not change our final decision, at least we can better appreciate the unintended consequences and maybe make it seem less arbitrary to the person on the receiving end. Regardless of our desire to be culturally sensitive, we always must ask ourselves "What's the best thing for the child?" I have to admit that sometimes learning this has forced me to move from rule following and precedent avoiding to thinking more specifically about what is best for this child, in this situation, at this time. We also need to always remember that we are in the business of putting the child first, not the parents.

While parent groups can be used in positive ways by the school to "get the word out" on particular topics and in communicating the school's mission to those whose English may not be as strong or who are new to the school, these groups can also be destructive if misinformation is disseminated as truth by someone higher up in the social strata. The advent of instant messaging services (currently WeChat in China and Kakao Talk in Korea) has amplified this situation, where a question becomes a rumor, and a rumor quickly becomes accepted as a fact. The sooner you can identify your Alpha Mom in any particular group (Seventh Grade moms, swim team moms, etc.) the more you can use these valuable communication tools to get the message out that you intend.

For children and young people in any culture, being accepted by friends is certainly important, especially as middle and high school students grow away from family and associate more with peers. For a Chinese or Korean child, not to be accepted by the group is doubly difficult. Mothers will work very hard to be sure that their child is not left out, whether this means buying the jacket, shoes, or book bag "style of the month" or giving large amounts of money to kids so they can take friends out to eat. Being excluded from the group can have serious and long-lasting consequences more serious than not being invited to the Hyatt next Tuesday. Children (and sometimes adults) will sometimes choose some unfortunate member who dares to be different and socially isolate them, sometimes actively bullying them. This goes far beyond a child simply being unpopular – it is deliberate group oriented discrimination and isolation of an individual. Koreans have a very specific word for a child who is victimized in this way: "wahng-ta." This is unfortunately also quite common in Japan, but interestingly, there is no equivalent word in Chinese.

"Wahng-ta" children may be teased, called names, become targets for lunch money extortion, find themselves purposely left out of games or other social events, or suffer physical or even sexual abuse. Parents and society recognize this social problem but seem helpless to do much about it. Both parents and students are fearful of reprisal and seldom speak up against this type of bullying and abuse (much as many American parents recognize the dangers of available street drugs, but are afraid to speak up for fear of reprisal and hope that somehow their child is immune). As with bullies around the world, today's "wahng-ta" too often becomes tomorrow's bully. The child (or adult) with no friends is more than just a "loner" in Korea; he or she is to be pitied above all others. Tragically, children who are isolated in this way sometimes simply refuse to go to school any longer, or choose suicide as a solution to their unbearable social position. Many a Korean TV documentary has highlighted this serious societal problem, noting recent cases of suicide. In cities this often involves children jumping off the roof of their apartment building. In

Japan, a rising phenomenon of children simply refusing to go to school any longer due to academic stress, bullying, or other social ostracism is called futoko.

In today's interconnected world, "wahng-ta" status can follow a child from school to school. I am familiar with a case in which a Korean-American middle school girl was enrolled in a Korean school when the family moved from the United States to Seoul. Because she was "different," or maybe because her English was so much better than that of her new peers, she quickly became a "wahng-ta" at her new school in Seoul. Things became unbearable, so the parents sent her to live with an aunt in Taegu, about three hours away by train. When she arrived at her new school she quickly realized that her reputation had preceded her, some students having already been notified of her transfer through the student grapevine. She was immediately cast into the "wahng-ta" role once again. Eventually she moved to an international school in Seoul where she fit in, and no longer carried her "wahng-ta" status with her.

College freshmen in Korea are often "initiated" into their new group by upper classmen and even by professors with nights of heavy drinking similar to some fraternity or sorority initiations in the United States. This tragically results in deaths by alcohol poisoning or drowning at the beginning of each academic year. Students who don't go along are seen as upsetting the harmony of the group, and avoiding bonding with fellow classmates.

Whether it is the family, the social group, the church, the company, the club, or the graduating class, Koreans seek out groups with which to identify to a degree most Westerners would think unhealthy. Subservience of one's own needs to those of the group, following the group's leaders, or following an undesired career path for the sake of the family are common themes in Korean society. Once again, we see a strong cultural characteristic (collective relationships) being evident in both Korean and Chinese culture, but to a lesser extent in

China.

CHAPTER XII: CONFUCIAN RELATIONSHIPS - WITHIN THE NATION

A Korean's relationship with his or her nation is also very deep and sacred. The pride of Koreans for Korea is the basis for many of the very positive qualities found in the country, as well as for some of the difficulties it faces when coming into contact with other nations. During the 1960's students were actually taught in school that after Germans, Koreans were the smartest "race" in the world! The fact that Koreans are very homogenous physically, that they have lived together on a small peninsula for 5000 years, that their written language was developed specifically for use with their spoken language and is used no place else on earth (except by expatriate Koreans), and finally that they have repeatedly been victims of hostile outside forces, has forged them into a proud, loyal, and solid people sharing a high degree of Korean "one-ness" and national pride. This feeling of collective nationhood is well expressed in the language; in Korean it is very awkward to say "My nation" as might be said in many other languages — it is always expressed "Uri nara" - "Our nation." (The solidity of the family unit is also demonstrated in this way; one always says "our family" rather than "my family.") This strong sense of "we Koreans" and "everyone else" is also apparent in the Korean word for "foreigners," which literally means "outside people." Koreans who emigrate from Korea are always thought of as "overseas Koreans" rather than as Canadians or British or Americans of Korean descent. When an ethnic Korean of foreign citizenship becomes famous in politics or sports in their adopted Western nation, he or she is considered by Koreans to be "really one of us." Bloodlines run deep: Koreans generally consider ethnicity rather than citizenship to be the basis of determining nationality. One interesting example of this occurred a few years ago when a U.S. citizen of Korean background rose quite high in the U.S. intelligence establishment. He came into contact with classified material (concerning Korea) that he illegally passed on to the Korean government. In explaining his behavior, he readily admitted that he had been spying. However, he excused himself by saying that there was no reason for the U.S. to keep the information from an ally, Korea, and therefore he was justified to pass it on to his "motherland." He failed to recognize that as a U.S. citizen he was no longer a Korean, and that his loyalties had to lie with the United States, not Korea – especially as a government employee and a trusted member of the intelligence establishment. The Korean press roundly supported him in this, saying that he really had a duty to help his motherland rather than the United States, which should have given the information to Korea, anyway. Most Koreans, having a very difficult time separating the man's U.S. nationality from his Korean ethnicity, thought he was completely justified in what he had done. Interestingly, the Korean government steered clear of this entire incident, wisely citing it as an "internal U.S. matter."

Another example of this strong connection with Korean heritage is the comment made on U.S. television by an ethnic Korean Chicago shopkeeper during the Rodney King riots in Los

Angeles in the spring of 1992: "If my family lives in America for five generations, we will still be Korean!" We can hardly imagine a first generation German or Polish American making such a statement. Although this was spoken nearly thirty years ago, the sentiment is still strong today. Among Asian immigrant groups, Koreans rank at the top of those who feel that they are discriminated against in the United States due to their nationality (again, this sense of victim-ness remains strong even in the face of the relatively amazing success of Koreans in the U.S. See the Pew Research study cited at the end of this section for more detail).

This characteristic of identification as a Korean and as a member of the Korean nation regardless of where life takes a person is an important point to consider in understanding our students. Firstly, it explains some of their tendency to stick together reported by educators in many schools. Secondly, it works to their detriment when and if they return to Korea, when they become "hidden immigrants" in a homogeneous nation. (see Pollock and Van Reken) Although they look Korean on the outside, they are exposed as pseudo-Koreans as soon as they speak another language. Ethnic Koreans who speak other languages in public in Korea are often ostracized. "Are you Korean or not?" is less a question than a rhetorical "What's wrong with you?", particularly coming from older Koreans. Children who have lived overseas are criticized by their grandparents for not speaking, bowing, or behaving properly, and a good deal of identity struggle often results. On one hand they are told not to forget that they are Koreans, and on the other that they are not very good ones. This will be discussed in greater depth later.

One consistent theme that is heard regarding students from South Korea is the intense pride that they have in being Korean. When I first taught at Seoul Foreign School in 1976, this was not the case. At that time, there were relatively few Korean "returnees." Students would deny that they were Korean, even if they had a Korean name, and would insist that they were anything but Korean. The Korean nation itself had little self-confidence or self-esteem at that time. However, beginning in the early 1980's, with Korean exports taking off and being recognized around the world, and the award-ing of the 1988 Summer Olympics to Seoul, national pride quickly bloomed. Being Korean was suddenly something to be proud of. This probably reached its peak during the 2002 World Cup hosted by Korea and Japan, when the city of Seoul and countless public squares across the country were awash in red T-shirts. This nationalism and pride is one of the fuels of the nation that keeps people working and studying amazingly long hours (which has made the country what it is today) but sometimes doesn't travel too well. One sign of this is common cliquishness shown by Korean students, not only in international schools but also at universities around the world, and often works against their integration into the school community. Graffiti that says simply "KP" is a sign of this nationalism as well; it means "Korea Power" and while not quite a territory marker (although it can be) it is certainly a secret sign of determined nationalism and belonging.

An unfortunate sidelight of this nationalism is that Koreans often pride themselves on their "racial purity." Certainly, a nation confined to a small peninsula, repeatedly being a vic-tim of surrounding powers, sharing a common language, cul-ture, and gene pool for thousands of years, has a right to consider itself a nation apart. However, what is frequently ignored is the fact that Korea, located at the crossroads of northern Asia as it has been, also has absorbed a huge amount of foreign influence, whether it is Buddhism and Confucianism from China, language from central Asia, or Burger King from the United States. In addition, the frequent ravages of war have brought invading and occupying armies with the unfor-tunate resultant addition of fresh genes – young, victorious male armies far from home have, throughout history, generally earned poor reviews in the area of ensuring the genetic purity of the conquered populace. Despite what Korean lore says about the virtuous women who flung themselves off the cliff into the sea rather than be ravaged by invaders (which did happen in the case of the Mongols in the mid-1200's) there has been a good deal of intermixing of foreign blood over the centuries.

Unfortunately, this focus on racial purity has resulted in a prejudice against anyone who is different, and until the past twenty years, particularly against any kind of genetic mixing of Koreans and others. In the years following the Korean War, mixed-race orphans were known as "dust of the streets." Even today there is no polite term in the Korean language for someone who is bi-racial; all terms are derogatory to some degree. Korean parents, even those deeply involved in the international community, often send a very strong message to their kids that they are expected to marry only "Koreans" – even if they are culturally foreign. In the past twenty years it has become more and more accepted, due to a shortage of Korean women, for Korean men to take foreign brides. Even in this case, ethnic Koreans from China (who are in fact quite Chinese culturally) are first choice mates.

Complicating this prejudice, many older Koreans still hold a low regard against anyone with darker skin. Some of this is due to the fact that traditionally lower-class laborers (farmers, fishermen, etc.) who worked in the sun became very dark, so darkness became associated with the lower classes, while higher class "scholars" who stayed indoors and studied, were inevitably lighter skinned. Korean woman are very sensitive to getting too much sun, and parasols and outsized visors are commonly seen in the summer all over the country. Korean women spend huge amounts of money on skin care products to keep their skin smooth and light colored.

In recent years the recruiting of African-American sports players onto Korean teams, as well as the wild popularity of some bi-racial entertainers, has helped to break down some of these prejudices. However, what might be fine on the basketball court or television screen is quite different from what might be acceptable when a daughter brings home a new boyfriend of a darker skin color or ethnic background.

The whole topic of ethnic identity and nationalism is more obvious when placed against a background of another culture, as happens with immigrant groups. An in-depth discussion of a number of variables that affect different Asian ethnic immigrant groups in the United States is found in a Pew Research Center 2012 study. For those interested in this topic, I recommend http://www.pewsocialtrends.org/2012/06/19/the-rise-of-asian-americans/.

South Korean Social Evolution: 1960-Today

As we look back over the history and cultural characteristics of South Koreans since 1960, eight years after the country had been totally devastated by the Korean War, we see a nation that is still dealing with the aftermath of 40+ years of Japanese occupation, even though that ended in 1945, more than 75 years ago. The experience of the Korean War, and moreover the legacy of a divided nation that it left behind, haunts Korean politics and even reaches into families split by the conflict. The grinding poverty of the 1950's and 1960's was slowly replaced by economic development, to the point that today South Korea is one of the very most technologically developed nations in the world, with its people enjoying a high standard of living. However, even people in their 40's remember childhoods marked by a much lower standard of living, and the legacy of a nation divided in two is still a daily reality.

Economic and democratic development were accompanied by tremendous social change as well, kick started by the 1988 Summer Olympics held in Seoul. Up until about 1980, South Korea had been mainly agrarian, with a growing manufacturing sector and a growing export market. However, rising educational levels and the lure of good jobs in the cities emptied many rural areas. Today the Seoul metropolitan area is home to nearly 25 million people, the fifth largest in the world. This move from country to city has caused huge social dislocation, particularly for older people who may have spent their entire life in a rural area but find themselves living with their grown children in high-rise apartments in large cities. Interestingly, the population of both Korea and the Seoul area are now in a gradual decline due to falling birth rates; this mirrors population trends in China and Japan.

This rapid urbanization, coupled with Korean integration into the world society and developing democracy over the past seven decades has brought about a gradual move from more traditional Confucian social norms and values to more Western Judeo-Christian values. South Korea is still struggling with this change, although this is not readily obvious to the casual observer or visitor to Korea. This nation (and its overseas sojourners, who many of us come into contact with in international schools) outwardly may seem very Western, boasting a population carrying the latest technology in its pockets, that travels widely, that has a high standard of living, exports its own culture to the world through food and pop culture, and increasingly has strong international language skills. However, traditional cultural values are still very strong among many Koreans. We clearly see this tension of the old pulling against the new in contrasting and competing educational forms and philosophies. The Korean and Chinese children in our classrooms, whether in Seoul, Shanghai, or Sao Paolo, are there because their parents want them to experience Western education, and escape the harshness and pressure of Asian education. Interestingly, often these families often bring with them the very habits and institutions that they are striving to leave – long hours of studying, after school academies (hakwon, in Korean) that demand hours of work on top of school, and a focus on entry to prestigious, "name brand" universities for their children.

Each of these major themes in Korean politics, economics, and society has greatly influenced the parents of the Korean children seeking Western education in our schools today. Only by understanding and acknowledging Korean's past struggles and successes can we begin to understand our students and their parents. The individuals we see today are only the latest version of who Koreans are – and for Korean students living outside of Korea; they also are impacted by the experience of being TCK's, or Third Culture Kids, and are thus affected by their host nation culture. We see kids who are Koreans at their core, with international veneers of various thicknesses, depending on where and for how long they have lived outside of Korea. Of course, this is true of their parents, as well, but to a much lesser degree. Finally, grandparents, who exercise a strong influence on their children and grandchildren from a distance, inevitably are very traditional in their values and attitudes, as most of their lives have been spent in a much different Korea than the one we see and hear about today. Thus, we teach Westernized children being raised by semi-Westernized parents, who in turn are strongly influenced by their own parents who may cling to the old, Confucian, "Korean way" of doing things. It should not be surprising that cultural conflicts occur in our schools. It is partly our job to be sure that we understand our students' backgrounds, and those of their parents, as well.

Mainland Chinese Social Evolution

The impact of Confucianism on relationships within the Chinese nation (Peoples' Republic of China) has many parallels to that of Korea. However, as has been noted earlier, China is much more ethnically and linguistically diverse, and is an immensely larger nation geographically. Left to itself, the centripetal forces pushing outward would rip the country apart, as it has repeatedly in the past 5000 years, even in the past 100 years. The glue that makes the PRC stay together in today's world is the authority of the Chinese Communist Party, mirrored in the Chinese government. While some may disagree with its methods, there is no doubt that it holds the nation firmly together. However, China suffers much less from racial discrimination based on skin color (although certainly that is a theme that runs below the surface of society). Perhaps the greatest dichotomy in mainland society today is between the rich and the almost poor, the urban and the rural. These will be discussed later on.

Hierarchy, Conformity, Identity, And Nationalism

By looking at the histories and cultures of Korea and China, we've been able to identify four major cultural themes that both connect and distinguish these two ancient cultures, all related to Confucianism: Hierarchy, Conformity, Group Identity, and Nationalism. Due to the distinct histories of these cultures, we see that each of these themes has developed somewhat differently. But why have we spent so much time investigating these areas? Because each of them directly impacts the people who are products of those cultures, and thus impacts how they, either as parents or students, react and interact with us and our Western style education. Many of the frustrations and challenges, as well as the very positive aspects of teaching children from these countries, have their roots in these characteristics. However, it is important to note that (again) due to differing histories, the degree of impact of Confucianism varies, depending on what country we are considering, as well as each family's unique history. The general rule of thumb is that however Confucianism impacts Korea, it also impacts other East Asian countries, but to a lesser degree. South Korea today remains, in my estimation, the most conservative and orthodox Confucian nation, with the possible exception of North Korea, which has such a thick overlay of Communism and rule by Kim personality cult that it is difficult to see what is underneath. Nevertheless, it is apparent that in today's North Korea the themes of hierarchy, conformity, group identity, and nationalism are very much alive and well, even if called by another name.

Let's add it all up. In East Asian Confucian societies (and Korean, Japanese, and Chinese communities in Western societies) we find the following characteristics:

Collective relationships. People tend not to think of themselves as autonomous individuals, standing on their own independently, but as members of one or more groups – be it the family, a church, a club, a school, a political party, or a nation. The maintenance of strong personal relationships, based on these groups, is very often the over-riding consideration when making decisions.

Strong ethnic and group identities. Related to #1, this strong sense of nationalism, on being Chinese or Korean or Japanese and a member of that ethnic group, is an obvious and integral part of how people relate to one another within the group, and how individuals relate to people outside their national or ethnic group.

A sense of victimization by outsiders. Again, both related to and strengthening national identity is the sense of national victimization and humiliation. When confronted by challenges, Koreans and Chinese still easily refer to the experience of first Western, and then Japanese aggression and colonialization (and in Korea, followed by occupation by U.S. forces, and the ongoing division of the peninsula that has resulted.) Koreans frequently talk about how they have "endured" the suffering imposed by others in order to remain Korean. While there is a good deal of validity to this argument, it is becoming harder and harder to see this as relevant faced with the reality of the vibrant, strong, and growing economic powerhouse that South Korea has become, which has taken an increasing role on the world stage in many areas. North Korea continues to blame its woes on discrimination and aggression by outside nations. The United States is the most convenient scapegoat, sometimes deserved, but often not. Taking this "victim" mentality to a personal level, teachers in international schools sometimes report that Korean students often do not want to take responsibility for their mistakes, instead blaming them on others. Parents often support this attitude by taking responsibility for their children's mistakes, as well, as we have seen above in the discussion about the role of the Korean mother. While certainly not unique to Koreans, this characteristic often appears as a sense of victimization, which doesn't always wear well in societies where taking individual responsibility for one's actions is highly valued.

The Peoples' Republic of China (mainland) continues to be sensitive to its past experiences with Western imperialism in the form of unequal treaties in the aftermath of the Opium Wars and subsequent "treaty ports" that were in effect colonies of Western powers scattered along the coast of China. Most notable today, and most sensitive, is the status of Hong Kong (both from Hong Kong citizens, and from the Beijing government.) Even the issue of the sovereignty of Taiwan is part of this legacy, as Taiwan was an early colony of Japan and remained that way for decades until Japan's defeat in 1945. It was only in 1949 that the Republic of China, formerly from the mainland, fled to Taiwan, and is now considered by the mainland to be a temporary "breakaway province" that is truly an integral part of China. Today, the Peoples' Republic of China is continually expanding its international political, economic, and military influence, and encourages a firm sense of nationalism based on the leadership of the Communist Party.

A high regard for hierarchy and respect for those higher up on the social or institutional ladder. Whether displayed as respect for teachers, for parents and grandparents (or anyone older), for anyone higher up in an organizational structure, or in China an expected respect for the "Party," hierarchy is always a factor either apparent or behind the scenes in any social interactions. Not coincidentally, the structure of the Korean language (primarily verb endings and some vocabulary) is determined by who is speaking to whom – looking up or down socially – a characteristic that makes the use of the Korean language a minefield of social faux pas for non-Korean speakers! Fortunately, Chinese grammar is much simpler and does not invoke a sense of hierarchy, at least in grammatical forms.

Related to this respect for hierarchy is a high regard for history and tradition. This makes change particularly difficult, particularly in the field of education, which is by nature tradition-bound and conservative in nearly any society. Looking to the past for answers, even if they are anachronistic, is very common. Reverence for the "sages" of the past is still important, even in the periods of social revolution such as Korea and China have experienced in the past 60 years. China took a less evolutionary route than did Korea, experiencing the decade-long Cultural Revolution, intentionally overthrowing the old Confucian relationships and traditions. However, a respect for the past is still an important part of Chinese culture, particularly in culturally Chinese areas (Taiwan, Hong Kong, Singapore, etc.) that were not affected by the Cultural Revolution.

Emphasis on harmony within the group. Whether the group is the nation, the school, an organization, or the family, there is a strong emphasis on maintaining group harmony through individual conformity. Not making waves, not complaining openly, not questioning authority, hesitancy to disagree with or question those "older and wiser" are all commonly cited as both positive and negative characteristics of East Asian parents and students. Unfortunately, once a group or individual has made a decision to disagree, the absolutes of Ying and Yang leave little opportunity for compromise and finding middle ground. This tendency to not complain and simply "endure" is usually less apparent among Chinese parents, who many Westerners have found to be sometimes quite confrontational, depending on which region they are from and their societal status. While the tendency to not openly disagree may save educators some headaches in the short run, in the end it can be counterproductive, as the discontent often just goes underground into social media. In China, for instance, the often unregulated and uninformed parental conversations on the WeChat social media platform have caused a good deal of difficulty for school administrators. The same phenomenon occurs in Korea with parents using the Kakao Talk platform. Some schools have had to develop an Acceptable Internet Use Policy for parents to give them guidance in how to communicate and share ideas in positive ways.

Obviously, in reviewing the above characteristics I have painted with a very broad brush, coming dangerously close to stereotyping. As in any culture, there are situations and certainly individuals for whom the above generalizations are not applicable. However, having some awareness that these characteristics, if not applicable to a particular situation, are widely recognized and accepted by both "outsiders" and "insiders" to the cultures, is helpful. And this is the reason that we should we be concerned about the general cultural characteristics of our Korean and Chinese parents and students. By having even a basic awareness and understanding of these characteristics educators can avoid some serious pitfalls. Western and Eastern cultures are literally worlds apart. We can support our students much better if we have some understanding of their cultural background, and more important, of that of their parents. While most of our students, daily immersed in the more Western milieu of many international schools, have distinct Western attitudes and characteristics, their parents may not. When our kids go home at night, they often shed the language and culture of their school day and re-enter their native culture. This, of course, is how true multicultural individuals are created.

In the next section we shall look at Korean and Chinese educational cultures, examine the childhood educational experiences of our students' parents, try to understand their views of education, discuss why Confucian-based education has evolved the way it has and see how it both conflicts with and supports the goals of our Western style schools.

Putting It In Perspective

The preceding sections have briefly described the foundations of Korean and Chinese histories and culture. It would be incorrect to give the reader the impression that every Korean or Chinese child or adult behaves according to traditional norms; far from it. During the past fifty years these nations and cultures have undergone tremendous changes. Firm Confucian cultural bases have been under attack by Western culture and values from without as well as political upheaval from within. The importance of family and of social harmony and stability have been shaken by an invasion of Western ideas such as individual rights, children's rights, and the rights of women. Cultures that have traditionally been based on respect to the oldest and reverence for the past have given way much more youth-oriented, commercialized, future focused nations. As young Koreans and Chinese have traveled more widely outside of Korea and China in the last few decades (Korea since 1980, China much more recently), they have seen that there are different ways of living and acting that are both frightening and attractive. These nations have gone from being primarily agrarian societies to urban, and the tools of survival and success have changed in one generation from ox-drawn plows and strong backs to cell phones and laptops. The Korean and Chinese parents and children we see in our international schools today are in the vanguard of those changes, yet beneath their cosmopolitan surfaces live the core Confucian characteristics described above. Therein lies the struggle of our students' parents. They are products of very traditional societies, the traditions of which are at the core of their identity. At the same time they are trying to balance that traditionalism with an international lifestyle and the knowledge that the longer they are away from their native cultures, the less their children will think and act like they and their ancestors have, in effect, losing their "Korean-ness" and "Chinese-ness." Conflict results from wanting their children to have the benefits of a Western education while not falling prey to what they consider to be the more dangerous sides of Western culture.

Interestingly, one area that continues to maintain traditional forms in China is education, as we will soon see. Rote learning, memorization, lack of emphasis on creativity or skills, and competition among students (and parents) seem to be increasing, although there is a growing interest at all levels in more progressive Western-style education. Government-approved bi-lingual and "experimental" schools are increasing in number as more Chinese parents choose a less traditional type of education for their children. Even these, however, are often "Western-style" in name only, and traditional methods and expectations remain in place.

An "Aha Moment?"

Stop for a moment and reflect on what you have read in the previous pages about Korean and Chinese cultures in relation to your students. What information is new to you? How does it fit with your experience? Where does it not fit? How might either of these depend on the past educational histories of your students and parents? Are they new to international education? Have they come directly from their home country? How might this new information affect your ideas and more important, interactions with these students and their parents? What is your "take away" for Monday morning?

If you are an international school administrator in China or Korea, how might some of this information apply to your management style with Korean or Chinese staff members? (We'll look more at this later). How might it affect your interactions with parent groups? With student groups? How would a tendency to conformity and harmony in groups affect your ability to find out what individuals are really thinking? How might you "get around" this hesitancy to share ideas in groups? How might what we have discussed above explain some of the emphasis on "name brand" education by parents, either at the international school level or in college and university choice?

Take a look at your own cultural identity. How strong is your own sense of personal ethnic or national identity? To what extent does it define you? To what extent is it irrelevant? How might the historical era in which your parents grew up have influenced their identities and values, and to what extend does that influence who you have become?

What are the basic values of your culture? If you are from a Jewish or Christian background, how has your religious background affected your core Western values? How might the values of your religion conflict with your culture? If you are not of a Jewish or Christian background, how have the teachings of these religions affected your culture, and in turn your personal values? How much are we products of our national cultures, and how much products of our chosen religion?

CHAPTER XIII: CONFUCIAN BASED EDUCATION – THE ONE RIGHT ANSWER

Earlier we examined Confucius' ideal educational system, developed in the Sixth Century B.C. in China. His goal was to instill the characteristics of character and integrity into youth by having them master the "Six Arts": computation, archery, music, calligraphy, chariot driving, and ritual. As Chinese culture and political influence spread throughout East Asia, many of these same ideas spread to Korea, just to the East. These ideas flourished in Korea, and as we have seen still exert a remarkable influence on the peninsula today. Ironically, today these ideas impact Chinese culture to a lesser extent than they do in Korea, due to a number of historical reasons. In the discussion of the characteristics of Korean education below, the reader can safely assume that many of the same phenomena and tendencies are very much alive in mainland China, just "less so" than in Korea. Taiwan lies somewhere in between Korea and Mainland China in terms of the contemporary influence of Confucianism on education.

Educational History And Origins

Formal education in Korea dates back to the Koguryo kingdom's Taehak state schools, established in 372 A.D., which provided select young men from the upper classes an academic and military education in preparation for careers in the government or military. Korea continued to have a strong tradition of education up to and throughout the Yi Dynasty (1392-1910 A.D.), albeit mainly for the male gentry. Traditionally, the hardworking sons of farmers and fishermen, even if they had the inclination and ability to study, had little time for such non-productive work. Thus, educated people, both teachers and students, traditionally came almost completely from the upper social classes. Teachers, as holders of knowledge, particularly came to be associated with the social elite, and were awarded high social status. The honorific Korean title for any adult, "sunsaeng-nim," literally means "teacher." This respect accorded teachers is still alive today and is one reason Korean children are often such a joy to teach.

This system of education for the elite remained in place in Korea until the arrival in 1910 of the Japanese, who imposed an educational system that was, although designed to keep Koreans in a low social, economic, and political status, at least not limited to the gentry. The imported Japanese educational system was also based on Confucianism, with a strong German influence as well. The traditional status of the teacher being the primary source of knowledge and authority, however, is still, 75 years after liberation from Japan, found in every classroom in Korea today.

Thus, the teacher/student relationship, like so much else in Korean and Chinese society, is based on original Confucian relationships, in this case the Father/Son relationship. The teacher is considered by both the child and society to be fulfilling very much a parental role, with the student taking on the traditional "son" role. The diagram below illustrates this relationship.

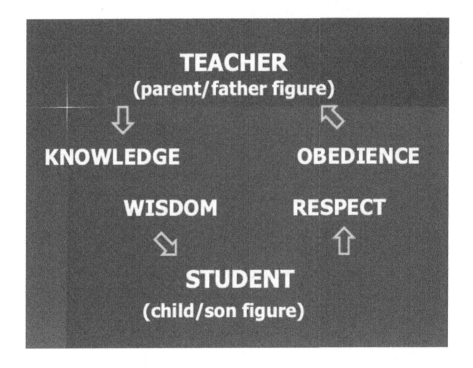

As in Korea, education in China historically has been the property of the upper classes for the reasons that 1) it afforded them a monopoly on power through the civil service exams based on Chinese classics, and 2) the working class simply didn't have time to invest in unproductive student years. Education became synonymous with wealth, power, and prestige. This explains the high social status and respect given to

165

teachers in Asia, even foreign teachers!

Traditional elitist Confucian education consisted primarily of memorizing how to read and write many thousands of Chinese characters and to read and understand the five classics of Confucian literature and teaching. As any student of written Chinese will attest, Chinese characters are learned primarily in one way — by memorization. There is no alphabet, although there are simple "radicals" with particular meanings that together may be used to build larger characters. There are 214 traditional radicals that make up all Chinese characters; the most complicated of which has no fewer than 64 strokes! It is a combination of four dragons, meaning "verbosity," which is perhaps appropriate given the amount of time it takes to write it. Google this for a deeper esplanation. (unfortunately, Kindle eBooks does not allow me to include Korean or Chinese script)

There is little room for creativity in writing Chinese; there is but one right way to write a particular character. For generations these characters have been written with each of the various strokes of a given character written in a particular order; to write them otherwise would reflect poorly on ancestors and great scholars who came before. Here we see respect for the past, conformity, lack of creativity, and following the teacher's directions to the "T" – or maybe we should say to the "stroke" – all a model for what a good Asian student should be.

One of the gifts that the Communist revolution gave to the new nation was to simplify written Chinese from the "traditional" characters (fan ti) to "simplified" Chinese (jian ti), which uses only 210 radicals to construct characters. However, traditional forms are still used in Japan, Korea, Taiwan, Hong Kong, and Singapore and generally any other areas where Chinese was spoken prior to 1949. This doesn't make learning written Chinese simple, only "simpler."

Given that a South Korean high school graduate today must learn roughly 1800 characters just to be able to read the newspaper, it is obvious that a great deal of time must be spent in memorization. In contrast, a Mainland Chinese high school graduate will know about 4000 characters, with a well- educated person being literate in about 8000 (there are about 80,000 characters in all!) Unlike China, however, Korea has its own excellent phonetic alphabet of 28 letters called Hangul, developed under the direction of King Sejong in 1433 A.D. Based on spoken Korean phonetics, it is relatively easy to learn, with few silent letters or esoteric forms. For hundreds of years the upper classes kept this simple and logical system from the masses, thus maintaining their monopoly on learning and power. Later on the Japanese outlawed the use of this system in their unsuccessful but methodical effort to eradicate Korean culture and replace it with Japanese. When Western missionaries first translated the Bible into Korean at the end of the 19th Century, however, they used only Hangul so that as many people as possible could read it; quickly the road to literacy and the road to the Gospel were one in the same, given the absence of public schooling at the time. As this widespread use of Hangul began in the late 19th Century; during the Japanese occupation (1910-1945), it was illegal to use Hangul, so the use of Hangul was driven underground; thus both Hangul and its ally Christianity became associated with anti-Japanese sentiment, which only encouraged the expansion of both! The same Christian missionaries who re-introduced Hangul as the language for the common man (and woman) set up some Western-style schools for children from all social classes, recruiting some students literally off the streets. Because of widespread fear of foreigners these schools did not receive much support from the upper classes despite the encouragement of the forward-looking, pro-Western, and rather anti-Japanese Queen Min, who was assassinated by the Japanese in 1895 on the grounds of Kyong-bok Palace in Seoul in 1898. During the occupation period, most Koreans were educated up through elementary school, and only in Japanese. Following the end of World War II and Japanese occupation, during the subsequent three-year rule by the U.S. military, universal elementary schooling in Korea was re-introduced, but using basically a Japanese system, as it conformed to both traditional Confucian ethics and values, and Korean styles of instruction.

Only since the Japanese departure in 1945 has Hangul been in widespread (and now legal) use, and it is rightfully a source of great pride to Koreans. In formal documents and in many Korean newspapers and magazines today, however, it is often still mixed with Chinese characters to clarify the meaning of Korean homonyms, although decreasing so with each generation. Interestingly, in North Korea Hangul is used almost exclusively without the mixing of Chinese characters still evident in the South. The teaching of Chinese characters (to supplement the Hangul) in South Korean schools has been an on-again, off-again phenomenon; the debate as to whether to continue to use Chinese characters (Hanja) mixed in with Hangul is ongoing. Thus, there are certain age groups among Korean adults today whose knowledge of Chinese characters is much more limited than that of others just a few years older or younger than they.

In Mainland China, education followed much the same path – for millennia it was the property and privilege of the gentry, and then, with gradual Westernization in the early Twentieth Century, a basic education became available to a wider and wider swath of the population. However, due to the societal disruption caused by ongoing civil wars during the first third of the century, followed by the War of Resistance Against Japan (1937-1945), immediately followed by the War of Liberation (1945-1949) between Nationalist and Communist forces, education for the masses was not consistently administered. (Peoples' Daily, December 30, 2000) Concurrent with the conquest of more and more area by the Chinese People's Army, the expanding Communist government quickly put in place an educational system for both economic and political reasons. This worked increasingly well until the Cultural Revolution, when for nearly ten years (1967-1976) schools were closed, and older students were sent out into the streets or to the countryside and teachers and the educated class were decried as "stinking intellectuals." There are many books written about the school-age experiences of young people during this chaotic era. One that poignantly describes what it was like to be a child during this tumultuous era is China's Son, by Da Chen (2001).

Korean and Chinese education today is little different in philosophy and methodology than it was twenty and thirty years ago, when the parents of our students went to school. Now, as then, memorization is the chief mode of transferring knowledge and information from the learned teacher to the supplicant student. More than a century after education stopped consisting almost solely of the memorization of Chinese characters and Confucian classics, the methodology of lecture and memorization is still firmly in place. Large class sizes (today still more than fifty students per class in urban areas of Korea; fewer in rural areas) also lend themselves to lecture rather than discussion. Student participation is often limited to whole class oral response to teachers' questions. Campaigns to integrate foreign language conversation and discussion classes, for example, fall flat in classes of fifty students in which the teacher wishes to maintain complete control. Similarly, constant public discussion about encouraging creativity, fostering thinking skills, encouraging inquiry, or rewarding initiative by students faces an uphill battle in a system that has long valued and promoted a "one right answer" ethos originally based on the "one right way" to memorize a character or a Chinese classic. Learning the right answers and agreeing with the teacher or with older students are valued characteristics. If the teacher, the book's author, the older student, or a parent or grandparent states that an answer is correct, then there is no more argument. There can only be one "right" answer. Lively discussion, creative thinking, alternative solutions, and intellectual independence are neither welcome in the classrooms of Korea and China at any level nor are they conducive to earning high grades or respect from the teacher. To conform, to harmonize, and to accept the status quo spells success in these educational systems. To come up with original ideas, or challenge the teacher in any way, is neither valued nor respected.

The Korean and Chinese educational communities are constantly working to adopt more Western methodologies and aims, but the inertia of traditional educational establishments is strong. Constant attempts at educational reform by the national ministries of education, where national educational policy is set, have met with frustration and resistance, even from teachers. Top down decisions have met serious resistance from below while militant teacher organizations (in Korea) put the blame for sluggish reform on the Ministry of Education above. It is interesting that even as Korea and China look to the West for guidance in the area of educational innovation, the West (particularly the United States) looks with envy on educational outcomes in countries like Korea, China and Japan, which appear to have such effective systems. The truth is that Asian education shines where memorization and "one right answer" styles of teaching and learning are most appropriate: in mathematics. Students educated in these tradition-bound systems do well in many other areas, but their success is based primarily on recall rather than on deeper understanding. Writing skills are often weak, as are thinking skills. Creativity is shunned; critical thinking is not rewarded. Independent research is absent. On the other hand, musical ability is often strong. Could this be because in order to truly excel in music a student needs to practice, practice, practice? Certainly the more Confucian educational style would foster strength in such an area.

Adherence to such a system is also encouraged by the fact that college entrance rests almost solely on nationwide standardized exams throughout Asia. Students' outside interests, talents, or abilities are simply not considered in the process of evaluation; success on these college entrance exams rests on memorization of the right answers for the test questions. Thus, the entire educational establishments, especially at the high school level, are test-driven. The more time spent in the classroom, it is thought, the better chance of high scores on these all-important exams. Truly, this is realistic when memorization is the key to success. Korean middle and high school students, particularly those at the top, spend nearly as much time after school each day in special institutes called "hakgwan" or with private tutors as they do in school. The long winter and summer vacations are opportunities for parents to enroll their children in special classes, lest they fall behind their competing peers. Children entering even second grade of elementary school are given summer homework and projects. One Seoul high school was known a few years ago to assign required "extra classes" for all but nine days of the five-week-long summer vacation! Elementary students usually are assigned extended projects to complete during vacation periods, as well. While this type of thing is looked upon with disdain by parents who want desperately for their children to enjoy some time of rest, they have no real choice but to go along, fearing that to buck the system might put their child at an educational disadvantage. Such single-minded focus on raising individual or schoolwide scores on standardized tests is neither unusual nor surprising. Education is both one of Korea's greatest assets and its greatest societal flaws. We could attribute this to contemporary Korea's race to be competitive in a global market, but this national educational frenzy is nothing new. Hendrik Hamel, a Dutch sailor who had the misfortune to be shipwrecked on Cheju Island off the southern coast of Korea in 1653, reported that Koreans indulged in a "national devotion to education." He reported that he observed both aristocrats and those of lesser status "take great care of the Education of their Children, and put them very young to learn to read and write, to which the Nation is much addicted." (Cumings, p. 60) Education has a long and sacred tradition in Korea!

Some idea of the modern version of what Hamel observed can be experienced best during the season of college entrance exams, or Suneung, occurring each November across Korea. (The Korean school year begins in February or early March and runs through the following December.) Below is a news article from November 2017 describing that year's exam. In the previous edition of this book I included a 1997 article – twenty years earlier – describing virtually the same exam scene, and expressing the same misgivings about the stress caused by the exam. A quick YouTube search will reveal any number of news clips describing the scene outside test centers in Korean on the morning of the exam.

South Korean Students Sit College Entrance Exam,
Aided by Chants, Prayers

Reuters News Agency ; 23 NOVEMBER 2017 · 9:32AM

South Korean students sat for their highly competitive university entrance exam on Thursday, a week after it was postponed for the first time ever because of safety concerns after an earthquake.

Schoolmates, teachers and relatives gathered in front of test venues early in the morning to cheer on the test-takers with hugs, chants of motivational slogans to the beat of drums and placards with messages of encouragement.

"I was a bit nervous, but I think I'm much better now and I have a good feeling about the exam", said 18-year-old Kim Chae-yeon, as she waited to enter an exam hall.

The test is life-defining for many high school seniors, as a prestigious university on one's resume is seen a minimum for securing a place in limited corporate jobs in Asia's fourth-largest economy, which is dominated by conglomerates.

More than 590,000 students are expected to take the exam, which stretches over nine hours and includes sections on mathematics, social or natural sciences, Korean, English, and a second foreign language, according to the education ministry.

Authorities take the grueling test very seriously, barring commercial flights from taking off or landing during the English oral section to minimize noise, and opening the stock market and banks an hour later to reduce traffic congestion. Police cars are even dispatched to pick up some students and ensure they reach exam halls on time.

Tensions had run high last Wednesday when the exam was postponed after a 5.4 magnitude quake, the country's second biggest on record.

"Last week was a tough period", said exam-taker Jin Yu-bin. "Some have their college interviews or writing tests on the same day of the exam due to the delay. I feel bad for them."

Elsewhere in the capital on Thursday, places of worship organized special sessions to offer prayers for the test-takers.

"Now the exams are happening, I hope he does not get too nervous and with the effort he has put in, just does his best with it," said Choi Byung-cheol, 55, after praying for his son's success in the exam at Myeongdong Cathedral.

(The Telegraph, November 23, 2017) http://www.telegraph.co.uk/news/2017/11/23/south-korean-students-sit-college-entrance-exam-aided-chants/

As we have seen again and again, we can find many of the same characteristics of Korean education alive and well in Mainland China, only less intense. Certainly the emphasis on memorization and the lack of emphasis on "21st Century Skills" is equally strong in China; what is evident to a somewhat lesser extent is the ubiquitous nature of after school academies, known in China as "buxiban." And where Korea has its Suneung college exams, China has it Gaokao. The article below from South China Morning Post (December 5, 2018) describes the Gaokao:

Gaokao: How One Exam Can Set the Course of a Student's Life in China

Despite its stresses and controversies, the 'high test' provides the only chance for less privileged students to make it to the top

PUBLISHED: Thursday, 08 June 2017, 6:50pm; UPDATED: Monday, 12 June 2017, 8:33am

China started its gaokao exam season this week, with 9.4 million Chinese students taking the annual national college entrance examinations from Wednesday. About 3.7 million of these students are expected to eventually enroll in undergraduate examinations after the exams this year, according to the Ministry of Education. The number will be nearly 10,000 more than those who enrolled last year.

Competition remains fierce to gain admission into the country's top universities, with authorities taking extra measures to prevent cheating, state-run Xinhua news agency reported. Since last year, cheating in the [exam] can be treated as a criminal offence. In China, the gaokao is widely considered to be the most important exam, which can make or break a young person's future. It is also intended to help level

JONATHAN BORDEN

the playing field between the nation's rich and poor.

We explain the significance of the college entrance exams in China, its history and the controversies surrounding it.

176

What is the gaokao?

Gaokao, literally "high test", is an abbreviation of the much longer official name, the National Higher Education Entrance Examination, the academic qualification test for almost all high school graduates hoping to receive an undergraduate education.

The first such standardized examination in the People's Republic of China was held in 1952 but halted 14 years later [when] chairman Mao Zedong decreed that educated youth – including current President Xi Jinping and Premier Li Keqiang – must be "sent down" to the countryside to "learn from the peasants".

The examination was restored in 1977 after the disastrous Cultural Revolution came to an end, making this year's test the 40th anniversary of the restoration of the gaokao. An age restriction on gaokao was scrapped in 2001 and anyone with a high-school diploma can now take the exam. A record of 10.5 million people sat for the gaokao in 2008 but the number has been declining steadily since then. This year 9.4 million students will sit the exam.

What subjects are included in the gaokao?

The examination covers three compulsory subjects – Chinese, mathematics and English – and one comprehensive subject depending whether the candidate chooses to major in liberal arts or the sciences. The whole examination lasts nine hours over two days starting on June 7. In a very few instances ethnic minority students will need to sit the test in their own language on the 9th.

Why gaokao is so important in China

The exam is considered the pivotal moment for Chinese secondary students as their scores in large [part determine their future – whether they can go to university, which institutions they will be admitted and consequently what careers await them. Candidates must perform well in the gaokao to gain admission to the better universities, where graduation guarantees a bright future with status, wealth and even power. For most Chinese, especially those from less privileged backgrounds, a high score in the gaokao is their only means to significantly alter their fate.

"It's a very narrow path but it was the only way for me to leave my rural area and prepare for the world," wrote Yu Minhong, founder of New Oriental Education, a major private language education provider in China. "The gaokao presents many opportunities for children, in rural and urban areas. Without it millions of children from rural backgrounds, including me, would have no hope."

How do students cope with the most important exam in their life?

The answer is to study, study and study some more, at every

possible hour. A lot of students finish their high school studies in the sophomore year and cram for the exam for the whole year. At Hengshui Middle School in Hebei province, where more than 100 students earned admission to the prestigious Peking and Tsinghua universities, students have been given IV drips as they study, believing that it will help them with concentration and focus. Girls are given contraceptive pills to delay their periods until after the exam.

How do parents and others pitch in to help while the gaokao is under way?

Parents are even more nervous than their children taking the exam. They book hotels near the exam centres so the children can rest between the two test sessions at noon or avoid being stuck in morning rush hour traffic.

Although it is common for local governments to make special gaokao arrangements, such as restricting traffic near test centres, there have been cases where worried parents in Anhui, Jiangsu and Shandong blocked roads for fear passing cars would affect listening comprehension part in English test. Square dancers voluntarily stop practising on test nights and noisy construction work comes to halt to give candidates some peace. Some mothers wear qipaos to the test centre for luck.

What are the controversies of the gaokao?

The fierce competition and emphasis on test scores have been criticised for putting students and even their teachers and parents under unnecessary stress, and denying teen-

*agers of getting a well-rounded education. University en-
rolment quota is distributed to each province or provincial-
level municipalities, such as Beijing and Shanghai, based on
the candidate's household registration, which leads to local
policies that forbid non-local students taking the exams in
the areas where they live as migrants.*

*This has led to protests by migrant working families de-
manding the right for their children to take the exams and
be considered for enrolment in Beijing and Shanghai. There
have also been protests by local parents in Jiangsu, Zhejiang
and Hubei against the Ministry of Education's scheme to al-
locate local enrolment quota to western provinces to promote
education fairness.*

*(http://www.scmp.com/news/china/society/
article/2097512/gaokao-how-one-exam-can-set-course-
students-life-china)*

From reading the above articles about the Korean and Chinese college entrance exams, we can see once again that while
the form of both exams are relatively the same, the intensity
of focus which the nation places on the exam is more extreme in Korea. Regardless of the comparative focus placed
on education between these two Confucian cultures, in either
nation the fact remains that the educational systems are test
based, with an extraordinary weight hanging on the results of
the exams. Why is there such an emphasis on education and
college entrance scores that airlines, the military, and police
become involved in Korea in creating the very best test environment for students? Why do Korea and China still experience the "addiction" reported by Hendrik Hamel when he was

shipwrecked on the shores of Korea 350 years ago?

The answer is simple. Today, as in the distant past, one who is educated has the doors opened to the higher echelons of society; an uneducated person is relegated to the very bottom of society. The only difference is that today the opportunity for education is open to all rather than just to the male aristocracy. Ironically, one reason for this emphasis on higher education is that the South Korean, and increasingly the Chinese populations, are over-educated. Without a college education, one can hardly get a clerk's job in a corporation or bank due to this education inflation. There is intense competition even for such spots, however. Only recently has entrepreneurship become possible and popular, particularly in the high tech area; joining a conglomerate for life, at least in Korea, is still the preferred route for many.

Not only is having a college diploma critically important, but also where that diploma comes from is critical to future success throughout Asia. As is true in the Confucian social structures, there is a strict hierarchy in the educational system. Ask any Mr. Kim (or Zhang) in the street which Korean (or Chinese) university is the "best," and he will undoubtedly answer, "Seoul (Beijing) National University." When considering which university would be best for their son or daughter, there is little consideration of his or her abilities, talents, or interests. Nor is there much discussion about the relative strengths or weaknesses of a particular department at a particular university unless one is highly talented in a specialized academic area such as art or music. What is important is the Name brand of the university, both to the applicant and to his or her worried parents: simply and finally, Seoul National is the "best." In mainland China it is generally Beijing University or Bei-Da, in Taiwan it is Taipei University, or Tai-Da; in Japan, To-Dai. Interesting and understandable is the frequent answer given when a Korean is asked what U.S. university is the "best." Without hesitation, he or she will impose the hierarchical (Confucian) model on a very un-Confucian U.S. system, and will almost certainly answer "Harvard." Other famous supposed "Ivy League" colleges are also acceptable, including Stanford and M.I.T.! Unfortunately, schools such as Dartmouth and Brown are not well known, and are often not considered to be "Ivy League," and are therefore not as high in the Korean and Chinese hierarchy. There is no question but that any non-Ivy League school would be considered to be of "inferior" quality. In Korea, just below Seoul National University in this strict hierarchy are Yonsei and Koryo Universities (and the all-women's Ewha University), with a few other Seoul universities following in third. You may you're your Korean students talk about applying to "SKY." This is shorthand for "Seoul National, Korea, and Yonsei Universities – collectively the "Ivy League" of Korea, along with KAIST, the Korea Advanced Institute of Science and Technology, and sometimes Ewha Women's University, which interestingly is seldom considered by Korean international school students.

Finally, there are the universities that are nearly everyone's third, fourth, or last choices. Until recent years, it was impossible in Korea to apply to more than one university in a particular hierarchical level in a given year. Thus, choosing which college to attend was an all-or-nothing exercise. Many students, failing entrance to the college of their choice, become full-time independent students for a year, spending the next twelve months cramming for the following November's exam in hopes that they can earn a higher score and just maybe a coveted seat at the school of their choice, possibly even a SKY school. I know of students who have tried three and four years in a row to get into a particular competitive university.

In China, this hierarchy is not quite as strict (not surprisingly); top universities are Tsinghua, Peking, Fudan, Jiao Tong, and a variety of others. All are held in very high regard and are extremely competitive.

Why is gaining entrance to a particular university so important? First, because once in a school, one does not transfer between universities. Just as people do not generally change companies during their career, students do not transfer; they remain loyal members of their university "group." Transferring is just not a ready option within the Korean educational system. Secondly, the name of the school on a diploma is very important to future life. Certain large corporations hire most exclusively from a particular university, normally the university from which the founder of the corporation was graduated. Earlier we mentioned the life-long importance of peer relationships made in high school and college. Given this importance placed on who you know, certainly, it would be more advantageous to build contacts and close interdependent relationships with those who are headed for positions of power and influence (from their elite university) than with people whose backgrounds were from lower down on the educational hierarchy. The selection of a university can carry directly over into future personal, as well as professional, life. When it comes time to choose a spouse (often a good number of years after college, after military service for males, and after getting settled in life), importance is placed on where one's prospective mate went to school. Graduates of a prestigious university would be marrying far "below" themselves if their intended partner were educated at a provincial or lower-level school.

In China, the name of the university is equally important in finding a job or finding a spouse. However, due to the size of the Chinese population, the proportion of the population who graduated from a four-year college is much smaller than it is in Korea, although the proportion of college students as compared to their age cohort is growing. Therefore, a college graduate marrying a non-graduate is much more common. According to the Ministry of Education of the People's Republic, in 1991 only 3.5% of 18-22 year-olds were enrolled in post-secondary education; twenty years later in 2011 this had risen to 26.9%; by 2014 the number was 37.5%. (Ministry of Education of the People's Republic of China, Gross Enrolment Rate of Education by Level)

Simply put, in both nations, which college one attends can and does have lifelong impact on future employment possibilities, future social status and prestige, and even future marriage partner possibilities. To a much greater degree than is common except at few very elite universities in the West, in Korea and China educational attainment represents more than an academic degree; it is without doubt a highly prized social pedigree. Where you went to university is an important badge carried with you throughout life.

It is interesting to note that although there is tremendous pressure in high school to study hard in order to get into an all-important name university, once a student enters, regardless of the prestige or name of the university, it is nearly impossible, particularly in Korea, to "flunk out." Professors are hesitant to fail students, even those who seldom show up for class. Little emphasis is placed on academics and a great deal on social life, that is, on establishing relationships. There are signs that this is slowly changing as there competition increases for employment after graduation, and employers are looking more and more closely at how well a student did at university (what he or she knows) rather than who he or she has gotten to know. Most college professors, though, could readily tell stories of pressure brought on them by those above in the university hierarchy not to fail students who did virtually nothing to earn a passing grade.

In Mainland China, top students are actively recruited for Communist Party membership as they near graduation. While there is no particular stigma attached to not accepting Party membership, to join the Party does open many economic and career pathways. Particularly, jobs in government often require Party membership.

Until these educational systems change in very some fundamental ways, there is no other way for a student to succeed but to compete; doing everything possible to get ahead of his or her peers. This competitive pressure-cooker atmosphere will most likely not disappear, or even lessen, until classes shrink to a size that allows discussion and the interplay of ideas, until Confucianism and the rigid respect for the way things have always been done is set aside, and until enough children and educators are able to experience Western education that parents won't tolerate this rigid system any longer. This is already being seen by the tremendous pressure for and interest in enrolling children in North American boarding schools, even at the elementary level, and high school exchange student programs, Perhaps some day Korean and Chinese educational cultures characterized by hard work, a structured curriculum, and a respect for teachers will be energized by a synergy with the Western characteristics of creativity, individualistic thinking, and encouragement of diversity. At that point Asian education may well have an unbeatable blend of the best of Eastern and Western education, and will present a formidable challenge to Western educational systems. In both Korea and China the explosion of international and quasi international schools, as well as the loosening of restrictions on local children attending such international schools, many of which are government sponsored, is a strong sign that governments are recognizing both the value of what Western-style education has to offer, as well as providing a pressure release to the growing numbers of parents who simply will no longer impose on their children educational environments and practices that they believe are harmful.

For much more detail on current statistics regarding the structure of the Mainland Chinese educational system, including information about students studying abroad, see the on-line article Education in China, World Education News and Reviews, March 7, 2016. https://wenr.wes.org/2016/03/education-in-china-2

How do such educational environments affect the Korean and Chinese students who are fortunate enough to be attending an international school? For students who are planning to attend university outside of Korea or China, the influence is indirect: their parents carry with them their own memories and attitudes of what a "good" student is, of what it takes to get into a "good" university, and what kind of name brand university is acceptable. They may not understand how non-Korean/Chinese higher education is different from what they experienced, and not realize that they are actually fostering habits and ways of thought that may be handicapping their children's present and future academic success. More on that later.

Further, for students who will be returning from overseas to Korea or China or Japan for university, conforming to the high-pressure expectations of their home countries is a reality. They truly do have to study long hours and memorize. They must cram for college entrance exams in their "home" country while also taking a full load of studies at an international school. They know that they will be "behind" their compatriots when they return home, even if they now have the very important skills of English fluency and the ability to "think outside the box." It is important for the international educator to understand that excelling and doing everything possible to come out on top is truly of crucial importance for these students. They are in many ways being handicapped by being in our schools rather than in their own local schools where their future peers are working overtime to earn coveted spots in top universities. The fact that often the methods they may use to get to the top conflict head-on with the goals and philosophies inherent in many international schools is of little concern to the student and parent. They know that their future lies "back home," and that they will not be ready for that future if they fully adapt to a Western educational philosophy. Thus, they carry two burdens, one to succeed in their international education, and a second to prepare themselves for an educational future in system that demands and values vastly different skills. This can be most easily realized by asking your Korean or Chinese students how many hours they spend at "academy" each week, and how many hours of academy homework they have. You may be shocked that the time spent in after school cram school "academies" rivals the load they already carry from your own international school.

Certainly, being an international Korean or Chinese student often provides some alternate methods of entry to Korean universities. Government rules are constantly changing, and individual universities frequently change their own requirements for "overseas" national students. We'll look at this a little later.

International educators must understand that parents will make tremendous sacrifices — financial, social, or otherwise — to get their child into the university of choice either in their home country or overseas. They recognize that their child's attendance at an international school gives them a chance to get into a Western university and possibly avoiding Korean or Chinese higher education, a chance they possibly never had. Given even a slight chance that their child might be able to go to Harvard or Yale or M.I.T., then, they will do everything in their power to be sure that that happens. Yes, the child might have to suffer long hours of study. Yes, the parents might go into debt. Yes, the child may be interested in something totally different than that which the parents have dreamed about, but if the chance is there, they will go for it. Unfortunately, many parents go about the college search in ways totally appropriate in Korea or China, but that sometimes result in frustration, failure or even tragedy in a Western educational setting. As educators who are working with the children of Korean and Chinese parents, this can become a challenge. In trying to instill such Western educational values as being a well-rounded individual, being able to think critically, creatively, and independently, and "following your dreams" we are confronting a Confucian educational culture five thousand years old. We can become frustrated, for despite our best intentions and sincere attempts, the tendency of many parents is to conform to Korean or Chinese educational norms and values, and to question our advice, however informed, in an area a crucial and life-defining as the choice of a university of career.

Parents quite often make critical decisions regarding the Western education of their children from very considered, very sincere, very serious, but very misinformed positions. We need to understand that when we deal with a Korean or Chinese family we may be dealing not only with parents and their child, but often with the expectations and dreams of grandparents, the demands of the extended family, and the consensus of their community, (particularly the mothers of that community,) as well as other "experts" such as a family friend who is current university student or an older friend whose niece went to a prestigious university. Notably, exorbitantly paid educational consultants, some quite knowledgeable but some whose experience is limited to simply getting into a well-known college themselves, are depended on for definitive advice, as parents believe that a school counselor is spread to thinly to adequately shepherd their child through the college application process. In order to save face for the school counselor, parents and students will often not admit that they have hired an outside consultant, making the entire process more complicated for school counselors. We often need to dig into where opinions or recommendations are coming from to put them in some kind of context, and to help parents and students do the same. Often, their actions and decisions would be very appropriate were they made within Korean or Chinese educational contexts. In the Western context, however, they are often very detrimental to the child and to his or her educational future. It is the responsibility of international educators to do their best to educate parents in these areas. This is not easy; in trusting us, a parent is putting aside what he or she knows to be true from their personal experience and from trusted others, gambling the future of a son or daughter on the words and opinions of a foreigner — an outsider – who may be here today, but gone tomorrow.

Usually, mothers are very well versed in the college application process in their own country. In Korea, for instance, the entire process of preparation for exams, choosing a university and department, completing and submitting applications, etc., etc., is performed by the mother. The child would be concentrating on his or her exam preparation, and not be distracted by the details of the application process. However, when that same parent is faced with the much more ambiguous and confusing process followed in many Western nations, she is likely to turn either to friends who have been through the process before or paid educational consultants. There is too much at stake to leave this process in the hands of their child.

The Role Of The Teacher

Given the Confucian background of Korean and Chinese educational models, we should not be surprised, as mentioned earlier, that teachers are highly esteemed by parents, students, and the community. To a degree that would be only a dream to a teacher in the United States or Canada, teachers are elevated in social status. Hence, the well-known Confucian saying "Do not even step on the shadow of your teacher!" As heirs to traditions thousands of years old, teachers are expected to be models of morality and sources of knowledge and advice, as well as partners with parents in both the educational and child-rearing process. Teachers are both respected and feared. If a Korean child misbehaves at home, for example, a common threat is to tell the child, "If you do that again, I'll tell your teacher!" Pre-school aged children in both countries are spoiled, as parents know that soon enough they will be straightened out and hammered into conformity when they start school. Korean and Chinese societies in general, and parents and students specifically, hold teachers to a high standard of behavior and wisdom, and reward them appropriately. Despite the social distance between teachers and students in Asian schools, students often do have real affection for many of their teachers. A special Teacher's Day is celebrated in both countries; in Korea some schools have reduced or no classes on this day, giving students time to honor their teachers. Students often write "love notes" or give gifts to teachers on this day in appreciation and recognition of their teachers. Some schools have gone as far as to arrange teacher foot washing ceremonies, performed by students.

Earlier I introduced my friend and colleague, Dr. Wang Su-yi, who has been a valued cultural informant for me for a number of years. Regarding the respect awarded teachers, Dr. Wang states,

"As you know, a teacher is regarded as important as the "Heaven, Earth, Emperor, Parent, Teacher" in the Confucius culture. This underlying belief defines the relationship between teachers and parents quite differently from in Western culture. That is why Chinese parents never feel at ease when meet with teachers or administrators."

Time To Think . . .

What educational characteristics mentioned here do you see in your students? Have any of your questions been answered? Have new questions been raised?

What can you learn from your students about what motivates them educationally?

What characteristics mentioned here don't fit some of your students? Why might this be?

Do you suspect that some of your Asian students are chronically sleep deprived? If so, ask them how many hours of sleep they get. Question as to what relationship this might have to academy (hakwon) attendance.

What do you know about the educational plans of your students after high school graduation? Are any headed back to Korean or Chinese educational settings? If they are headed to North America or Europe, what are their plans? Can you or your college counseling department help them to make good choices? How much are they making decisions based on reality, and how much on parental dreams?

How do the educational characteristics of your ethnic Korean and Chinese students affect the academic climate of your school? What opportunities do they present to the school? What challenges do they bring? How might you address these challenges?

The Sacrifice Of A Korean Mother

Born in Japanese occupied Korea in 1920, Kim Soon-im was for many years known to this author as a stately and confident, yet very tired Korean grandmother. She gave birth to three sons and two daughters, and raised them well while being a caring and dutiful wife, as expected of all Korean women. What amazes me, though, is the dedication that she showed her and her husband's extended families over the years as the next generation pursued a quality education. While she had a full house of her own children, throughout her marriage she was also "mother" to 26 other relatives' children for months or even years at a time. Although her husband was well employed as an engineer, sometimes there were not enough rice bowls to go around, and the children had to eat in shifts.

Why was her house so full?

Kim Soon-im and her husband had left their childhood homes in the deep South Korean countryside to move to the port city of Masan shortly after the Korean War. There her children had access to city education, which in those days was much higher in quality than the "country" education she had received. Country relatives sent their children to live with the family to share in this urban educational opportunity. There was little in the way of payment other than an occasional bag of rice from a farm; after all, everybody was "family." It never occurred to her to say that the house was full enough. Relatives would do the same for her children were the situation reversed. She had what her relatives lacked: keys to a city education and a brighter future for her children. She had a family obligation to share those keys. She fulfilled her role with dignity, and it is her proud legacy.

CHAPTER XIV: INDIVIDUAL EXPERIENCES

Sojourners, Immigrants, Returnees, Local children, and TCK's

Up to this point we have discussed the historical, cultural, and educational backgrounds common to the majority of our ethnic Korean and Chinese parents and their children. Now, however, we will look at external influences that affect only certain of our students. The only way to know which of these experiences apply to whom is to ask the students themselves:

Are they "sojourning" Korean or Chinese citizens, coming directly from their home countries but living overseas with the intention of returning home after a few years? (Example #1: A Korean Mom works for Samsung and gets a three-year assignment in Manila. Example #2: Winston Ng is attending boarding school in the U.K. for his high school years and plans to return to Hong Kong to take over the family business some day.)

Are they first or second-generation immigrants who have no intention of moving to their parents' country of origin? (Example: Mr. and Ms. Zhang emigrated from Taiwan to Canada; their children were born in Vancouver. All are Canadian citizens and have no intention of returning to Taiwan.)

If you are teaching in Korea or China, which of your students are "returnees" to the home country of their parents (and who are bi-cultural or wholly Westernized) (Example: Susan Wang, born and raised for many years in Chicago, is living with her parents in Shanghai, the city of their birth and where they have returned to live to care for Susan's aged grandparents. They have no plans to live outside of China in the future, although Susan would like to attend the University of Michigan.)

Which are local children who are simply attending your international school in their home city or country? How do these Western educational experiences mold these children and their parents? (Example: Mr. and Ms. Chao are native Beijingers but want their daughter Xixi to attend English-language Beijing International Academy.)

Are they Third Culture Kids (TCK's) who have lived in a number of countries, following their parents' careers? (Example: Tom YK Kim's dad works for Hyundai and has lived and gone to international schools in Manila, Dubai, Atlanta, Tokyo, and Shanghai. He has never lived in Korea for more than a few weeks at a time, although he has visited his grandparents there once or twice a year.)

Let's look at each of these possibilities in detail:

Children As Sojourners

"Sojourners" are by definition individuals who have left their home country and culture with the intent to someday return – in three months, three years, or even three decades. They retain their native culture, although they may also take on characteristics of the host culture in which they live.

In examining the huge numbers of Asian young people who are leaving their native educational system in search of a Western education, the phrase "Exodus from Excellence" comes to mind. These young people for one reason or another see a brighter future, or possibly a less dark present, in changing to more flexible and open systems that will depend less on conformity and more on individual talents and goals. Although Asian education has gained an international reputation of some renown, as we have discussed, and many have experienced, high scores and Harvard acceptances is only a very small part of the story – perhaps the bright top if the iceberg. For one reason or another, unless you are teaching in a completely local school, your students have chosen your school as an attractive alternative to the education available to most people in their home country.

While there is a plethora of statistics regarding the number of university level students from Korean, China, and Japan studying abroad, there is much less information available regarding middle and high school students who have chosen the same path. Of all international university students in the United States, China, India, and Korea are consistently the top three sending nations, although in very recent years the numbers from Korea have been dropping somewhat. Both independent and public schools in North America are host to many thousands of students who come from East Asian nations. In addition, there are also thousands of East Asian students living outside their home countries either in boarding programs or with one parent (or in some cases, no parent) at international schools, primarily in East Asia. As is true of most students attending international schools around the world, many of these students are following their parents whose jobs are taking them to other nations, and as a result East Asian students end up attending Western style international schools, although larger cities, such as Shanghai and Beijing, are also home to Korean and Japanese schools. The Western educational experience is thrust on them, although they may have rather continued with their national system of education. However, just as some students specifically are sent overseas to Western countries to study outside of their home country, a check among the Korean or Chinese students at any international school will likely show a considerable number who are living overseas specifically in order to receive an international, Western style education. It is very common, for example, to find Korean students living in China or the Philippines, attending international schools, and living with one non-working parent. Normally dad remains back at "home." Koreans even have a term for these dads: "Gireogi Appa" or "goose dad," given the fact that he often flies back and forth to see his family. Unfortunately, complaints are also heard from international school teachers in countries like the Philippines that in fact some Korean students, even in elementary school, are living in boarding houses run by Koreans while attending international schools, having been admitted under the understanding that they would live with at least one parent.

Added to these students who are physically living outside their home country for the sake of getting a Western education are local students attending "international" programs that are exploding in both China and Korea. Some of these are international divisions of well-regarded indigenous schools (for example, Shanghai High School International Division) or branches of or joint ventures with well-known schools in Western countries. Many have proliferated in larger Chinese cities, many with relationships with both North American and European, particularly British, institutions. (I have my own theories as to why Korean and Chinese parents might prefer British to American style education, mostly to do with curricular structure.) The Korean government has been sponsoring for some years the Jeju Global Education City on Jeju Island in Korea, which currently hosts four international schools – one each from Canada, the United Kingdom, and the United States, as well as a second campus of the indigenous Korea International School.

Sojourning students are not simply taking a "year abroad" to experience a different culture and educational experience; they and their families have made an intentional decision to leave the familiarity of the educational system of their home country to embark on a life-changing Western educational experience. Whether a student is going across the world or across the city to attend an international school, however, the question remains: Why make such a life-changing decision? Why leave behind the familiar culture, language, and educational system that parents grew up with, and through which parents can guide their children, to an unfamiliar system fraught with huge linguistic and cultural barriers, not to mention the fact that parents are now putting their children's education and future in the hands of unfamiliar foreigners? To what degree are the educational advantages of an international high school diploma (with possible hopes for entrance to a Western university) behind such decisions, and to what degree are families escaping their own system? Certainly both of these forces are at work, pushing students away from Confucian-based education while simultaneously pulling them to Western education, to varying degrees for different families. The literature and media are rife with stories glorifying the high academic standards and achievements of Chinese and Korean students, as well as stories (and statistics) highlighting the high levels of stress, suicide rates, and general unhappiness that cloud the lives of many Chinese and Korean students. The competition and stakes are so high for Asian students to succeed within their systems that young people are judged more on their identity as students (successful or not) than they are on what kind of individuals they are becoming in terms of character and life skills. This author, in counseling families who seem torn apart by teen/parent conflict, has often found that the conflict almost completely is centered on academic achievement. I have challenged parents by asking them when was the last time they had a meaningful conversation with their child about something other than grades and schools. Sadly, often the parents could not recall when that was, nor can the child. Too often a child's identity and worth is tied to their academic prowess – or lack of it. I remember distinctly a parent conference with a Korean dad, centered on his son's declining grades. As we were lamenting the boy's less than stellar grades and study habits, the dad suddenly exclaimed "He is a bad son!" When I pushed him as to why he said this, his reply focused entirely on the son's academic issues. It was a struggle to get the dad to understand that while he might be a less than top student, he could still be a good son (and a decent kid). While parents grieve over seeing their children one-dimensionally, they also feel caught in a self-imposed win/lose competition among students (and parents) for the "top" grades in a class – an important measure in hierarchical Asian schools.

Another "pull" to move overseas is related to the relatively recent diaspora of Korean and Chinese workers and missionaries; mirroring the exponential economic growth in their own countries. Since the mid-1980's Korea and Taiwan, and more recently Mainland China, have become increasingly important and involved members of the international community. Korean and Chinese conglomerates have plants and offices all over the world, staffed by Korean and Chinese executives and engineers who bring their families with them. Korean Christian churches are sending out missionaries by the thousands, as well. In recent years South Korea has had roughly 20,000 missionaries serving overseas; Chinese Christians are aiming at that number by the year 2030. (Christianity Today, January 1, 2016) Many of these missionaries have children who wish to attend international schools. In many cases, these missionaries are serving in very low-key roles in Arab or Moslem majority nations (as are foreign Christian missionaries in mainland China). In addition, thousands of adult Korean and Chinese students and educators are studying and teaching around the globe. The children of many of these expatriates are found in international schools. In some locales there may be only one or two ethnic Korean or Chinese families. In cities or remote work sites where an organization or company has a substantial presence, however, they may make up a large proportion of the student population. Stories of small missionary schools suddenly becoming inundated with Korean students when Samsung opens a new factory in town are common, seriously impacting the culture of a school, not to mention the demands of potentially large numbers of ESL students.

The "Third Culture Kid" Phenomenon

Many of these children that we find in international schools become what are known as "Third Culture Kids," or "TCK's." TCK's are defined as being either 1) mobile children who are growing up in cultures different from either their nation of citizenship or that of the culture of their parents, or 2) those who are growing up in an international school environment and social culture even though they may live in their parents' home culture. For example, a Korean child living in Uzbekistan with his missionary parents is a TCK. An American or German child growing up in Korea would similarly be a TCK. An ethnic Korean child attending an international school in Korea would also be a TCK by virtue of the fact that he or she is experiencing a mobile, international culture. Conversely, a girl from Shanghai attending an "international" division of a local school that enrolls a very small proportion of non-Chinese would not normally be considered a TCK, because no second culture (a mobile multinational student body) exists at that particular school. (The classic source for information about the characteristics of TCK's both as children and later as adults is *The Third Culture Kid Experience: Growing Up Among Worlds, 3rd Ed.*, by David C. Pollock, Ruth E. Van Reken, and Michael V Pollock. The international world owes a huge debt to these authors and leaders in the field of TCK education and socialization. These authors describe a number of characteristics shared by most TCK's, whatever their national background. One would ask – "So what is this THIRD culture?" Think of Seung-ho Kim, a Korean boy who lives in Toyko and goes to an international school there. Seung-ho shares his FIRST culture with his parents – Korean; he speaks Korean fluently. His SECOND is the host culture, in Seung-ho's case that would be Japanese because he is living in Tokyo. However, Seung-ho attends an "American" international school in Tokyo that enrolls students from 45 different nations, and his best academic language is English. Is his school completely American? No. It is Japanese? No. But it does have a "third" culture that is uniquely international by virtue of its student body and the mix they all bring to the school. After a while, Seung-ho takes on this THIRD culture – he is no longer 100% Korean, and neither does he become Japanese, although maybe he can speak Japanese fluently and can "pass" as Japanese. Seung-ho is a classic Third Culture Kid – his culture is now international, and he will retain some aspect of that internationalism throughout his lifetime. When asked where he feels most at home, he doesn't talk about a place, but about being with a certain group people – his fellow TCK's – wherever in the world they may be spending their childhoods.

We will see in later on that, as is true for most TCK's, an overseas experience for a Korean or Chinese child can be a double-edged sword. For example, by attending an international school, the child avoids, at least for part of his or her education, the grueling Korean or Chinese system. While this is a real plus in many ways (one which is the envy of many or his or her cousins back home) it is also a real negative if and when the child returns to his or her homeland and enters a local school. The very rigidity of the Korean and Chinese systems and the difficulty these systems have in accepting diversity work against the re-entry adjustment of returning students. In addition, the more the child or family has acculturated to the foreign or international culture, the less "Korean" or "Chinese" they become and the less fit they are to return to a stricter Confucian society, with its emphasis on conformity. Conversely, they will eventually be more able to succeed in the larger international community as adults. Children may lose their sense of being Korean or Chinese and find themselves experiencing an increasingly wide cultural gap with their parents. Their parents may fear that their children are becoming too "foreign." In fact, their fears may be valid, and in large part we, their teachers, are responsible.

As mentioned earlier, the gurus of the Third Culture Kid experience are David Pollock and Ruth van Reken. I offer a special tribute to a good friend and international colleague, Dave Pollock, who introduced me to the whole idea of Third Culture Kids too long ago for me to admit. Dave counseled thousands of TCK's himself, and was visiting a school in Vienna when he tragically and unexpectedly passed away. I was attending an international Christian schools conference in Vienna at which Dave was expected to speak, and many of the participants were former missionary kids who had known him all their lives. The international world lost a wonderful friend and confidant with Dave's passing, and he has been missed greatly. His work continues, however.

TCK's exhibit a number of interesting characteristics as a result of their mobile, international lifestyle. Pollock and van Reken note a number of these characteristics, particularly in relation to Korean and Chinese young people, but we should remember that TCK's come from many countries of origin.

1. Most TCK's have an opportunity to learn a number of languages, including English. This is a real plus for children returning to their parents' home countries to study. Foreign language institutes are found in almost every neighborhood in Korea and in Chinese cities, and children as young as three and four are enrolled in English language programs. Asian countries are trying hard to communicate with the rest of the world to gain a more equal standing. In truth, bilingual adults have an advantage over their monolingual (English-only) counterparts across the negotiating table, whether the discussions are political or economic in nature. Returning to Korea or China from their international experience fluent in English can give students a real edge in school, although they may be held suspect by their foreign language teachers whose language ability is often far below that of their returning students. This can cause some uneasiness and even jealousy for teachers who are accustomed to being the unchallenged font of all knowledge. Overall, however, high English scores on the all-important college entrance test give students a strong advantage, and may help to balance weaknesses in other academic areas. Korean students living in China have an added advantage – it is quite easy for Koreans to learn passable Mandarin due to the fact that a good proportion of Korean vocabulary is based on Chinese, at least in written Chinese. While the two languages don't sound the same, there are

enough cognates to provide a good foundation. In addition, most Chinese would look at a Korean child and expect them to speak Chinese, so there is an added cultural incentive. Thus, when a Korean child moves from Shanghai or Beijing into Korean education, they come with fluent English, Mandarin, and perhaps another European language, in addition to their native Korean.

2. Most TCK's develop cross-cultural skills, a high degree of cultural flexibility, a three-dimensional worldview, and an international orientation to world issues. Today, increasingly Asian nations are becoming involved, respected, and powerful members of the international community. For this new status to continue to grow these nations need individuals who can operate from a wider perspective than that of someone who has always lived in a small, mono-cultural nation like Korea or a historically isolated nation like China. While returned TCK's eventually become vanguards in the national race for internationalism, the TCK experience may in the short term be responsible for these young people's not fitting in well in nations rife with nationalism and xenophobia; this is particularly true in Korea. Having cross-cultural skills and an international perspective often means being able to see an international conflict from both sides. However, being able to express other than purely national perspectives on issues may land the young person in hot water with new friends who may see him or her as being disloyal to "our nation" and its position in world affairs. They are not unique among TCK's in this regard, who often experience this problem when they return to a "home" where they may have never lived and where they feel like outsiders, with perhaps a more balanced, international perspective on national issues.

3. TCK's tend to be mature for their age due to their experi-

ences. This is a real plus if the student returns to college in their cultural homeland. Often, native students in China or Korea have had one goal in life up until the time they enter college, and that has been to be a top student. Life skills, independence, personal initiative, and common sense are often lacking. They all too often simply look to their "seniors" for clues to how to behave. However, many TCK's of whatever nationality are more able to resist temptation, make informed judgments, and behave in mature ways than their peers who have never lived outside their home country. On the other hand, if they have not lived in Korea or China during their teenage years, they may be naive to the youth culture and be unaware of ways to stay out of trouble. Just as a Canadian TCK might feel "out of it" and uncertain when moving to Canada, so might a Korean TCK upon "returning" to Korea. He or she must quickly learn to "be Korean" in order to fit in and not be the nail that sticks up. While China is a little more tolerant of people who don't fit in culturally, much of the same phenomenon is true there as well, as it is to anyone who has spent most of his or her life outside of their "home" country where others assume they belong.

Although mature, TCK's can also be quite naive. Some well-traveled TCK's can tend to be what I call "world smart; street stupid." Most are completely comfortable hopping on a plane and flying half way around the world to meet an old friend or go to summer school. They know how to book a plane reservation, use a credit card, book a hotel, and figure out what to do when a flight is cancelled. They expect jet lag, and know how to deal with it. They can travel to a country where they don't speak a word of the language and figure it out. I know personally of a middle school girl who "ran away" from home – or more accurately, flew away from home. (I have changed some details of this story for obvious reasons.) One long weekend her father called me, her principal, asking if I knew where she was. Through the help of a friendly school travel agent, we tracked this young lady from Shanghai to Amsterdam to Atlanta, where an aunt eventually intercepted her. In the course of a four day weekend, she had gone to the airport, purchased a ticket to Amsterdam, taken a taxi to a downtown hotel to spend the night, eventually booked another flight to Atlanta to see her aunt, and found a way to contact her aunt when she got there. All this before the days of email, on-line ticketing, texts, and cell phones. When I talked to her after this saga, I asked her if she felt any fear during her excursion. "No," she replied. She was completely comfortable, at the age of 12, with making these travel arrangements, using a credit card, and flying around the world. What worried me (but not her) was the fact that she was a young Asian girl, traveling alone, arriving in a strange city in the middle of the night, asking a taxi driver to take her to a hotel, checking in to the hotel, etc. etc. Her confidence in traveling was extraordinary and today serves her well as an adult; her lack of awareness into the danger of being a lone middle school girl in a strange European city at night was completely lost on her. Many international middle schoolers would think nothing of traveling from Asia to Europe or North America on their own, but wouldn't understand that walking across their Boston summer school campus alone in the dark might not be a good idea. World smart, street stupid.

4. TCK families tend to be close, especially if they have moved from country to country. Due to the fact that often TCK children may move from country to country more regularly, family bonds can be closer than more stationary families. They have experienced a lot of adjustment together, and need to depend on one another when they first arrive in a new country. Home, whether an empty apartment or a hotel room becomes their temporary safe haven because that is all the family has for the moment. Asian families are already often close, with strong parental/child ties, a tradition of caring and

respect, and a sense of history tied to ancestors. However, other dynamics may come into play that work against family cohesion. Primarily, growing cultural differences between parents and children take their toll on family ties. While it would be unfair to say that Chinese families are not as close, the very common phenomenon of both parents working long hours outside the home, and the children being brought up and nurtured by grandparents (who are often very much a part of the nuclear family), works against very close child/parent relationships; this is particularly true of Chinese fathers, who can be quite distant emotionally from their children (as can Korean dads). Every family's relationships and dynamics are unique, of course. The phenomenon of the bicultural family – with the parents being culturally from one society, and the children, while certainly influenced by the parents' culture, being primarily molded by the international/Western (school) or host country culture – is very common. Often when we speak of a bicultural family, we assume that the two parents are from different cultures, which may indeed be true. However, increasingly the "bi" part of bicultural refers to the parents' original culture and children's international culture.

5. TCK's tend to make and drop friends easily. Due to their sometimes frequent moves, or the coming and going of other TCK friends, they (and their adult counterparts) tend to develop strong people skills, and can easily make friends quickly. They seem at ease meeting new people, and are open to new friendships. Unfortunately, these friendships often are quite shallow because they have learned that it hurts too much to say "goodbye." The converse of making friends quickly is also true – because they have "lost" friends so often, they also develop a sort of "quick release" mechanism for friendships. I have found myself doing the same thing as I have experienced new teachers coming and leaving every year. The good news is that technology now means that "Goodbye"

doesn't mean forever; it means until we FaceTime as soon as we get WiFi, wherever we land. So much of young people's lives and relationships are lived on line that it makes long distance relationships much easier to maintain.

The Immigrant Experience

As noted earlier, many ethnic Korean and Chinese children living outside Korea or China, and most hyphenated children (Chinese-Canadian, Korean-American, Taiwanese-German, etc.) students, are the children of immigrants. The parents' and children's views of their own identities have been molded by their immigrant experiences, whatever their adopted country may be. No longer do they see themselves as purely "Korean," or "Chinese" although they may identify themselves as such. The longer they or their parents or grandparents have lived outside of their ethnic home country the more they have become acculturated to their new country and to the Western culture, particularly after beginning school as young children. Schools have always been, both figuratively and literally, any nation's cultural classroom. In nations nourished by recurring waves of immigrants, schools have been the primary acculturating structure and influence for newcomers.

Whether currently living as immigrants outside their native countries or having now returned to their native countries either temporarily or permanently, bringing with them their culturally foreign children, these individuals — many of whom are our students' parents — have had or are having the experience of being new immigrants. For most immigrants, their adopted nations lured them as "lands of promise" rather than "lands of opportunity." They have suffered the long waits and not infrequent indignities during the immigration process, from standing in long "visa lines" in Seoul or Beijing to a possibly less than friendly welcome in their new neighborhood. For example, those who have gone to the United States might have had a Hollywood image of the U.S. before departure, which of course may clash with the reality of long work days and difficult living situations in their new homes.

They may have expected instant riches, as well as gunfights on every corner, but have found neither. Job discrimination, usually based on cultural differences or lack of English ability, but sometimes blatantly racial, may have kept them from advancing through business ranks unless they limited their sights to strictly ethnic-run businesses. It is not unusual to find a graduate from a "top" Asian university operating a grocery or liquor store to support the family, with all of the family working 18-hour days, struggling to ensure that the children receive a "top" American education. Although initially after immigrating they might have felt that they were advancing quickly through the economic ranks, eventually they may have reached a point of economic frustration, a glass ceiling beyond which they could not go. This often occurs about fifteen years after arrival, and can lead to frustration and depression at the lack of unlimited opportunity in their new country. The individual may become convinced that the "promise" of the adopted land was a sham. Most, however, decide to stick it out and dream of their children fulfilling their own now frustrated aspirations. They want to live out their dreams of the West vicariously through their children.

The history of Chinese immigration to the United States is long and winding, not without its chapters of legally codified racism as well as eras of periodic discrimination. Chinese began to come to North America in the 1850's both to mine gold (as a result of the 1849 California Gold Rush) and later to build Western railroads, as well as to work in factories and in agriculture. However, due to blatant racism and fear of the numbers of Chinese entering the United States, from 1882 to 1943 Chinese immigration was severely limited, with final barriers (shared with various other immigrant groups) lifted in 1965. Today Chinese are the third largest foreign-born immigrant group in the United States, falling behind Mexican and Indian; in 2016 there were more than 2.3 million Chinese immigrants in the U.S., mostly skilled or highly educated workers, and mostly located in New York State or California. For in-depth data on various aspects of Chinese immigration to the U.S., see "Chinese Immigrants in the United States," Migration Information Source, Sept. 29, 2017).

Korean immigrants (who from 1910 to 1945 were considered Japanese citizens due to Japanese colonization of Korea) faced many of the same discriminatory legal and cultural limitations, as did the Chinese until 1965. For the most part, Korean immigrants to the U.S. have been both driven from Korea and attracted to the United States by political, military, and economic ties and opportunities. In 1970 there were approximately 39,000 Korean immigrants in the U.S.; by 2015, nearly one million. Since 2010, however, the numbers have actually decreased due to the rise in standards of living in Korea (as discussed earlier) that both reduced outflow from Korea and increased reverse-migration. Many of the children of these "reverse migrants" find themselves attending international schools in Korea, in some cases because they are too Westernized educationally and socially to attend Korean schools, in some cases because parents intentionally want their children to continue to experience Western-style education.

Many Korean immigrants to North America in the 1970's and early 1980's became quite acculturated to their adopted society. There were few Korean communities, and learning English and adopting local cultural norms was imperative. In more recent years in the United States, however, as the number of ethnic Koreans has risen it is becoming less and less necessary for Korean- Americans, especially in some of the larger Korean communities such as in Los Angeles, New York, or Chicago, to become acculturated. They may tend to "ghetto" themselves, living totally "Korean-style," neglecting to learn English, even holding on to those Korean values and expectations which might be hindrances to success in America. Their children follow generations of immigrant children who suffer both generational and cultural gaps with their parents. Relationships with parents may become problematic: as the children grow up proficient in English, they sometimes lose respect for their parents as parents come to depend on them for help in English to survive. An interesting subgroup among immigrant teens and young adults is what is called (for Koreans) the "il-chum-oh," or "1.5" generation. They belong to neither first nor second-generation immigrant groups, having immigrated as teenagers. They have a core of cultural values and language learned in childhood covered by a veneer of Western characteristics learned after immigration. They do not fit in comfortably with either their parents' generation or other new immigrants, who seem old fashioned or "too Korean/Chinese." On the other hand, they do not fit in with their much more Westernized younger siblings or peers who entered their new country at a much younger age and who lack cultural and linguistic roots of their nation of origin. Often their English is imperfect, yet neither can they speak, read, or write age-appropriate Korean or Chinese. They may find themselves only partially literate in two languages, and completely literate in none. They may find solace with other 1.5's, and find themselves in conflict with both first and second-generation immigrants. Unfortunately, these "in between" immigrants are often the source of ethnic gang related groups as they struggle to work out their personal identity as well as carve out a place for themselves in their new host culture as they conform to neither their original nor their new country's cultural norms.

Most immigrant parents expect their children to become active participants in the culture of their new country, wherever it may be. A minority, however, want their children to retain their native culture, living as cultural expatriates while being naturalized citizens. They want their children to keep native culture and values alive, to speak their parents' language fluently, and to marry same-culture spouses, all the while profiting from greater economic and educational opportunities than those they may have left behind. While the desire for many Koreans and Chinese to expect their child to attend only an "Ivy League" university (a term that is used with great ease and greater misunderstanding among many Asians, as we saw earlier) is well documented. In fairness we must state that this phenomenon is not limited to Koreans and Chinese; many Vietnamese and Indians also share this characteristic, and previous groups of immigrants whose cultures have held education in high regard (earlier Jewish immigrants, for example) also held such high expectations. It is interesting to note that such very high educational expectations for any immigrant group have generally lasted only one generation; it remains to be seen whether newly immigrated ethnic Koreans and Chinese will follow the same path.

For those readers who are teaching immigrant children or foreign-born children of immigrants, the degree to which what you have just read applies depends on a variety of factors: the age of the parents at immigration, the age of the children at immigration, whether or not the family plans to return "home," whether the family lives in an ethnic community or has more fully acculturated, parents' educational level, and many other factors. Getting to know the children and their parents, their history, and their backgrounds is crucial to understanding the children as students, as it may well affect their current academic habits and eventual educational aspirations. Talk to your students; ask them questions about their backgrounds and future plans.

The Returnee Experience: "Coming Home" Or A "Hidden Immigrant"?

Many overseas ethnic Korean and Chinese families return home to live either temporarily or permanently. What are the reasons for this "return migration?" There are as many answers to that question as there are families. Some who went to the West to study for a few years as undergraduates or graduate students just stayed on, married others of the same ethnic group, and settled down in their new countries, becoming "educational immigrants." Others who intentionally emigrated to the West may have tired of or grown frustrated with the immigrant experience, as discussed earlier. Their dream of success in their adopted country may have gone sour, or a sense of duty to aging parents may have demanded their return. As they enter their mid-thirties, their parents would be approaching sixty, the age at which their parents are retired and are considered honorable elders. They may expect their adult children to return home and care for them. Others may return due to the lure of new job opportunities, free of the social burden of being "immigrants." Others may simply be homesick. Of course, for many overseas non-immigrants the reason for going overseas was job related and their term of a few years of overseas service has simply ended. These are the "sojourners" discussed earlier.

Whatever their reason for returning home, both parents and children share certain common experiences. For example, children are often considered by parents and extended family members to be "returning" home, but in fact they may have never lived there. They are, unlike their parents, moving to a foreign country, although one which they may know a great deal about. They may fit in easily, or may suddenly find themselves (once again) immigrants in their own country or origin. Ironically, parents who have worked very hard to be sure to carry on their culture and traditions with their children may find that, due to the rapidly changing cultures of Korea and China, they are more traditional than their relatives and friends they meet "back home" where things have changed dramatically in the previous twenty years.

The child faces a difficult situation should his or her family, for whatever reason, return to their homeland. He or she has been exposed to the pluralism of Western culture, lifestyles and standards, and has acquired fluency in English. He or she has truly become a hyphenated Asian, a mix of rich family cultural characteristics and valuable Western characteristics and attitudes. Many of the qualities that meant "success" in the Western/international culture or international school environment were fostered and cultivated by parents and the school. Some of these characteristics become negatives, however, when the plane touches down at Incheon, Shanghai, or Hong Kong. The firm Western handshake or look in the eye may offend grandfather. Grandmother may consider a girl's wide smile and ready laugh or dark makeup to be unladylike - "nice girls" don't do those things. The Korean child's practiced bow of greeting may not be quite deep enough for the grandparents; his spoken Korean possibly childish (which makes it rude due to the levels of Korean language) and unacceptable; her hairstyle or clothes too extreme. He or she may not have learned the more polite formal body language a native-born Korean child would have learned naturally. The Chinese child may have taken on Western attitudes of independence and styles of dress that don't sit well with grandparents. His or her outgoing, gregarious, confident, fun-loving and inquisitive nature may not be appreciated in a nation where children are to be first and foremost successful and serious students. Children may make negative comments about their "backwards" country cousins. Suddenly these well-adjusted young people may find themselves the objects of well-intentioned but undisguised ridicule by relatives and neighbors, and quickly realize that being American or Canadian or German or having lived overseas is not appreciated or valued in Korea or China, and in fact may be the root of social unacceptability and an embarrassment to parents. He or she is not considered to be a "foreigner" by relatives (which would possibly result in them being given a little cultural slack), but rather a poorly mannered and ill-adjusted Chinese or Korean child. Parents often become the object of blame — "Why did you bring me here?" is a common theme. The children quickly become what Pollock and Van Reken call "hidden immigrants." They look like they belong, they are treated as if they belong, but they do not belong – and they soon realize this – but these are cultures in which belonging is of tremendous importance. Complicating this is that as parents realize how different their child really is, they may do everything possible to re-acculturate them by enrolling them in special institutes or by hiring local tutors. Many are enrolled in local schools and are just expected to "sink or swim." Some swim, but many do not. Many of these children end up in our international school admissions offices. In Korean international schools, ethnic Korean children have long been the majority ethnic group, often by a very large margin. In some international schools in Korea, the only Western children are those of faculty members! As the Chinese economy takes off, and government regulations loosen, China is also following this pattern. In fact, many international schools in China are purposely enrolling more culturally Chinese children in order to stay afloat financially.

The phenomenon of the "hidden immigrant" is not limited to Asian children. Most hidden immigrants speak his or her native language fluently, but conversely has more trouble "conversing" culturally in any fluent way. He or she feels an odd sense of being apart from the culture, and observing what is going on without truly participating. He or she learns to bite their tongue sometimes when they feel the urge to say something that would be culturally unpopular, or just inappropriate. Many of us who have lived overseas for any length of time – sojourners ourselves - have been caught in such situations. At a summer seminar during my Ph.D. program with Walden University, I was attending a session dealing with multiculturalism. When I arrived I realized that most of the participants were African-American or Puerto Rican. Somehow I had expected a room full of Asians and Europeans (American culture shock #1!) "Multiculturalism" to me meant international, which this group clearly was not. During the discussion among this group of well-educated doctoral students, the conversation came around to the difference between deep human values and cultural values. I offered the thought that "Actually, despite what we were taught as children, perhaps we AREN'T really all the same under the skin." The room went silent. People turned around to look at me as if I were some kind of ignorant redneck from the backwoods. The hostility was palpable. My attempt to engage in a deeper, doctoral-level, value-free discussion of deeper cultural realities was interpreted as a racist rant. I tried to rescue my words, but without success. I had clearly taken my 30+ years of international living and dropped it into Middle America, although a very educated sample of it. My words did not resonate, they did not bounce. They dropped like a rock into a bottomless quarry. I soon found an excuse to leave the room and escape the increasingly warm environment. It was an unforgettable "hidden immigrant" moment for me, not one I want to repeat.

Perhaps is an extreme example, but I think we've all been caught in conversations in which we have nothing to add because we know nothing (and maybe care not at all) about that TV show or movie or latest sports scandal, or perhaps rather than risk the humiliation of exposing the fact that "self-checkout" at the supermarket might be a challenge for us. Or, as I have done, politely handed cash to a clerk at Wal-Mart with both hands – as I would have done in Korea – and gotten a somewhat quizzical look. Sometimes just not saying anything and making a quick retreat is the best strategy, although it doesn't advance our quest for acculturation.

Not only are the children "hidden immigrants," facing culture shock and possible ridicule upon return to their "home" country, but parents as well are suddenly expected to act totally Korean or Chinese, and possibly take on the role of obedient children to aged parents. For fathers, life may become more pleasant, with new opportunities for professional and social advancement opening up. However, the Asian business culture demands long hours, including working until seven or eight o'clock at night (or until the boss leaves) and a half day on Saturdays, with business "golf" meetings on Sundays. After work, there are often obligatory dinners out with fellow workers or visiting customers, not ending until everyone has had far too much to drink. More then one "returnee" marriage has reached a crisis when for the first time dad starts to come home drunk in the wee hours. The Western family tradition of "dad home by five, dinner at six, and some family time afterwards" too often quickly disappears, with dad seldom (and unpredictably) returning home before very late in the evening. Only recently has there been a growing realization in the Korean business culture that husbands have responsibilities to the family in addition to bringing home a fat paycheck, but this is only slowly developing. Too often a couple who has developed and grown into a Western-style marriage finds that due to the husband's job demands, their marriage is taking on a less intimate, sharing atmosphere. Children see less and less of their fathers, and mothers take on a much more central and "Korean mother's" role with the children. Often the breadwinner, who was sent to Korea or China by a Western company, is quickly recruited away by a local company, with the loss of an international compensation package, including international school tuition. This same phenomenon takes place in China, but to a lesser extent, in large part due to the more equal status of men and women.

The situation for mothers may be more difficult. If a woman never became acculturated to the West, it may be easy, even a relief, to come "home." If she became somewhat Westernized, however, she faces a cultural dilemma, realizing that she no longer really "fits" in. Many are the returnee moms who have admitted, "I always felt like an outsider in America, because I knew I was different. Now I feel like an outsider in Korea, because everyone else tells me I'm different. I'm not sure that

I belong anywhere." A young Canadian-Korean teacher states, "It's ironic. I find that I feel more Canadian when I'm in Korea and more Korean when I'm in Canada."

Old college friends tell the returning mom that somehow she is different, that she speaks and dresses and holds herself like a foreigner. Other mothers' intense discussion of their own children's education and upcoming exams and expensive tutors makes her realize that she has little in common with them, and she may begin to feel guilty that by taking her children overseas she has put them behind the children of her old friends, and has robbed them of the pride of being Korean or Chinese. In China, where most women work, there is less time for socialization (except through social media such as WeChat), so this pressure to compete is somewhat ameliorated, but is still apparent.

Changing Roles For Returnees

A further dynamic for "returning" mothers, particularly in Korea, is that often they must resume the role of daughter-in-law that they have not practiced since they left Korea, possibly as young brides. Due to the tremendously inflated real estate prices in Korea and in larger Chinese cities, many returning families who lived well overseas may be forced to live with in-laws for a while until they can afford their own apartment. In Korea, given the very strong bonds between a son and his mother, even in adulthood, a whole new set of family dynamics may emerge, particularly if the mother-in-law does not understand the cultural changes that her son and his wife have experienced while living abroad. This may bode ill for the daughter -in-law, particularly if she becomes the object of blame for not bringing up her children "properly," adding to her feelings of alienation and incompetence. In China a much less hierarchical relationship between parents-in-law and adult children, but it is very common for returning sons and daughters to move in with parents, most likely in greatly reduced living space. Suddenly the head of the home is an aged grandparent with no international experience or understanding.

A result of these radical changes in lifestyle is that the somewhat Westernized mothers often turn to others who will understand their predicament — others who are suffering the same adjustments. As mentioned earlier, teachers and administrators in international schools may realize that informal grade level "Korean/Chinese mothers' clubs" develop as support groups — both to help members deal with their alienation to their old homelands and to provide information and support in matters related to the international school system into which they have placed their children. If these moms are knowledgeable about the school's culture, aims, and values, positive communication can result, with those less acculturated to Western education benefitting from this interaction and learning from those moms who are better informed. However, quite often peer pressure and age-based (or husband's position-based) hierarchies develop within the groups that may result in a solidarity of opinions regarding schooling, based on misinformation or misunderstanding that may not be healthy for either the school or the children. A teacher or administrator, in trying to deal with a difficult academic or behavioral situation, may find that he or she is not just dealing with the child's parents, but with the solidarity of opinion of the mother's social group to which she may have gone for advice. These groups may become vehicles for comparisons of report card grades, honor role status, and SAT results, even of the children of moms not in the group. Gossip regarding teachers and other families can rage, not so much about personal family issues (as might be true in the West) but about whose child is at the top of the class, who got in trouble at school (and thus who to keep one's own child away from), who got accepted at what college (and who didn't), what teacher is the "best" in the seventh grade, etc., etc. This unhealthy situation can and does result in a great deal of competition among mothers based on children's grades, summer school plans, and college acceptances. The need to conform to the opinion of the group in order to be accepted may be overwhelming for some mothers. Unfortunately, the ease of communication and sharing information with many others simultaneously made available by social media platforms has greatly exacerbated this problem for many schools. WeChat (in China) and Kakao Talk (in Korea) have taken the place of the Tuesday morning coffee group, but can get out of hand even more quickly.

It is important to remember that each returning family's priorities and dreams are different. One family might wish to remain as Westernized and international as possible while being in Korea or China, and plan on the children going to university in the West and eventually settling there. They want their children to attend an international school where they can continue to enjoy the benefits of a Western education and learn to be truly multicultural. Alternately, they may send their children to boarding school in the country they lived in rather than bring them "home" with them. Others want their children to learn to become Korean or Chinese, but realizing the demands and limited opportunities of the local educational system, and recognizing that their children could never survive entering at the middle or high school level, they wish to enroll their children in international schools. We can hope that they choose to give their children an international school education for all the right reasons. However, for others, many of their core values and plans for their children's future may be at odds with those of international, Western-style schools. They may be in disagreement as to standards of discipline, study habits, teaching styles, or expectations of individual freedom and responsibility. With such basic differences, why would they send them to international schools? There are many motivations, but one prominent one is that they may simply want a faster and easier route to Western higher education and its status than Korean and Chinese systems easily provide.

Other families may want their children to go to local schools to "learn to be Korean/Chinese" while maintaining their Western language and cultural background. If such a family maintains contacts in the West, visiting during school vacations, going to camp or summer school, watching English language television, and reading age-appropriate books, these children can become truly bicultural.

Still other families may have never planned on staying out of their country as long as they did, and consider themselves and their children to be completely Korean or Chinese. They have no intention of their children remaining Westernized. Alternately, due to citizenship issues, many Korean or Chinese families returning to their home countries today do not have the choice of choosing a Western-style education; children who are Korean or Chinese citizens may find themselves required by law to attend local schools. Although the national governments have recently taken some steps that open up the option of international education for a few "international" returnee children who have spent an extended time abroad, most must attend local schools.

Whatever the reason for attending local schools after returning to their home countries, many of these children often adjust quite well in local schools and quickly take on new cultural identities. Others, particularly if they have become totally Westernized, suffer difficulty in academics as well as harassment by other children and even teachers who do not understand that they are going through a major adjustment in culture and identity, and view them simply as uncultured and rude by local standards. Often these children suffer terribly.

Changing Educational Systems: A Life-Changing Decision

Almost all students, regardless of culture or nationality, face some type of transition during their educational journey. Some of these transitions are relatively smooth; others are life-changing. For Asian students, some of the most common transitions are these:

Moving from their home country to another with a similar culture (A Korean student moves from Korea to China and enrolls in Chinese school. Apart from the language adjustment, the common Confucian structure and expectations of the two systems are very similar.)

Moving from their home country to an international school where they will attend school with a vastly different educational culture. (Like our little friend Charlie at the beginning of this book, moving from a Taiwanese educational environment to a Western international school environment, simultaneously learning a new social and academic language)

Moving from a local school to an Western-style school in their same country (a student moves from a culturally Chinese school in Shanghai to an international school in China, possibly even in Shanghai)

Moving from a Western-style international school to their home country school (a Korean "returnee" student attending international school in China moves home to attend Korean school in Korea – a twist would be if that student moved from an international school in China to a Korean school in China)

Moving from an international school to their home country university (a Chinese student from an international school in Japan returns to China for her university education)

Moving from a Western-style international school to a university in the West (a Chinese student who has been educated in an international school in Korea enrolls in a university in Boston)

A locally educated student returns from experiencing a Western university education to their home country (A Chinese student, educated in the Chinese system, attends the London School of Economics and later returns to Beijing to work)

A move from a Western educational environment to their home country's military (A Korean or Taiwanese student, having attended an international school or university, moves to their home country temporarily to fulfill their military service responsibilities)

Each of these moves has many variations depending on the culture of the student, how long they have been away from (or living in) their "home" country, and their various language abilities. There are many variations on a theme – I knew many Korean students in Shanghai who had never lived or attended school in Korea, and who were fluent in Shanghainese dialect, Mandarin, Korean, and English. They felt most comfortable in Shanghai. Moving to the US for a university education and dorm life was an adjustment, and after two years moving to Korea for two years to serve in the Korean army was another adjustment. Finally, returning to the US to finish their university education, now as former Korean soldiers, raised in China, and speaking four languages, they were the quintessential international student.

Whatever type of schooling parents choose upon return to their home countries – boarding school, international school, or local school – this decision will have lifelong ramifications for their children and their family. A primary school student, even if his or her Korean or Chinese is limited, can most likely make the transition to the local school system and see success within two or three years. However, an older child may have a great deal of adjustment to make, both academically and socially, to the local school culture, as we have seen above. Korean and Chinese schools create Korean and Chinese adults; international education creates either Western adults or multicultural adults who eventually are at ease in both the East and the West. Which route to take is a critical family decision affecting not only the child but also the family and the family's future. It is a question of whether or not future generations of the family will remain Korean or Chinese – or join the ever-expanding international community.

Regardless of where they go to school, however, many young people find themselves caught in difficult educational and cultural dilemmas upon "returning" to Korea or China. Their parents are themselves working hard to become "Korean/ Chinese" again, and they are pulling their children along with them. Local society, from grandmothers to taxi drivers, demands that these young people act and speak the local language in the best Confucian tradition. The longer they remain in their old/new environment, the more outwardly acculturated they probably appear.

"Returning" students may feel alone and alienated from their families, as well. Identity issues that emerge at middle and high school age for all children are confounded by additional ethnic or cultural questions. As they constantly try to balance conflicting Eastern and Western values, they may temporarily completely reject their cultural identity, or conversely become "Super Koreans/Chinese," rejecting their Western identity. Other culturally ambiguous young people like them, caught in the same dilemma, become their soul mates. Close and lasting friendships develop based on a shared, often painful, experience. Much as their mothers seek out others with similar backgrounds and challenges, understandable group survival strategies appear among their children. Unfortunately, to Western educators many of these characteristics appear to be cliquishness, exclusivity, or alienation, particularly among ethnic Korean students. One frequent complaint of Korean students in international schools is that "the teachers don't understand us." We have to ask ourselves – Are they right? If so, what are we doing about it?

Local Students

We've looked at Immigrants, Sojourners, Returnees, and TCK's, who make up the majority of students in many international schools. However, many international schools for a variety of reasons find themselves educating the children of the local elite who can afford a Western education. This has long been the case in many schools in Latin America, and is becoming increasingly common in Asian countries. This brings a somewhat different set of challenges to foreign teachers and administrators at international schools.

First, the overwhelming majority, with the possible exception of a few faculty kids, are locals. They all share the same first language and culture. They are not the "visitor" to an international setting, the teacher is. This may put the teacher at a distinct disadvantage, particularly if education is not particularly valued in that culture. The local culture may overwhelm the more North American or European school culture, not only in terms of language and pop culture, but also in values and work habits. For example, many parents may be planning on sending their children to university in an English speaking country, and see attendance at an international schools as their ticket. They may not value hard work, or promptness, or individual initiative as much as the school might expect. (Of course, this can work in the opposite way, as well!) If the majority of the students in a school are "local kids", they speak the same social language and may have little use for English outside of their academics, hindering their English language acquisition outside the classroom.

In other international schools, the local student may be the exception rather than the rule. In this case they may feel particularly out of place at school for a few months, returning to the safety of home each afternoon. If English is not spoken at home, they may have little support with homework, and language development may be slowed, particularly if they spend the vacation months with family. The school may find itself spending a good deal of energy educating the parents to Western educational values and habits. In Asia, for example, educating parents in the areas of sleep science, of 21st Century Skill development, of the necessity of exposure to English beyond the school day, and the importance of involvement in extracurricular activities in sports and the arts, and in the entire college application and choice process may be necessary. Local students may be more likely to be living with grandparents, who may well be the decision makers in the family in regards to a child's education, but who may have no experience or understanding of what it takes to be a successful student in a Western school setting. Pre-college social counseling may be more necessary than for students who have been exposed to Western culture.

Whether a school is primarily composed or local students or just a few, teachers and administrators, particularly if they are new to international education, must carefully consider what they need to do differently in order to support their students as much as possible. This takes knowledge of the local culture, which can unfortunately be sorely lacking in the international school community. Hopefully this book will help some, particularly those teachers in Asia.

Kentaro's Story:

Third Culture Kid, Sojourner, Returnee

I'd like to share with you the story of Kentaro, who I knew as a middle schooler in Seoul when I was middle school principal at Seoul Foreign School (SFS). Kentaro had left Japan in early elementary school when his dad was assigned to Germany, and then in 7th grade moved on to Seoul. Kentaro was filled with bountiful energy and an interesting sense of humor. He expressed himself often (and always with a smile), and paid about as much attention to his appearance as most 7th grade boys. We loved him; everyone knew Kentaro! He was anything but the stereotypical serious Japanese student, and completely embraced the freedom of Western education and Seoul Foreign School. Entering 9th grade, he returned to Japanese school in Tokyo. As he left SFS, we were concerned about his adjustment to a much more strict Japanese school environment in which the very characteristics that we so appreciated in him and served him so well in an international school environment could backfire in Japan – a fear that we soon learned was not unfounded. I am still in touch with Kentaro, and he gave me full permission to share with you an email he sent me about six months after he moved "back" to Japan, saying that hopefully my sharing his message of suffering will help kids in similar situations today. His message was filled with the anguish of a TCK, a hidden immigrant, and a returnee, and resounds with cultural dissonance. I share his email with you in part; I have included grammatical errors as they help to more fully express what he was telling me.

November 17, 2002

Hello, Dr. Bordan, How are you?

This is Kentaro writing from Tokyo on Sunday afternoon!!

Well, anyways I am very sorry that I didn't send u any mail for such a long time. Well u see it doesn't mean that I was forgetting about SFS or something like that. Actually I miss SFS SOOOOOOOOOOOOOOOOOOO much because my new school in Tokyo is literally S-A-D compared to SFS!!

Well you see, in my school we do some Army-like assembly every week and forced to wear this sad-looking uniforms in the most neatest way as possible (well, we have to wear the uniform inside school campus too and it is VERY uncomfortable).

Also most of the students in my school don't have much morals) guess because nobody have any Religious belief type moral) and International Sense. And even the teachers are not international and teaching some WRONG things, which really makes me ANGRY everytime.

From those things, wut I hate the most is that in school we don't have much right to say about wut we thinks, so for example if teacher say to you to say YES, no [matter] wut you things u have to say YES, otherwise the teacher gonna get angry. Well I think tis is not good, because doing this makes the students loose the ability to "THINK" and "SAY YOUR IDEAS", so I always fight against the teachers about this INJUSTICE and ask them to CHANGE IT!! (still nothing really changes....they don't even do a debate.....)

One more sad thing is that there is a teacher who teaches the students [things] which ain't true, like for example one teacher always says bad about Christianity and america (because she is believing in some nasty religion) and always criticize me when I say things which I did in SFS FOCUS group (small Christian student groups] and so on (well, because of that I even think to turn myself to Christianity and become Christian).

So of that, I always say to the teacher that wut she says is wrong.   And in SFS I guess most of the other students gonna say so too, but sadly because of the sad Japanese schooling system, no other students in my school say a word to a teacher or worst they go to the teacher's side and blame me for stopping the class!!! (Because they are scared of the teacher writing bad comments on the grade sheet). OOOOOHHHHHHHH!!!, Going to this school makes me feel like I am living in some school of Dictators. And there are more and more bad-news to tell about here but I just don't way it because it brings my baaaad memory back. Well seriously when I was in korea I thought I could blend back to Japanese school easily but now I am totally disappointed or is this something called the "Culture shock!?" and I don want to become like on of them so I have to get out of this miserly as quick as possible. [at this point Kentaro goes on to talk about wanting to attend an alternative, more international high school, and how he is currently studying for its admissions exam. Unfortunately he never did gain admission to that school. He closes his long email by saying... "i am thinking to visit SFS, so I hope I can see you and other dear teachers and friends!!!!!!!!!!

"Well anyways, the letter is becoming quite long so I will quit around here.

So anyways,

"HAAAAAVVE A NICCE DAY111['{}'}/ FROM KENTARO KATORI!"

Kentaro's story points out what some of our students face when they leave our international schools and "return" to Asian style schools. His may have been an extreme case, but I know of other students who faced the same challenges and angst; he simply expressed it so eloquently in is own way – thus the reason I have kept his email for 18 years. Sometimes I wonder if we are doing any favors to our kids who we know will return home to their national systems, with our emphasis on free thinking and expression. Are we setting them up for a really difficult re-entry? Do we have a choice, as their parents are in fact paying for a Western educational experience? Moving from one culture to another can sound exciting and mind-broadening, and it is, but it can also cause a great deal of pain, particularly for young people who are still trying to sort out their identity apart from the challenges of changing cultures at an unsettling time in their lives.

Thankfully, Kentaro's story ends well. He completed high school, and eventually earned a Masters degree in "Classic Japanese poetry in the Middle Ages." He is now (2020) living in Tokyo and has a successful banking career that gives him an opportunity for some international travel and interacting with non-Japanese. Thank you, Kentaro, for letting me share your story and your words. They will make a difference in other kids' lives.

Additional Comments Regarding Returning Students

As noted earlier, most students of Korean and Chinese citizenship are required to return to national schools upon their return to Korea. Until a few years ago, there were so few returning children that they were quietly absorbed into the Korean educational system with little or no consideration for their background, special talents, or difficulties. However, in the last decade or so the ministries of education have recognized that such children are quite different than most local children, both culturally and in their academic backgrounds. The general attitude has been to re-acculturate them as quickly as possible, although there are very few special programs for them. Most enroll in Korean and Chinese schools and do the best they can. Both Korea and China have local schools with "international divisions" such as Shanghai High School International Division in China, but these tend to be quite traditional (local) in pedagogy. Classes may be taught in English (of uncertain quality), but often by local teachers. There are increasing numbers of English language options designed for local Korean and Chinese students (for example, those in Jeju Education City in Korea, and Dwight International School - Shanghai) that may be appropriate for returnees. It is hoped that continuing with English language and Western type education will be increasingly available to returnees.

At this point in time (2020) a Korean child who has attended international schools for five or more years outside of Korea is legally eligible to attend international schools in Korea, but due to the high demand by expatriates for spaces in international schools, particularly in Seoul, this is not always an option due to space. Chinese citizen children are restricted from attendance at international schools except under special circumstances (again, related to the number of years they have lived continuously outside of China). The best advice international educators can give parents when they have questions as to their child's educational options in Korea or China is to have them contact the education office in the city to which they will move, or individual international schools if they are looking at that option. Laws and regulations change frequently with political winds and cultural change, and anything printed here could soon be out of date.

While the "overseas" door may be open to more returnees at the college level, the landscape continues to change rapidly. Again, it is best for parents to contact individual international divisions of colleges to which their sons or daughters wish to apply. Some universities in Korea are very open to visits from international school (outside of Korea) guidance counselors; if your school has a large enough Korean population, and can afford it, you may consider arranging a trip for two or three counselors or administrators to visit popular universities such as Seoul National, Yonsei, Koryo, and KAIST.

Finally, a word about Asian students studying in Western universities. It is no secret that many Western universities (and independent secondary schools) stay afloat by admitting large numbers of full fee paying international students, many from Asia. Currently (2020), the largest number comes from Mainland China. Many of these students face serious cultural and educational adjustments; about 25% of Chinese students studying in the US eventually leave before finishing their program. Why do they drop out, walking away from a lifetime of family dreams? Of this 25%, 58% simply cannot keep up their grades, either due to language ability or inability to adjust to a new educational style and expectations. 23% are expelled due to issues of academic integrity (one would assume because they either didn't understand the importance of the rules of academic integrity, as has been discussed earlier, or they simply didn't follow the rules.) 10% withdrew due to attendance issues – they simply didn't go to classes. One has to wonder if this isn't due to the sudden freedom of an American college campus, combined with the fact that their mother was not there to get them up in the morning, or prepare their meals, or organize their day, as they had for the previous 18 years. (South China Post, 29 May 2015) The remaining 9% apparently dropped out for other reasons, perhaps visa or financial issues, or any of the other challenges facing those of us who choose an international lifestyle.

CHAPTER XV: SMASHING STEREOTYPES - LOOKING AT INDIVIDUALS

Up to this point, ethnic Chinese and Korean children have been described as being the products of their parents' historical, cultural, and educational backgrounds. We have also taken a look at the experiences of international life as well as those of returning to their parents' home countries for the first time. A stereotypical picture has been painted of children who are being molded by many of the same forces and turning out all the same. This is hardly the whole story, however. While it is true that the backgrounds of many such children have some striking cultural similarities, it is just as true that the foreground of each child's life is painted by his or her individual experiences. To what extent any set of parents or any child reflects the characteristics discussed up to now is a result of any number of factors. In working with these young people we need to keep this in mind at all times, lest we paint them all with the same brush. Each child is an individual and deserves to be treated as such. Some children act and think like they never left Cleveland; some act like international TCK's. Others may seem like they never left Seoul, Shanghai, or Shenzhen. As educators we need to ask ourselves some questions about each and every child who comes into our classrooms if we are truly interested in discovering the answer to the question "Where are they coming from?"

Some of the variables that will upset our stereotypes are found below. As you get to know each child, do a little research and find the answers to these questions. You may be surprised at the variety of backgrounds, and you will be able to better meet each child's emotional, social, and academic needs.

1. Is this the first overseas experience for the family? Are they "real" Koreans or Chinese who are only sojourning in another country for a few years, a short flight away from being "at home"? If so, much of what is included in this book will apply. Conversely, if they have always been living internationally, have the children completely absorbed the international educational culture, and not share many of the cultural characteristics of their "home" country at all? In an interesting twist of this phenomenon, I remember very well a bi-racial middle school boy who transferred to my international school in Seoul from a public school in Korea Town in Los Angeles. His report card was written all in Korean, and all of his teachers had Korean surnames. He had lived in L.A. all his life with his Korean mother and grandmother, and his English was very broken and heavily accented. This boy, despite his mixed ethnicity, Western-sounding name, U.S. passport, and history of living in the United States, was both culturally and linguistically a Korean child. This was a reminder to me that kids and their backgrounds come in all kinds of combinations, and it is our job as educators to put our assumptions aside, get a firm understanding of each child's characteristics and needs, and meet the student where he or she is in their educational and cultural journey.

2. How long has the child been out of Korean or Chinese schools? Was he or she sitting in a local classroom in Busan or Beijing last week? Or have they always attended school outside of China or Korea? Don't expect them to be too "Korean" if their only contact with a Korean school was to go to Korean (or Chinese) Saturday school in New Jersey or Orange County. Conversely, if they have always gone to "local" schools, don't assume that they don't have a firm grasp on English or Western thinking. Some parents are very proactive in providing their children a rich array of international experiences. Once upon a time it was the rare Korean or Chinese child who spoke reasonable English if they had never attended an English language based school. No more is this true; there are ample opportunities for kids to develop a good command of English without ever leaving their home country. Korean "hakwon's" and Chinese academies abound, and while many provide little value added, some are quite good in establishing a base level of conversational English.

3. What is the proportion of Korean/Chinese students in your school, or more important, in a particular grade level? How strong is the Korean or Chinese community in your city? If the children live in an ethnically restricted neighborhood (Korea Town/China Town) then they may maintain many of their families' characteristics to a much greater degree than if theirs is one of only a few Korean or Chinese families in a larger international community. If there are just a few students from any one culture in a school, they will acculturate quite quickly to the general international school environment. However, if there are enough students in the same age group of a single culture to support a viable social group that can survive without interacting with the wider school community, they may choose to isolate themselves socially and linguistically. Unfortunately, Korean students' reputation to isolate themselves culturally is not completely undeserved, whether at an international school or at the university level in North

America or Europe. Chinese tend to mix somewhat better, coming from a less homogeneous culture that takes a more accepting view of people and customs that are different from their own. What is the magic number at which group identification and self-isolation tends to occur? While it would depend on the size of the school, I have found in visiting schools that generally, if the percentage of Korean students in a given age group reaches over about 40%, they may begin to group themselves and resist integration into the larger school community. However, there are many other factors that can influence this dynamic. One quick and unscientific measure of such isolation is the degree to which kids tend to isolate themselves in same-language groups in the school cafeteria. Are there "Korean tables" or "Chinese tables?" Conversely, do they feel completely welcome to sit with others outside their ethnic group? Interestingly, it is also readily observable that teachers and staff often self-segregate by language in the cafeteria – Korean or Chinese staff; Korean or Chinese teachers, Filipino staff and speakers, Anglo teachers, etc.

4. Are the children hyphenated Koreans/Chinese? (Korean-American, Korean-Brazilian, Chinese-Canadians, etc.)? This is not a question about an ethnically mixed family, but of a family that emigrated to a foreign country, and whose children are citizens and members of the culture of that nation. If so, the longer the parents lived there, particularly if they emigrated before they entered their teens, the less Korean or Chinese they will be culturally. Sometimes the parents grew up as Third Culture Kids who may find themselves to be "hidden immigrants" in the country of their ancestors, and don't behave as expected to by peers or grandparents. Just because they look physically Asian on the outside doesn't mean that they are culturally Asian on the inside, of course. It's very easy to make assumptions about people's culture based on their ethnicity; we need to guard against that.

5. What is the educational level of the parents, and where

were they educated? Many of the parents of the children we find in our schools were educated, at least in part, outside of their country of origin. They may have strong understanding of Western education due to their own experiences, and be totally "on board" with the philosophy and methods of the school – that's why they chose an international education for their children. Conversely, many with high educational aspirations for their children may be willing to sacrifice for their children to attend an international school – but look at it primarily as a ticket to a prestigious Western university. Their Western education may have been limited to university, or even graduate school – hardly the best examples of progressive pedagogy. They may have no idea what Western pedagogy is all about; they may assume an international education as simply a traditional (local) education taught in English; certainly there are many opportunities for that if that is what they are looking for. These are often the parents who have the greatest number of questions and complaints about Western pedagogy. Quite simply, they are getting a different and more life-changing educational product than the one that they intended on buying. The story below will illustrate this; the reader can probably provide his or her own examples.

I remember a phone call I received as principal in Shanghai one day, and realized quickly that this Chinese dad was less than happy. He immediately demanded that his daughter be moved from her history class to another teacher's. When I asked him what the problem was, he stated simply that the teacher didn't teach his daughter. When pressed for details, he declared that just the day before, his daughter had asked the teacher a question, and the teacher replied that it was a very good question, and that she should do a little research and report back to him. "See," the dad continued," he was so lazy that he would not answer my daughter's question. Furthermore, my daughter says that he never lectures; he just has students work in groups among themselves. How can she learn if he never lectures?" I invited the dad in for a discussion about what Western education is, and whether it was the right fit for his daughter. I'm not sure he was ever completely convinced that we were doing the right thing for his daughter, but I didn't change her teacher, and he didn't withdraw her from our school. In the end, she went on to a large "name brand" university in the United States, where I'm pretty sure he was more comfortable with the pedagogical style!

6. Is the family sojourning overseas for only a few years, or is this a permanent move? As mentioned earlier, the family that expects to return to Korea or China has a much greater stake in maintaining their home culture both socially and educationally than the family that has left home with no intention of ever returning. If they are focused on a new, international future, they will approach what an international school has to offer with more enthusiasm than if they see it as an interruption of two or three years in their child's "real" education, and expect their child to fit back into their local educational system when they return. Their primary focus may be maintaining their child's native language at age-appropriate levels, and preparing for a future in their home country's educational system. Your international school may well be a second choice for them, if no Chinese or Korean (or Japanese or German) school is available in your city.

By researching the answers to these questions you can more fully understand some of the factors that make each child unique — how much of "who she is" is a product of birth, of conscious parental decisions, of perhaps capricious decisions of a company or government or mission board, or of sometimes unintentional decisions made by parents? Each family and its history is unique, as is each child's. Past experiences have molded them into the families we meet and the children we see in our classrooms each day. They are special and unique families and children, headed in many different directions after spending a few years with us, and deserve to be treated as such.

Looking Back, Looking Ahead

At the beginning of this book you were asked to jot down some characteristics that you personally attributed to ethnic Korean or Chinese children. You were asked to be honest with yourself, noting both positive and negative characteristics, and to also write down a few questions you might have about these children. Before we go on to discuss how we might be able to make the Western educational experience more positive for them, look back to see if some of the characteristics you noted earlier make more sense now, if only partially.

Think about your own students – do you see them reflected in these pages?

Think about what you have read regarding the historical, cultural, and educational backdrops sketched here. Consider the individual life experiences of some of the children in your classroom or school. Are things starting to make sense? Are some as confusing as ever?

How can you best help students new to your school with their transition? What are some of the "pieces" of that transition that may cause challenges for the student?

Have some of your questions been answered and maybe some pieces of the puzzle falling into place? Are you experiencing any "AHA!" moments?

Do you have new questions? How could you get the answers?

CHAPTER XVI: WORKING WITH KOREAN AND CHINESE PARENTS

Now that we've looked at the backgrounds and general characteristics of many of our Korean and Chinese parents, as well as Confucian thought as it applies to education and child-rearing, it may be helpful to operationalize these concepts and examine some ways in which we can better work with Asian parents in ways that both honor their backgrounds and history, and support the educational lives of their children in our international schools. Below are some practical suggestions that may be of help.

1. Build the teacher/parent relationship. All human contacts in Confucian cultures are based on some type of relationship, be they positive or negative. Sitting down with a parent to conference and "getting right down to business" without some "getting to know you as a person" time will be offensive or uncomfortable for many Asian parents, particularly Koreans; Chinese tend to be more matter of fact. When meeting parents, especially for the first time, exchange name cards if you have them (they most likely will); look at their name card and acknowledge the company or organizational connection. (No mention of the position is necessary.) Spend some time talking about the family. Show an interest. Ask about their recent move. Remembering some of the things you have read about in this book, ask some questions to try to see what this family is all about. Ask about the child. Find out where they are from. Where do they consider "home"? What language is spoken at home? Tell about yourself and where you were educated. Are you married? Do you have other children? Where are you from? For Chinese, knowing whether they are Taiwanese, mainlanders, or from Hong Kong or Singapore is important and will tell you lot. Let them know you know something about Korea and China – where have you traveled? What do you like to do? They will be much more likely to share their ideas and feelings after a few minutes of small talk, finding a few things in common, or sharing a cup of coffee to establish a relationship. Things go much more smoothly after that, and it is time well spent. Encourage your school to provide enough appointment time on conference days so that, especially early in the year when you may be meeting the parents for the first time, the conferences are not rushed. Don't be afraid to share something of yourself early in the year through email or some other means of communication. Let them know where you have lived. Have you ever visited their home country? How long have you been overseas? They may be interested in where you attended university, but there is no need to share that unless they ask – remember that they may be trying to fit you into some kind of "teacher hierarchy" based on your educational choices. Do you have children? What are your personal interests? Sharing some of this information will open up areas of conversation so that you can more easily build a relationship on more than what Mimi got on her last math test.

2. Don't read too much into the word "yes" in Korea. In talking with native Korean speakers, understand that "Yes" does not necessarily mean agreement, but only indicates understanding. Much as in English we might say "uh-huh" to indicate that we are following the conversation and understand the speaker, in Korean one uses the same word as for "yes." When this is translated into English, it comes out "yes" instead of "I see," or "Uh-huh." In addition, in the interest of maintaining harmony, a parent might not say "No" outright, but would hint around it. (A hint of disagreement could often be if the parent says that something would be "really difficult." That usually means "No.") Don't be afraid to ask for clarification. Another frequent source of misunderstanding is that in English, we have a confusing habit of asking questions in the negative, such as "Your child doesn't speak English, does she?" In Korean and Chinese, negative questions like this are answered by "Yes, I agree" or "No, I don't agree." For example, if you ask this question the parent might answer "Yes," which in this case means "Yes, you're correct, she doesn't speak English." Conversely, a "No" answer would mean, "No, you're mistaken, my child does speak English." This confusion can be avoided by simply asking only positive questions — "Does your daughter speak English?" — for simple "Yes" or "No" answers.

3. Find ways to help Asian parents understand the Western philosophy of your school. If you are a counselor or administrator, work to develop a pamphlet that briefly describes what a Western education is – and what it isn't. Print it in English, Chinese, and Korean. One school in Korea has published an excellent pamphlet entitled "Understanding a Western Education." Think of the questions you often ask about parents – the frustrated "Why don't they understand that we don't . . . ." and structure your own pamphlet around those. Some areas might be as follows:

a) what it means to teach the "whole" child,

b) what "21st Century Skills" are and how these skills focus more on academic and life skill building than they to on the warehousing of information,

c) why and how you develop the use of higher level thinking skills beyond memorization of facts,

d) how you involve parents in the educational process,

e) how you use technology to organize and support teaching and learning,

f) how the school handles discipline with an eye towards fairness and consistency,

g) how parents can develop a realistic level of emphasis on grades,

h) how you use a variety of assessment tools (beyond pencil and paper tests),

i) what they can expect from homework – and what they should NOT expect,

j) realistic college selection in the Western context,

k) the importance of their child using English both in and out of the classroom.

l) the importance of continuing to develop their native language skills in reading, writing, speaking, and listening.

Each school will find different areas of misunderstanding or even conflict with parents, and will wish to develop such a pamphlet of their own, being sure to have it translated into Korean or Chinese by someone with a strong understanding of both the school and Western education and good translating skills; if the translator doesn't understand fully what you are trying to convey, you may be inadvertently spreading misconceptions about your school. I have developed short Keynote presentations for use with both Korean and Chinese parent groups using the table in the next section, "The Roots of Confucian and Western Educational Practice," and followed up with Q and A. Such presentations have gone a long way towards helping parents understand where the school is coming from pedagogically, and explaining what their child is experiencing daily – and why. Seeing and hearing it in this format helps parents to structure their understanding beyond simply relying on a litany of stories from children or friends describing moments of incomprehension or frustration.

Identify a member of staff, or parent, who has a firm understanding of both types of educational systems, and can express it in the parents' language. Feel free to translate the table that follows:

The Roots Of Confucian And Western Educational Practice

CONFUCIAN-BASED EDU-CATIONAL SYSTEMS	WESTERN STYLE BASED SYSTEMS
Measures of student success are competitive; the individual student is compared to peers	Individual student growth against standards is the focus of learning
Academics dominates school live and the definition of an education	Wider school curriculum is based on the development of the "whole child," including the arts and sports
Assessment is primarily exam-based	Assessment based on projects, research, participation, presentations, as well as exams
Curriculum is primarily based on mastery of facts rather than skills	Learning goals include skills such as communication, collaboration, creativity, research, and independent thinking
Focus on learning "the answer" through memorization	Facts are important, but understanding "how and why" is emphasized. There is no "one right way" to learn or succeed; creativity and thinking skills are highly valued
Outcomes are performance focused: grades, ranking, honors	The process of learning is important as well as the factual learning itself; reflection is valued
Hierarchical ranking of schools and universities	Emphasis on the "best fit" for university depending on stu-

with an emphasis on "name brands"	dent's talents, skills, interests, and personal needs

Obviously, the chart above is simplistic and is based on broad generalizations. Just as every student is unique, so is each school unique. There are Asian schools with philosophies and practices that are much less rigid than described, and there are many Western teachers and schools that are much more traditional and "Asian" than is noted above. What I have described are general tendencies and characteristics of most schools, most of the time, in philosophy if not always in practice.

Assuming that most readers are familiar with the extent to which Western schools are described by the right hand column, we won't discuss these in detail here. However, taking a much closer look at what the left hand column means in actual practice would be helpful. Even if the reader is not teaching in an Asian style school, he or she most likely has students in the classroom that have spend some of their previous educational experience in such an environment, as we have seen earlier. By understanding where students have come from, both figuratively and literally, we can better meet them where they are and bring them towards a more Western outlook on education. Children are quick to pick up the differences between their previous Asian experience and their new Western experience, and usually find the differences positive. Parents, however, are not experiencing Western education every day and may have a much more difficult time understanding the depth of the differences between the two systems, and may focus their goals on English acquisition and acceptance to a brand name Western university, among other characteristics. It behooves us to be sure that they understand, before enrolling their children in our international schools, that these deeper differences are real, and will affect the expectations put on their child. This cultural conflict between educational philosophies is often at the root of some of the strains between our parent communities and our schools.

Let's look at some of the areas of greatest difference between the two educational philosophies. The "hidden curriculum" of Western education includes a number of Western values, including: the following:

Help parents understand the concept that Western education focuses on competition of the individual against him or herself rather than against peers. In most Western nations, there is opportunity enough in higher education for any student who has the academic credentials, the money, and he desire to attend college. While not everyone can get into the most prestigious schools, few who truly aspire to higher education go uneducated if they are willing to work for and have the time and money to invest in it, which unfortunately not everyone has. The emphasis is on doing one's personal best, discovering and developing one's individual talents, and setting realistic goals, rather than on competing against peers or being number one in the class. How one compares with classmates has very little lasting meaning or prestige in the Western educational setting. For parents who might have only experienced an intensely competitive Asian educational system, this is often difficult to understand and might even be interpreted as encouraging laziness or a lack of ambition. Conversely, a student with little competitive spirit who returns to a Korean or Chinese school may be severely handicapped and become overwhelmed by the atmosphere of competition, where competition is valued for its own sake. I remember talking with a Chinese mother one day who was planning on transferring her child to another school in Shanghai. When I asked her why, she responded that our campus was not competitive enough. Not understanding what she meant, I pointed out that our students achieved high SAT, IB, and AP scores, and they could and did certainly compete very successfully in the college acceptance game. "Oh no," she replied. "I know that. What I want for my child, though, it to learn to complete with her peers and be at the very top of her class. Your school simply doesn't provide that level of competition." This mom was not unusual in her aspirations for her child; she wanted the school to encourage competition for the sake of developing her daughter's competitive nature. On the other hand, I know many Asian parents who have chosen our international schools primarily because they realize that their child can succeed and go on to quality universities without suffering through four years of unrelenting competition. This focus on competing against the group rather than developing one's strengths, weaknesses, and talents harks back to the Confucian focus on collective relationships (and the Western focus on individuality). However, we can also see that within that sense of collectivity there can also exist a high level of competition, just as in Western cultures we can see examples of high degrees of cooperation and collaboration. Perhaps it is easier to collaborate when there is less focus on competition?

One example of how we unwittingly may contribute to competition among moms is our tradition of posting or publishing Honor Rolls. While it's always good to recognize academic success, our middle school honor roll in Seoul became over time a bottom threshold for acceptable academic work. In the days before on-line newsletters, we posted the High Honor and Honor lists on the office window, which was across from our entrance staircase. After a while, I started to realize that the moms almost all made a beeline for the Honor Roll list before they went anywhere else. Why was it such a big draw, even more than other posted announcements and information? To assure themselves that their child was on the list as they should be? To see if someone else's child was not on the list? I more and more doubted the efficacy of posting the list. The camel that broke this camel's back was when a mom came in to see me, the principal, and commented on the Honor Roll list, and then quickly added something to the effect that there were no non-Korean names on the list (which was true that quarter). The lists came down that afternoon, much to the consternation of moms who must have missed its reassuring message.

When I was a high school principal in Shanghai, annually we identified the class Salutatorian and Valedictorian, those with the second-highest and highest GPA over their four years of high school. They would be publically congratulated and acknowledged at the graduation ceremony. However, normally the difference between the two students would be in the range of hundredths of a GPA point. Given that the students inevitably had taken different programs, and maybe even different numbers of courses, it was easy to see that this very small difference in GPA (but a huge difference between being #1 or #2) was meaningless. Needless to say, eliminating this mark of success did not meet with unanimous approval by parents (or some students) who for a year or so mourned the identification of a #1 student, even though nearly everyone understood the inaccuracy of such an honor. However, we weathered the storm and designed instead GPA bands identified by Cum Laude, Magna Cum Laude, and Summa Cum Laude, with those groups choosing their own speaker who represented the entire class. This further eliminated one more cause for stress and competition, while continuing to honor academic achievement.

An emphasis in Western education on the development of a well-rounded student; the "whole child," rather than a one-dimensional individual who only knows how to study, may be a new concept to many parents. Whereas in Korean and Chinese education expertise in the arts or sports is given a nod, for most "good" students academics is all-important. Local schools do not generally have sports teams (unless they are special sports high schools), bands, or other such extracurricular activities. While a rich club program may be emphasized at the middle school level, usually these clubs all meet at the same time on specific afternoons each month. In high school they are noticeably absent, and any involvement would certainly not positively affect college admissions decisions. Sports, drama, forensics, robotics, or other extracurricular activities are similarly absent. For our children whose educational futures lie in the West, parents need to understand that "straight A's" and a perfect SAT score won't get Kyung Min into Harvard; top schools want more than just a bookworm. Unfortunately, parents often hear this to mean that Kyung Min must also be captain of the basketball team, sit first chair violin in the school orchestra, be president of the Student Council, and get the "A's"! (again, focusing on the competition) On the other hand, if the student is returning to Korea or China, we must realize that while all these activities might make the child a much more well-rounded individual, it generally won't help him or her get into Seoul or Beijing National University. Possibly in this case the most realistic long-term solution would be to let Kyung Min and YiYi keep their noses in the books. It might be against our educational philosophy, and clash with what we know is "right" for their development as self-realized individuals of character who are following their dreams, but where they are headed our philosophy, while popular in theory and hopefully the wave of the future, is not yet a reality in Asian universities.

The Western focus on the application of a developmentally appropriate curriculum rather than simply pushing kids as fast as they can manage through curriculum levels may not be shared by many parents. In a highly competitive system, the student who goes the fastest and farthest wins the race. In a system that emphasizes memorization to the detriment of understanding, prefers conformity to the development of creativity, and prizes getting the "right answer" to the development of a critical mind, this often translates into a dependence on memorization and a heavy reliance on "authorities," be they the teacher, the after school academy tutor, or the textbook, as has been discussed previously. For example, it is no secret that Korean, Chinese, and Japanese children far outpace children from the United States on standardized math tests in high school. By high school, they may be years ahead of their Western counterparts. However, if we accept Piagetian theory and research in cognitive development (as well as our own experience), we know, for example, that it is not possible for most middle schoolers to understand higher level algebra. Yes, they can memorize formulas and theorems and apply them to specific types of problems, but real understanding in depth is beyond all but a portion who might be exceptionally mature cognitively. Following a more traditional educational philosophy, crunching the numbers is more important than becoming a thinking mathematician. Students can sometimes be pushed, step by step and chapter by chapter, beyond what would appear to be their levels of ability, and they may even earn good grades. However, often a review a year later will show that there has not been corresponding retention and understanding, even for very talented students. It makes sense that such pressure to advance rapidly would be effective in a system where memorization, a very low level thinking skill, is used and valued so widely. The fact that higher level thinking skills are stressed in Western education, and that these thinking skills in large part hopefully relate to natural stages of cognitive development, needs to be impressed upon parents who may be thinking in terms only of learning (memorizing) more and more information rather than developing higher level skills such as analysis, evaluation, and application. If we accept Bloom's Taxonomy of learning objectives and skills, we can quickly see that memorization and fact recall, while important, are found in only the base of the pyramid. (see https://bokcenter.harvard.edu/taxonomies-learning) If we want students to rise above this level, they must be challenged with learning tasks that demand more than memorization of facts. Western education, over time, demands these higher levels; by and large Asian education does not. The result is that the Asian system produces young people who are very good at being students – individuals who are skilled at learning what they are told to learn. However, the system does not produce very good inquisitive, intrinsically motivated, lifelong learners. This causes problems for them if and when they move on to higher education in the Western world, and certainly if they try to succeed in the world of Western society and work.

Conversely, while we may decry the force feeding of higher level math upon upper elementary students, if they are planning on returning to Korea or China they must learn (that is, memorize) this material if they are not to fall far behind when they return "home." Whether or not your school allows this is a philosophical question worth some serious discussion and soul-searching. Don't worry that you are setting your students up for failure if you refuse to put fifth graders in high school algebra classes, though! Korean and Chinese parents may, and often do, subscribe to monthly home study practice and advanced math programs called in Korean "kong-mun-su-hak" that keep students abreast, and sometimes ahead of, their peers at home. Such programs are widely used in both Korea and China. Ask your class how many attend after school or weekend "academy" in math. You may be surprised at how many do. You may be interested in seeing some of the materials they are using. Don't be afraid to ask to see them. We'll revisit the topic of academies later.

I have found that introducing Bloom's Taxonomy to parents is a helpful and informative exercise in parent education. Asking a group of parents which level most accurately describes their own high school education, many will see that they fall into the lower levels. Asking them what they would like for their children, and they will have much higher aspirations. You can tie this into why teachers use various methodologies and stress certain skills; this is an opportunity to introduce the concept of 21st Century Skills as well. Additionally, I try to lead into a discussion of sleep habits, often a real problem with kids (and parents) who think that the more you study, the better you will naturally do. Koreans have an expression "Sleep four hours and pass; sleep five hours and fail." While this strategy may (questionably) work better before an exams based on recall of information, it doesn't bode well for a student headed into an assessment that demands higher level thinking skills on Bloom's scale, as a student will more likely find in a Western style school. More on this later.

Parents should understand the high value placed on cultural diversity rather mono-culturalism. Interestingly, this is one of the most difficult challenges facing schools anywhere that have a large number of (particularly) ethnic Korean students. A national history of persecution, a strong group identity, and a shared experience encourages them, to a degree somewhat beyond that of many other ethnic groups, to stick together in groups and exclude others, as noted earlier. This may be natural in a population that comes from a small, cohesive nation. While not necessarily "gangs" in the traditional sense, the sense of group loyalty and nationalism is often strong. Evidence of this might be to find the graffiti "K.P." scrawled on the walls of the rest rooms; it means "Korean Power." This phenomenon is unfortunately found on college campuses in the United States, in public and private schools outside of Korea among first and second-generation immigrants, and in international schools in Asia and elsewhere. It is not a characteristic that lends itself to fostering inclusiveness, acceptance of differences, and internationalism, and does not reflect well on Korean culture.

This strong collective sense seems very natural to Korean parents. While they may have chosen to send their child to your school to learn English, to rub elbows with children from other nations, and to learn Western ways, they do not understand that the experience of attending an international school or attending school outside of Korea will necessarily slowly create in their children identities that may be less than Korean. When parents see this starting to happen, they may steer their children into choosing only ethnic Korean friends. Seldom is this expressed aloud, but it is there nonetheless. Often, it is just based on parental fear of the unknown, or some idea that Western children are not diligent students and lack manners. In fact, overall Western families may not stress academic competition to the level that many Korean parents do, and certainly Western children do not normally exhibit Korean manners, including automatic deference to authority. Korean parents need to understand that the school is consciously working to have students mix with and learn from each other both academically and socially, and that it actively encourages mixing among national and/or ethnic groups. This naturally may conflict with traditional norms. Normally, this is not much of an issue in elementary school, but as the children get older, usually between grades six and eight, the ethnic separation begins. Parents may get particularly involved at the high school level if and when the danger of inter-ethnic dating begins. They may react by forbidding their teenage children (particularly daughters) to date at all or if they do, to date only other ethnic Koreans. Possibly fear of perceived, stereotypical Western immorality is the real issue. Frequently other Korean students will ostracize anyone who dates outside their group, and a non-Korean interloper, either boy or girl, trying to date a Korean may be scared off by their Korean peers. The fact is that even today in Korea, marrying a non- Korean often causes severe family strife and rejection. Bi-racial children who attend Korean schools are still the victims of taunts and name-calling. Such prejudicial attitudes are both the root and the result of this kind of discrimination. Additionally, it is a sad fact that while romantic contact between Korean and Caucasian young people is often strongly frowned upon and may bring shame on the family, such contact with students of African heritage is often truly abhorred. Koreans have unfortunately had little contact with people of color, and that which they have had is often limited to twenty-year-old American GI's posted far from home – probably not a fair cultural sampling. Such ethnic preferences may be considered simply signs of a healthy Korean national identity, but when stripped of their Korean-ness they simply racism and xenophobia. These characteristics are negative enough within the boundaries of Korea, but perhaps more important do not travel well overseas. The more Koreans travel, the less of a problem this has become, but it is still alive and well.

This exclusiveness can be particularly troublesome when the vast majority of the students at an international school are Korean. Unless the Western child has a particularly charismatic personality, or is particularly talented in a valued sport, it is very difficult gain a seat on Student Council or be chosen to lead a team. I know of more than one international teaching couple in Korea who has left their school, where they were very happy otherwise, when their child reached middle school age and began to experience exclusion. I remember meeting with a Korean couple whose child was new to the school, but simply not advancing in English. I asked them if their son ever had Western friends visit their home. There was an awkward silence and the mom said, "The American kids have no manners!" When I probed her about this, she said that when an American child came to their apartment, the child did not respectfully greet her, bow, and thank her for her hospitality – and do it again when he left. I can well imagine that the child did not do this, and I can also imagine that the mom felt disrespected. All children need to learn that when visiting the home of someone from another culture, they need to follow a little bit of the "when in Rome ..." philosophy. As an aside, "sleepovers" are very rare in Asian youth culture, where in Western culture they are seen as an important step in learning independence. My wife and I very often found a pile of male teen bodies on our living room floor of our on-campus home the morning after an evening school function, but very seldom were either of our sons invited to spend the night at a friend's home. Perhaps parents thought that their child staying over at the "principal's house" was a safe bet, and better than going off with friends to the local teen hangouts nearby.

The Western concept that education is an individual process, not a series of performances, is a fundamental difference that parents may have difficulty understanding . Korean and Chinese parents tend to see a report card as a final sentence, a blot (or star) on the future. That children are "not done yet," that their children are growing in many other areas of their lives than in academics, and that a grade report is a milestone rather than a finish line, must be repeatedly stressed to parents. "Yes, Soo-young had a difficult job on her research project on dinosaurs, but she learned a lot from her mistakes" will receive a nod but not be really understood as a learning experience, but more as a failed performance. That fact that Soo-young earned a "C" on the project might instead result in demands for extended homework hours, the hiring of a tutor, mom helping just a little too much on the next project (to ensure a good grade) or even physical punishment. The grade is seen, quite simply, as being more important than the learning that has gone into it. It is a true "mark" on the person and their future, as well as on the family. In Asian education, that unfortunately is quite accurate.

In the overheated competitive atmosphere among many Korean moms, comparisons of students is perhaps inevitable. Korean and Chinese cultures are by nature competitive, as we have discussed earlier. Any posted honor roll list will attract immediate attention, and you may find out that some of the moms are more aware of who is on the honor roll (and who is not) than the counselor is. Comparisons among parents of their children's standardized test results, college acceptances, S.A.T. scores, and report card grades are common. Good scores are as much an achievement and ribbon for the mom as they are for the student.

Western educators ideally believe that every student is unique, with his or her own strengths and areas for improvement. Parents (of whatever background) often have difficulty understanding that kids have areas of talent (or lack thereof), just as adults do. Once in a while as principal I would get into a discussion with a group of parents about grades, and they would be shocked to learn that only a very small percentage of students in our highly academic high school earned perfect grades. They wondered aloud what the school could do so that so many students didn't do "so badly" and not get all A's. I would then ask them who among them got all A's as a high school student, and usually only got a few hands. I then asked them who as an adult was strong in writing, math, sports, science, humanities, a second language, etc. No one would put up his or her hands. So then I asked, "While it might be expected that your child got perfect grades in elementary school, at what age do you no longer expect your child to be a perfect student?" Grade 9? Grade 12? When, between the end of elementary school and adulthood, is your child no longer expected to be perfect?" This normally resulted in a rather excited conversation, but I think it got parents thinking. Maybe they only thought they should try to get a new principal! While they understood my point, they still wanted their child to graduate at the top of his or her class.

The point is that often parents have difficulty understanding why and how a child may have academic strengths and weaknesses in different cognitive and affective areas. This makes a certain amount of sense if you remember that Asian education stresses memorization of content – a low hanging fruit on

Bloom's Taxonomy. Pretty much any student can memorize, if he or she just spends long enough doing it. More study equals higher grades when memorization is the goal. The concept of multiple intelligences and natural talent is foreign to most Asian parents. Perhaps in the West we too easily chalk up poor grades to lack of innate ability in a specific subject area. Certainly some Western kids could do better if they just put in more time; and certainly a case can be made for more focus on academics among many Western children. However, international school teachers often find themselves facing parents whose expectations of their child's performance is simply not realistic, for whatever reason. We'll discuss this in more detail below.

Complicating this is the entire area of legitimate learning differences, which are only beginning to be understood in Asian societies. Parents simply do not have the vocabulary or concept structure to understand that different people learn differently. Difficulties in school are almost always considered to be either innate ability or lack of motivation: Min-ju is either stupid or lazy. "Min-ju kong-bu moteh-yo" – "Min-ju doesn't study well," is the way it is expressed. If the school suspects some kind of learning difference in a child, this should be approached very gently with parents. Even if the parents can be brought to understand the nature of the problem, they may refuse treatment or even diagnostic testing due to fear of possible social stigma. Should testing not be available in your city, it is available on a limited basis in Seoul and other large Asian cities, where it can be administered in Korean or Chinese. You may have to help parents make those connections. You should consider insisting on such testing by a qualified and certified educational psychologist or psychiatrist as a condition of continued enrollment if you suspect a serious learning difficulty that is hindering progress. Insist on having the results translated and signed by the doctor and a copy sent directly to you. Unfortunately, I have seen too many kids and parents return from a visit to a local doctor who simply says that yes, children this age often have trouble paying attention, and no intervention is necessary. The school is then placed in the uncomfortable position of indicating that the Chinese/Korean doctor's letter is not good enough; you need a Western trained doctor. This can get embarrassing and even ugly. Avoid it up front by requiring a Western certified and trained educational psychologist (because yours is a Western school); there are so few local ones that the parents will be forced to find a Western trained one well versed in educational differences. Don't be afraid to recommend one yourself; better yet the school should develop and maintain a list of reputable educational psychologists.

Teachers, counselors, and administrators would do well to keep the following in mind when working with Asian parents:

1. Parents may want their child to be placed "ahead" of others in grades or subject level. Parental demands that a child new to a school be placed in a grade or level ahead of where the school may feel is appropriate may also occur. Remember that because the Asian school year ends in February (actually effective instruction ends in December, followed by a long vacation before advancement to the next grade) admissions personnel in Western-style schools following a Northern Hemisphere calendar will have to decide whether to put the child "ahead" a semester or keep them back and have them repeat the second semester of the same grade level. Parents will be very anxious that their child will "be behind his peers a year when he goes back to Korea/China" if he or she has to repeat a half year in your school. (Remember the importance of hierarchy, most often in school established by age and grade? A child "a year behind" upsets this harmony because he or she would be a year older than classmates.) This is true, and if they are going to return within year or two, it is probably better to let them have their way. Otherwise, the child may be truly ostracized when he or she returns to his or her old school. However, if the family plans to stay overseas or be in your school any longer than that, particularly if EAL help is necessary, do not be afraid to insist that the child repeat half a year. For example, if a child entering your school in February or March has just completed Grade 6 in Korean/Chinese school, placing the student in Grade 6 and having him or her "repeat" the end of the year is probably preferable to having them skip half a year by placing them midway through Grade 7. For high school students, I have sometimes had the student audit that repeated semester, which also gives them a running start in English and getting used to a new system, and takes off the immediate pressure of earning grades. Conversely, it must be remembered that a child entering in August or September will have only completed half of the school year back in Korea/China – and the parents may want you to put them ahead a year. Don't be afraid to stand up to parents' pleas to put the child ahead. They may not have any appreciation or understanding of the social, academic, and linguistic challenges that lie ahead for their child, although they may insist that this can all be overcome by ensuring you that the child will "study hard."

At the middle or high school levels, there may also be excessive pressure on the school to place a child inappropriately in an advanced section of a class, particularly in mathematics. It takes a strong and principled teacher or counselor to stand up to such pressure. Schools need to establish guidelines (placement tests?) for level placement of students, and stick to them regardless of parental pressure.

2. Parents may, as mentioned earlier, provide excessive help with homework or projects, not in any attempt to cheat, but just because a good grade is so important to them. Extra tutors may be hired unbeknownst to the school who may also "assist" in completing assignments. Expectations for college acceptances at only the very "best" colleges may be placed on students, and many children from prominent families may even have their future role in the extended family business mapped out for them in elementary school. Counselors need to be aware of this, whether or not they agree to such practices. I know of one prominent Korean family where various offspring had future roles all outlined for them – this one would become the family lawyer, that one the family doctor, etc., while the children were in elementary school. This may have worked in the end if they went to local schools, where following parental instructions is highly valued. However, by sending a child to an international school where we teach them independent thinking and a "follow your dreams" mentality for twelve or fourteen years, this may eventually cause some friction at home when the assigned brain surgeon wants to become a rock musician! This assigning of professional roles has not been a problem in China due to the one-child policy, but certainly the expectation for a single child to become a doctor or lawyer or prominent in business or the sciences is common.

3. Parents may place on their children a level of expectations and pressure that many Western educators would consider excessive. Students may be shamed by their parents or even physically punished for less than perfect grades; more than one middle or high school student has been seen dissolving into tears on report card day because of the expected reaction at home to the one "A-" that mars an otherwise perfect report card. That fear of punishment may or may not be well founded. Other common punishments meted out by parents are for a child to be told to sit outside on the apartment or house steps all night (later let in by the other parent or grandparent), being given the "silent treatment" for days by a parent, or having the threat of "I'll send you to Korean/Chinese school if you don't do better" hang over heads. Parents can be brutal in shaming their children: "Die!" "You don't deserve to be my son!" or "Fool!" are common shaming comments. Physical punishment is not unknown by any means. The love is deep, though, and the child knows that the parent really doesn't mean it, shocking as it can sound to the Western ear. Koreans and Chinese can sound quite harsh in their interactions. If art is any reflection of culture, try watching a Korean TV serial drama and note the amount of shouting and demeaning behavior that occurs within a family. Drunken behavior is also commonly seen in these dramas. Certainly this is exaggerated, but it does reflect to some extent cultural reality. Conversely, you will seldom see the level of violence or sex you see on Western television.

4. Parents may not be familiar with age-appropriate, acceptable Western social behavior. Remember that these parents grew up in a turbulent, but very socially protected Korea in the 1970's and 80's, or in the case of mainland Chinese, in the aftermath of the very puritan Cultural Revolution (1966-1976). In their childhood days drugs were the toys only of organized crime; only adult men and elderly women used tobacco, and drinking was strictly limited to college and beyond. Boys and girls were strictly separated until college, attending segregated middle and high schools. Sexual contact among young people was almost unknown, except for maybe among high school dropouts or other "misfits." Parents may not realize that these attractive dangers are very available to their children and to their children's peers, depending on where they live. Furthermore, parents may not be aware of how to have parental radar turned on for signs of social problems. A few strange smelling leaves in a bureau drawer will be assumed to have come off In-Young's socks; alcohol on the breath can readily be excused away as mouthwash, and stale cigarette smell on clothes can be blamed on a smoke filled taxi. While we don't want to alarm parents unnecessarily, we do owe it to them to let them know gently if we believe their son or daughter is showing signs of anti-social or self-destructive behavior that parents might simply think is a result of normal acculturation. On the other hand, China and Korea are two of the most wired and internet-savvy nations in the world, and young kids can be much less naïve than their parents in some areas. Gaming addiction is quite common and is recognized as a social ill, and is a major cause of incomplete homework for some students.

In Mainland China, among both Chinese and Western parents there is an assumption that due to China's strict social mores, alcohol, tobacco, illegal drugs, and prostitution are not readily available. This is not true! The school has some responsibility to educate parents that in fact a fourteen year-old foreign looking child has no problem ordering a beer in a bar, nor does he have any problem going with friends to a massage parlor and ordering up a "happy ending massage." The police generally are not too concerned about these issues, particularly if it only involves foreign citizens. Marijuana is also readily available on the street in China – just do a web search. Harder drugs are said to be available in bars frequented by foreigners. There are very strict laws against drugs in China, but for foreign citizens, a few nights in jail and a one-way trip to the airport would probably be the result unless it involves Chinese citizens. There have been cases where entire expatriate families are given the choice of wading through the legal system, or leaving the country within 24 hours with a ban on returning. On the other hand, while both Korea and China are assumed to be very conservatively sexually, particularly in China there are few moral or religious inhibitions against premarital sex. Unbelievably, the age of consent is 14 in China and only 13 in both South Korea and Japan, but this hardly reflects the conservative sexual mores of those cultures.

In the area of sexual awareness, young people in both Korea and China are often lacking in basic knowledge. Sex education in school is limited to "plumbing," outside of school it is limited to the wisdom of older friends and the internet, especially pornography. Parents generally do not discuss sex with their children. Despite censorship of on-line pornography in both countries, which many parents expect will protect their children, nearly every foreigner in China has VPN access to get around the censors. The school has two responsibilities: to provide age-appropriate sex education programs to young people, and to educate parents about the real (and digital) world that their sons and daughters are very aware of, and may be enjoying. Complicating this is the fact that there is a wide range of tolerance of alcohol use and sex by teenagers among the various cultures found in international schools – so less permissive parents can't always depend on the fact that "a parent will be at home" will provide an environment that would meet their own standards of "clean and safe" for their own teenagers.

Although Korean and Chinese societies openly acknowledge some of these "Western" social ills that have infected their nations, they may, like many parents, be naïve as to their own children's involvement or exposure. While parents certainly care about their children getting involved in these types of social ills, they may assume that as long as their child is polite and gets good grades, there is nothing to worry about. They are often shocked to find that in fact their children are involved in things they would never have dreamed of when they were young themselves.

5. Parents of EAL/ESL students may require their own acculturation to the new educational environment. An interesting phenomenon in many international schools is the reluctance of parents to have their child receive second language instruction in English. Keeping a child in EAL after a year, especially when a younger friend has exited from the same class, may become problematic for everyone; to have a younger friend or sibling "pass" an older student in EAL class can cause a good deal of anxiety among students and parents. At its core, it is not a question of academic readiness, but a matter of individual and family "face" and shame. EAL departments should work with counselors and administrators to help parents understand the realities of second language development so that parents can know what to expect in terms of language development – and that it not simply a matter of their child "studying harder." Perhaps, when they studied English as an academic subject as a student, that would work. However, parents need to realize that their children are not just learning about English, but learning to use English in their every day lives. Conversely, when the school finds itself re-assigning a child to EAL classes year after year, at some point the question needs to be asked whether or not an EAL diagnosis is possibly masking some deeper learning issue. In that case, diagnostic testing is most likely in order. Continuing to address a learning difference with EAL strategies is not fair to the child and denying him or her the possibility of appropriate help.

One of the things that can retard second language acquisition is long summer vacation! Not only do students often take the summer off from speaking, reading, writing, or listening to English, but also parents often will use this time to return to their home country and enroll their children in native language classes, which can further erode progress made during the school year. Simply reading English language classics (a common parental requirement) simply doesn't do the trick! Parents should be encouraged to ensure that their child has plenty of English language listening opportunities; I have usually suggested watching programs like National Geographic or the Discovery Channel, either on DVD or cable. These shows have visuals to support the narration, and the level of English is high but usually "kid appropriate." Students should be allowed to video chat with friends (in English), or be enrolled in a summer class that includes native speaking teachers and plenty of reading and writing (SAT prep does not do this particularly well, as these courses are often taught in Korean or Chinese.)

Summer vacations can also be used to advantage. For a student of middle or high school age who is progressing well but simply needs some language immersion, I have often recommended summer programs in an English speaking country, of which there are ample in North America. However, some words of caution are appropriate here. Lacking some guidance from the school in choosing a summer program, parents may default to asking friends to recommend a program. Often, popular programs are held at schools that have name recognition in Asia. The result too often is that Min-ju might go to Exeter or St. Paul's summer program in order to be immersed in English, but in fact find that most of the students are from Korea and China (this happened to my son; I didn't do my research very well!) Other parents, concerned that their child will get homesick, will organize a group of eight or ten friends to go together to learn English. In both of these cases, the kids have a great time, and do attend solid academic classes taught in English, but end up spending the summer in a linguistic and cultural bubble – the very one they are paying to escape! I would suggest helping the parents to find appropriate summer programs, using following criteria:

Find an accredited program that has a long-standing program for English language learners. There area a number of resources that can help you do this; check out catalogs such as Peterson's Guides on line. They have an excellent summer program catalog; there are many others. If they use the PSAT for middle schoolers as an admission or placement test, it's best to avoid that program or school. They are most likely using the test results to sift applicants down to a reasonable number; the PSAT is a completely inappropriate test of any knowledge for a middle school student. Smaller, less academic programs will provide a better immersion experience, generally.

Contact the summer program director to find out what proportion of their enrollees in the child's grade level also share the same native language as your student. Certainly they will have two or three, but if there are many more than that, you can be assured that the child won't be forced to actively participate in an immersion experience after they have sought out and found same-language friends for the summer. The school should also assign roommates with different native languages, who are forced to use English.

Choose a small school. The large, popular programs from brand name schools will necessarily have many Asian students enrolled. Avoid them, not because they are poor programs (they aren't) but because the child needs to be forced into using English constantly.

All recommendation forms for students should be channeled through your guidance department and guide parents away from sending a large group of kids to the same program. Whether this is for an EAL program or just an academic enrichment program, students will have much more to gain by not attending with a bunch of friends.

"Sell" this to parents not only as an academic opportunity, but also as a way for their child to learn independence and self-confidence in preparation to later university success. I have seen mothers pool resources to send one mom with the students to rent an apartment for the summer outside the school gate, to be sure that they were well taken care of, to wash their clothes, and to check on them frequently. This of course is not how kids learn to be independent. Of the many dozens of students I have arranged to go to EAL summer school, I only had one complaint, that from a Vietnamese mom who told me in September, "My son learned lots of English, but what I didn't like is that he is now so much more independent. He went rock climbing and kayaking, and even saw a bear in the woods!"

A counselor or administrator should be willing to be a go-between in the initial application process. Sending a child half way around the world by themselves to spend the summer in the sinful West is a scary proposition. You can even help by ensuring parents that if the school says it arranges for airport pickup, it will. I found it helpful to establish a long-standing relationship with one or two summer programs for EAL students that I really felt comfortable with. They trusted my recommendations; I trusted that they would take care of the child. I could monitor how many students applied and attended, and could help kids to arrange to fly together, or with one parent. Schools would be honest in their feedback about academic and social progress. This also cut down on an annual search for new schools every year. One was close enough to where I spent my summers in New Hampshire (USA) that I could (with permission of the school) drop by and surprise the student sometime during the summer, which the kids actually appreciated very much.

6. Asian parents may need some instruction on how they can prepare their child for higher education in a Western country. Asian culture tends to keep children dependent on their parents well into adulthood. Parents need help in understanding how difficult this kind of dependency may make it for their children to succeed on their own in a Western university environment. Korean and Chinese students are supposed to be just that — students. They are not supposed to have to worry about the other time-consuming duties of life. Thus, Asian children generally do not have chores to do around the house, even simple things like making their own bed or taking their dishes to the sink. Teachers might be surprised to find that their middle or even high school Korean/Chinese students have never washed a dish, made a bed, or thrown a load of clothes in the wash. It's not that it is below them, they simply have never experienced the need to do these things. Mom (or the maid) does these things and are literally shooed out of the kitchen. The child is to spend his or her time with his or her nose in the books. While this does not cause any particular difficulty for the university, except that it makes if very difficult for a young person who struggling to both adjust to a new academic and social culture, and having for the first time in their lives to take care of themselves. Lots of Asian kids simply have never developed basic survival skills. In addition, children may have never had to work for money, and may have been given a generous allowance with no responsibilities attached. Even after students have gone off to North America or Europe to university, more than a few mothers "commute" from Korea or China every month or so to check up on their son or daughter, clean their room, make some of their favorite food, and generally be sure that Choon-ho or Shi-Shi is being taken care of. Boys in particular may be considered to be in need of a mother's attention. Schools can help in this situation by providing parents with lists of skills that their child should learn by the time they graduate from high school. Alternately, the school could provide a "senior seminar" to introduce graduates to college survival skills. For example, using a washer and dryer correctly in order to avoid pink underwear, cooking simple meals beyond holding an instant noodle cup under the hot water dispenser, food safety tips (don't eat the pizza left on the window sill overnight), cleanliness routines (When he returned to Shanghai from the U.S. for winter break, I asked one Chinese young man, completely educated at our international school, whether or not he had some kind of laundry service for his sheets and towels or did them himself. Incredulously he looked at me and said, "You're supposed to wash them?") Handling money responsibly is another important area for kids whose money management skills have been limited to asking mom for more cash.

The dropout rate by Chinese students attending Western universities is about 30%. There are multiple reasons for this, including running into issues of academic integrity (some intentional, some a result of cultural differences) and limited

English language ability (how did they gain admission in the first place?). However, a very common reason is that the students simply lacked the life management skills to take care of themselves. Their every need has been taken care of for so long by doting parents and grandparents that when they are on their own, even in a college dormitory, they often cannot manage both being a student (difficult enough in a foreign language in a foreign system) and managing their daily lives.

Another example of prolonged dependence, noted earlier, is the tendency for parents (either mother or father) to "take responsibility" for their children's actions. "It's my fault, maybe I'm a bad mother; don't blame him" is all too often heard when a Korean or Chinese child gets in trouble. You can be sure that justice will be meted out at home (the family has been embarrassed, after all) but any type of punishment that may be found out by other parents is avoided at all costs. Administrators need to assure parents that just because Yung-jin is being suspended for two days, you will not publicize it. They may well ask if this incident will be put 'in his record' and beg that it not be. There is a good deal of public shame suffered by the parents when a child gets in trouble. I have had parents ask me to guarantee that no other students will find out about the misdeed – days after it occurred, two student news cycles ago! It takes backbone to stand up to pleas to not discipline Yung-jin this time in return for a promise from his parents that it won't happen again. Don't except the excuse that he didn't know any better, and that it is just the result of bad parenting. That is seldom the truth, and Yung-jin still has to be disciplined at school!

7. Western educators should be aware that parents may also try to take responsibility for a child's academic success or failure by promising better grades or greater success in the future. The chance of retention or academic probation may be perceived as a family shame rather than any shortcoming on the part of the child. Again, while the child will bear the full brunt of the responsibility when he or she gets home, parents will want to avoid any chance that other parents will find out about the situation.

We can help parents by explaining that although we all want their children to do as well as they can in school, by pampering them, by not allowing them to fail once in a while (and thus learn that it is they, not the parents, who "own" the grades), by making life too easy, and by making excuses that they are raising children so dependent on them that they will have a very difficult time surviving on their own in a Western college or university where personal self-survival skills are so important. Baring such support, to succeed in university outside of Korea students need to be much more than great students - they need to become independent people able and willing to take care of themselves.

We've all heard about helicopter moms who circle overhead to be sure that no disaster strikes their child while also being on hand to redirect and guide their little one should he or she stray off course and be distracted from their all important studies. Less known is the snowplow parent, who goes ahead of their child on the academic journey, clearing any obstacle that might cause the child to suffer inconvenience or emotional or academic stress in any way. The old adage "what doesn't kill you makes you stronger" isn't well accepted in Asia. On the other hand, today's parents had to struggle mightily against great odds to be where they are today. If they can ensure that their child can also succeed, but without suffering the pain that they did, they will do their best to make that happen.

Mee-jung, an only child from a very wealthy Seoul family, was one of the smartest girls in her prestigious private Korean elementary school, and was consistently at the top of her class. Her mother, a woman of culture and intelligence, hired an English-speaking Korean woman married to an

American teacher to tutor her daughter with the goal of eventually gaining entrance to a private American boarding school. Mee-jung studied hard and stayed at the top of her class throughout middle school. The tutor felt tremendous pressure to ensure that her young charge scored top marks on any test. Mee-jung was well supported by her mother; she sent Mee-jung to the tutor's home by car and driver, and whenever she arrived at the tutor's home, she sat in the back seat and waited for the driver to open the door for her and carry her books to the door. She worked hard until she was chauffeured off to her next art or ballet lesson. Her every hour was carefully scheduled by her mother, who was providing her every opportunity for success. Eventually, the tutor and her husband were able to help her gain admission to a very prestigious New England boarding school for ninth grade. She seemed headed for every future success. Unfortunately, what Mee-jung possessed in intelligence she lacked in common sense and independence. Her life had been so totally organized for her (violin and piano lessons, art lessons, English lessons, etc., etc.) that she didn't know how to wash her clothes, cook a bowl of ramyon, or pick up after herself. More crucial, she didn't have the self- discipline to organize her own time or get herself up in the morning, and quickly fell into a spiral of academic difficulty. For the first time in her life, her mom couldn't manage her life and ensure success, and she didn't have the skills to do it on her own. Unable to manage both academics and life, within two years she and her mother were searching for another school. Eventually she returned to Korea, her American education a failure not due to any academic limitations or even English language difficulties, but to a dismal lack of self-motivation, independence, survival skills, and common sense. By being everything a good Korean student should be she never developed the abilities necessary to fulfill her parents' dream for her of an American prep school and college education. More to the point, her mother, by being everything a good Korean mother should be, raised a daughter so dependent and lacking in maturity that she simply could not survive in an American educational and social environment, where independence and self-direction are demanded.

In some parents' eyes, academic success or failure is tantamount to success or failure as an individual of value. This equating of academic prowess and personal worth is one of the pressures that pushes students to excel academically, and one of the most difficult things to understand for many Western teachers. I wrote earlier of the Korean dad who kept insisting to me that his seventh grade son was a "bad son," in front of the child. When I challenged him, he very frankly stated that he was a bad son because he didn't earn top grades. This idea is not a new one; it is well expressed three decades ago by the authors of *Handbook for Teaching Korean-American Students,* p. 29, (1992) published by the Bilingual Education Office of the California Department of Education. This observation, made about Korean immigrant parents, still holds true today.

"Parents in Korea generally support the schools and hope for fulfillment of their own lives through the success of their children. Parents instill in their children very early the idea that parental acceptance is contingent on high performance in school. The Korean community as well as family and relatives often give prominence to and recognize high academic performance. When the report card is sent to parents, they often call each other to compare their children's grades, knowledge of which is shared by parents, relatives, and neighbors. Korean children feel obligated to receive high grades and are imbued with the notion that their academic success is linked to the family's reputation. Students learn early that they are working not merely for themselves but for their family as well. Keenly concerned about their performance, they become competitive not only for their own sake

*but also for their family's prestige. Low performance levels
elicit parental disapproval, criticism, disappointment, and
sometimes shame among relatives and friends."*

**8. Parents may look to you for advice and help; they see you
in partnership raising their kids.** Don't hold back. Korean and
Chinese parents view the school as a partner in the raising
of their children, taking seriously your "parental" Confucian
role. Teachers have always been held in very high regard
in Asian countries. Sending their child to an international
school is quite a gamble for them, as they are entrusting a
major part of their child's upbringing to foreigners, who they
may not completely understand and who must seem like it-
inerant globe- trotting migrant workers who will most likely
not be around in a few years. One example of this is in the
area of discipline; in Chinese and Korean families, parents are
often not the ones who administer discipline to their own
children. Quite often the school is expected to provide this.
Parents can and do threaten their children that they (the parents) will report bad behavior to the child's teacher (a 180-
degree switch from what many of us are used to!) When a child
gets into trouble on the streets, the police often contact the
school before contacting the parents. Korean schools have at
least one faculty member on duty 24 hours a day, seven days a
week, for just such emergencies. Teachers are expected to play
an active role in the moral upbringing of their students beyond the walls of the classroom. Therefore, do not be hesitant
to counsel parents and help them in cross-cultural situations,
but be sure not to end up being the heavy in the family. They
will be truly grateful for your help and insight.

Late one rainy Shanghai night I was awoken to my phone
ringing. It was the school CFO, who had just gotten a call from
a police box downtown. It seems that two of our high school
students had been picked up by the police for some indiscre-
tion, and wanted someone from the school to come down to

the station, about a 30 minute taxi ride away on this dark night, to identify the students. Once they had been positively identified, the police captain had said, then they would be released to my custody as their principal. Along with the school security officer, I dutifully went down and visited a rough and beat up police station, a visit that ultimately ended at about two in the morning with the release of the students and a lecture from the police captain. When I arrived, I was amazed to find the mother of one of the students already there; when I called the other she asked if it was really necessary! What surprised me was that the police would not release even one of the students to a parent, but would release her to me, the principal, as the "responsible party" representing the school. I could then "release" the studentst to their parents. In the case of the student whose mother refused pickher up, she went home with the other mother for the night. This incident reminded me of a lesson I thought I had learned years earlier in Korea: it isn't just the parents who consider the school as a partner in raising their child, the entire society, even the legal system, has the same understanding.

While parents may not accept all of your advice, you can be sure that as an educator you are held in higher regard as an expert in child rearing than you might regard yourself, even if you have no children of your own. The very honorable status of teachers in Asia will most likely be applied to you. This status is based on your education, morality and leadership. You may be approached for child-rearing guidance, especially in matters related to school or acculturation. If you feel confident in this area, don't be afraid to offer help. Remember, however, that in their eyes you are still a foreigner. In really important matters, family friends, and especially grandparents who may have very little understanding of a Western-style school situation, are also very influential. While you are interacting with the parent, there is a host of silent partners who also have a strong voice in the upbringing of the child.

These situations can be very frustrating until you realize that while parents may be listening to you and outwardly agreeing with what you say, you may never meet the real decision makers. Cultural conflicts can be frustrating when you realize that the parents are coming from a completely different child-rearing background. Hopefully this book will give you some greater level of understanding.

While in the West there is often pushback against the school "pushing its values" on students, Asian parents expect this, and see the school as a vital partner in the moral education of students. In Korea this is often expressed through classes that specifically teach Confucian cultural values. In Mainland China, this "moral" education is often mixed with political (Party) indoctrination, as well. A colleague of mine at another international school in Shanghai, a principal, told me about a situation that happened to her. A high school girl with traditional Chinese parents had lost her lunch card at least twice, not an unusual occurrence. The first time it was returned without incident; the second time it was repeatedly used by another student to buy her own lunches before it was "found." The school was able to identify the culprit, and a confession and apology were forthcoming and appropriate discipline administered. However, this was not enough for the parents of the victim, who insisted that the school (the principal) was not taking strong enough action. When she pushed them on what they expected, they repeatedly demanded that the principal "instruct" all high school students not to steal. When my colleague suggested that high school students (including the thief) already were well aware that stealing was wrong the parents disagreed, asking how the students would know if the school did not teach them. The principal asked them "Do you want me to gather all the students in the auditorium, and tell them that stealing is bad?" She explained that students (and quite possibly their parents) would find this kind of instruction, at the high school level, insulting and even laughable.

That was exactly what the parents expected, and demanded that if that did not happen, then they would go to "higher authorities" at the school, which the principal welcomed them to do. This incident was an example of serious culture clash, with 1) parents expecting the school to be the first line of defense in moral education, and 2) expected it to be done in a way (gathering all students together and lecturing them) that simply does not work in a Western educational environment. (I'm not sure it is very effective in an Asian environment, either.) The parents also demanded to know the identity of the student who had used their daughter's lunch card so that they would "instruct" her themselves. That, too, was refused. The result was very frustrated parents who believed the school was being negligent, and a very frustrated school administrator who realized that the cultural friction of this situation would most likely never be soothed, however hard she tried to explain to the parents that she was not operating by Chinese rules.

9. Parents may opt to enroll their children in after school academies. An integral part of this competitive drive for more and more education, earlier and earlier, is the phenomenon of the after school academy. It is not at all unusual that a middle or high school student may have scheduled twelve or fifteen hours at various academy classes weekly – plus the homework that goes along with each class. For children in the local school systems, most of these classes parallel the regular school national curriculum, but are taught a few weeks earlier to prepare students for the "real thing" in school. Because the class sizes in academies are usually smaller than in a public school, the instruction for the individual student is quite possibly even better than what they will get in school. This often renders the regular classes in school redundant. It is not unusual for students to spend more time and effort on their academy classes than their regular school classes. Mothers feel compelled to enroll their children into academies so that they won't fall behind other students. The financial burden on families is heavy; in Korea, even among low-income families, the average percentage of household income for a family of two school-aged children spent on after school private instruction is over 10%. Note that this is an average – which means half of all families spend more than that amount.

Although many parents choose an international education to avoid this type of pressure-cooker education, you will find that the guilt, worry, and habits that they are trying to avoid follows them into your school. Expect that many, if not most, of your Korean, and very many of your Chinese students, will be attending after school academies. The irony is that while these classes are supposed to prepare students for their "real" classes in school, because international schools don't normally follow any common national curriculum, the classes don't really prepare the kids for much of anything applicable to their schoolwork. The time, money, and effort spent on after school classes could be much better applied to their regular homework. I have often counseled families whose high school son or daughter was simply not doing his or her schoolwork. One of the first questions I asked was how many after school academy classes the child is scheduled for. Inevitably, the mom will reply that it is minimal. I ask them to write it all down for me. Between SAT prep, English composition, Korean or Chinese math, Korean language, Chinese characters, violin, and tennis (or some similar menu) it often tops ten or more hours, which the parents don't see as excessive. When I ask about the homework associated with these classes, the number often doubles. Then, I ask about the schedule, and find that often that student may not get home from academy classes on weeknights until 10:30 or 11:00pm – and then begin their school homework. Weekends are often reserved for the "recreational" tennis or soccer, along with the practice that goes with these activities. Korean Christians may also spend the better part of Sunday, and even Wednesday evenings, at church activities. Unscheduled time is considered wasted time. Is it any wonder that creativity suffers?

For students eventually returning to Korea or China from overseas, some type of preparation is inevitable and necessary. It is a well-accepted fact in the ESL world that a beginning language learner will not be able to advance in the new language beyond the level attained in the native language. Therefore, a Chinese or Korean (or French or Italian) English language learner should continue instruction in their native language, both for identity and cultural reasons as well as to ease the learning of English. However, what is not necessary is for a student who is not doing as well as mom would like in math (always an area of concentration) or English to go to academy or have a private tutor for these subjects in order to raise school grades. Math is taught in Asian countries much differently than it is taught in Western schools, and the advanced academy instruction will have little impact on school grades because the two systems don't match. Going to English classes at an academy to raise a grade is similarly off target. Often the emphasis is on vocabulary and grammar development, and in any event is not taught by a trained, native-language English teacher. Even if the teacher is a native English teacher, normally he or she has no teacher training, simply went to a brand name university, or is teaching the required curriculum of that Chinese/Korean owned academy. The idea that just because a tutor attended (graduated?) from a well-known university somehow makes them an excellent instructor is of course ludicrous, however much sense it might make to some parents. A degree in English literature similarly does not guarantee the skills necessary to help a child with assigned schoolwork. The child would be much better served by having a trained teacher from the school, or from another international school, tutor the child. At the very least, any tutor (and this is more difficult in an academy environment with multiple students) should be communicating with the classroom teacher so that they can support the schoolwork rather than detract from it by spending the student's time on other topics. Also, it is quite possible that a tutor or academy has been scheduled because the student's grade has fallen to an A- or B+; hardly the territory for academic triage.

So given that tutoring and academies are going to happen for many students regardless of what you say to a family, how can you handle this challenge? I would suggest a number of things:

a) With the family, do an audit of the actual number of hours, including transportation that their child spends on scheduled private education of one type or another. Then, reviewing each class estimate the number of hours spent on homework for each class. Add it up. How does it compare the same type of hours/activities related to their regular schoolwork? Is this reasonable? Add that total to the transportation, in-school time, and homework from their "regular" school. Is this total reasonable for any young person?

b) Again, look at each academy class. Are there any that are unnecessary? A tutor for a student who is struggling in English class, who will communicate with the teacher and coordinate efforts, may be a good investment. However, simply enrolling a child in an English academy that will provide a program with no relationship to current schoolwork is probably a waste of time, money, and effort, and may be counterproductive in terms of school grades. For a student heading for Korean or Chinese university, native language preparation classes are probably not a bad idea. But lets drop the extra tennis or golf lessons (unless the student really enjoys it), and for a high schooler probably ongoing violin lessons (if the child is already taking orchestra in school, or unless the child is really passionate about violin) can be ended. As much as this may make mom unhappy, by the age of 15 or 16 the die has probably already been cast as to whether or not we have the next

YoYo Ma on our hands. How many adults really will pull out their violin or sit down at the piano and play some Brahms or Schubert at a dinner party? Maybe a switch to jazz piano, if the student wants to continue, would be more useful so they could enjoy it for a lifetime in less formal environments than a concert stage.

c) Look critically at popular SAT prep classes. Classes that focus on test taking strategies is probably not a bad idea – once – but simply memorizing vocabulary is not of much value, unless the academy instructor really focuses on word roots, prefixes, and suffixes, which can of course then be applied in different situations, including the SAT. The school can preempt some of this by intentionally focusing on PSAT results, which today provide an individualized diagnostic of weak areas, as well as access to Kahn Academy remedial lessons as needed. The ongoing debacle of leaked SAT test questions and cancelled scores will never end until the College Board stops re-using questions, and tightens up its own security. I speak from personal experience as a school administrator in China! Simply taking the ACT instead of the SAT will not solve the problem in the long term, only move it over to the ACT. Scholars in both Korea and China have reached the same conclusion that until high stakes, standardized college entrance testing is a thing of the past, as it is with increasing numbers of U.S. colleges and universities, the impulse to hyper-prepare for years before the test, and use less than legitimate means to gain some small advantage over the kid sitting in the next row in the test center, will never end. The situation in large cities in both Korea and China is similar.

d) Investigate how academy attendance is affecting sleep. The Korean Journal of Pediatrics reports that " Chronic sleep deprivation among adolescents inhibits pre-frontal lobe functions, such as working memory, judgment, and insight, resulting in impairment of learning and school performance." (Korean J Pediatr. 2011 Jan; 54(1): 29–35). This should be no surprise to teachers, of course. The occasional incidence of a child falling asleep in class should probably be ignored, but when it becomes habitual it's time to ask some questions. Quite probably, for middle schoolers the issue is a combination of 1) academy work eating into their late evening hours, and 2) gaming, chatting on line, or some other less wholesome internet activities. For high schoolers, it is most often due to staying up too late studying, at least on weekdays – a problem compounded by academy attendance, as noted earlier. For some of our students who have a more "active" social life than others, they may be burning the candle at both ends by studying until the wee hours (the Korean high school "bedtime" average is roughly 1:30AM for high schoolers) and by staying out late with friends on weekends, stealing away their one chance to rejuvenate. The average number of hours a Korean high schooler sleeps is 5.5; Korean's have a well known saying "Sleep four hours and pass, sleep five hours and fail!" The message here is that sleep is optional in the minds of both parents and students. While a lack of sleep may affect learning efficiency on the bottom of Maslow's pyramid to some degree, as we go up the pyramid we can assume that sleep would take an ever-increasing toll on learning and comprehension. Certainly, it is easier to memorize vocabulary words when sleep deprived than it is to perform complex mathematical operations or analyze a piece of literature. As Asian education is highly fact/memorization based, it might make some sense in that environment to equate hours studying to increased academic success. Certainly we quickly get to a point of diminishing returns where increased study/lack of sleep contributes to academic difficulties.

e) Discuss with parents how the pressure to succeed, exacerbated by academy attendance, might be affecting their families and parent/child relationships? The on-line data reflecting legitimate research into this area is well established for Asian countries, particularly Korea. Governments and Ministries of Education wring their hands about academies and testing and the toll it takes on young people's lives, emotional wellbeing, and sustainable educational attainment. Parents decry the emphasis on testing and study, and in fact may have transferred their child to your international school to escape this environment, although they often can't quite leave it behind. Students are miserable; most young people do not enjoy living lives focused only on education, although they may know nothing else. Walking the streets of urban Korea or China, or joining vacation-goers in those countries reveal an interesting phenomenon – there are very few middle or high school students enjoying time with friends or family members. In the early morning, late afternoon, or late evening you may see students hurrying to of from their appointed places of study, but you will seldom see high school kids enjoying a weekend afternoon or a vacation with their family. They are home, somewhere, studying. Students report high levels of stress, most often related to grades. Excellent is never good enough; taking a break triggers guilt. The result of this narrow lifestyle is the fact that South Korea now has the highest suicide rate in the world. While we cannot change this in Korean or Chinese schools, we can affect individual kids in our own schools by working with their parents and trying to negotiate a livable, balanced lifestyle for their children that will still ensure an enriching and fulfilling future, both during and after their academic journey. Another price of this emphasis on education is that the idea of curling up with a good book, even for adults, is anathema in Asia. Reading is closely associated with study, and after 16 years of education, people are done with study.

Excessive pressure, including the use of academies, can have very negative effects on parent/child relationships. Parents often decry the fact that their high schoolers are drifting away from them emotionally. They complain that their children are argumentative and grumpy much of the time. I often ask them if they are also grumpy when sleep deprived, and then remind them of how little sleep their child probably gets. Then I ask them a question that often results in a very quiet room. "When was the last time you had a meaningful conversation with your child that was not related to their schoolwork or educational future?" Tragically, it is the rare parent who can answer this question in any meaningful way. Coupled to my earlier comments about a child's "worth" as an individual being related to their academic prowess, and we can quickly see why family relationships are often strained. Combined with the intercultural issues ("Of course I have to go to Academy, I have a Chinese mom!") we see lots of opportunities for teachers and counselors, and sometimes principals, to involve themselves in culturally sensitive ways with families in crisis. If kids and parents can hold all this together, and have fulfilling lives, be strong students, and get into great universities – GREAT! We know there are some blessed kids who can do that. But for the large majority, even among our naturally talented international school students, this does not happen. We have a lot of stressed out kids in our classrooms, and as Western educators we have a responsibility to do what we can to mitigate that.

f. Discuss with parents the importance of after school activities for the development of a healthy mind and body. Is academy attendance disallowing involvement in sports, the arts, and other extra-curricular activities? While academy classes normally meet a few hours after school activities, there are only about so many hours in a day. When it comes down to a choice between playing soccer or being in the school musical or going to academy, academy often wins due to the fact that in the eyes (and experience) of many parents, involvement in such activity doesn't contribute at all to a college application portfolio, and in fact may detract from it. Unless the child is a golf prodigy or the next K-pop star, parents may see these activities as a waste of time. It is imperative that parents be shown how activity involvement is 1) important to the development of healthy minds and bodies, 2) may actually help to improve academic success (lots of research on this in the area of music), and 3) if the child has any possible future in Western universities, it is imperative that they chose a few activities and stick with them.

g. While at school you see a bicultural, or even totally Westernized child, parents may see a 100% Korean or Chinese child at home. They may need help to recognize that their child is not totally Korean or Chinese any more, but is evolving into a new multicultural individual. It was mentioned earlier that generally (in particular) Koreans' sense of national identity and "groupness" often make it difficult for them to see shades of Korean-ness or recognize or appreciate biculturalism. While they will readily acknowledge that their child now is fluent in English, or now wears different clothes, or has different tastes in food, they still quite naturally still think of their child as being really Korean rather than bicultural or a TCK. Helping them to understand this sometimes causes some degree of regret or guilt on the part of the parents, but it may well help parents to understand their children better, and vice-versa.

While the chances are good that most parents understand that they are paying for more than English fluency or a "ticket to Harvard" by sending their child to your school, whether it be an international school in Beijing or a "year abroad" in Boston, what they don't expect is that there is a whole hidden "cultural curriculum" that Western education teaches kids. This is taught through disciplinary policies, encouraging involvement in extracurricular offerings, social freedom to mix with kids of the opposite sex, support for creativity, and running elbows with kids who are different from those they would find in their national schools. Attitudes and behaviors towards others who are "different," whether in culture, skin color, language, religion, talents, or sexual orientation change over time, often in ways that parents would not approve of were they to realize what was happening. The stereotypical example is of the Korean girl who talks her parents into letting her go to the prom, in itself quite possibly a hurdle for parents to conquer. The fact that "everyone else is doing it" is perhaps the most convincing argument in a conformist society. However, when the girl's date shows up on the doorstep and for the first time the parents realize that he is African American, or Asian Indian, or even (for some more traditional Koreans) Japanese, things can get very uncomfortable for everyone involved. Parents may realize for the first time that their daughter has learned more at her new school than they thought they were paying for, and that their "Korean" daughter is no longer completely the young person they thought they had been raising. Increasingly younger parents are more understanding and are more accepting of differences, but older parents, and particularly grandparents who may be living with the family, may have much narrower and more traditional definitions of "normal-ness" and social acceptability.

10. Many ethnic Korean parents may see themselves as outsiders from the Western school culture. This author, even after living in Korea and China for more than forty years, was still considered an "outsider." The Korean and Chinese words for "foreigner" are "a person from outside"; this is not just a linguistic form but reflects a real perception. In my case, my inability to become anywhere near fluent in either Korean or Chinese may have had something to do with that, and I accept that responsibility, but I know Westerners who have grown up in Korea, elected to go through the Korean army, have predominantly Korean friends, speak, read and write flawless colloquial Korean, but are still considered "foreigners" due to their ethnicity. Ethnicity and nationality, being one in the same in Korea and much of China, are concepts that are difficult to separate in more mono-ethnic societies like those of

Korea, Japan, and (to a lesser extent) China. An overseas ethnic Korean or Chinese, then, may naturally project their own definition of "foreigners" on themselves and expect that he or she is considered an "outsider" by host country nationals (which may be accurate in areas of many host countries) or by the Western school community (probably not as accurate, especially when host country students - Korean or Chinese - may be in the majority.) Sensitivity to this perception, and a conscious effort to include ethnic Korean and Chinese parents in school events and activities, is welcomed and helpful. Help them get involved in the PTA, ask them to be room mothers, get them on the governing board, or find some committees on which they can serve and contribute a different perspective. They want very much to be involved, and can and will be a really positive, involved, and hard-working force in your school. While "ethnic" food days are most often a welcome and tasty opening to intercultural interaction, involvement should go beyond that level. Your parent organization can be a very effective vehicle to help them get involved. As mentioned earlier, I found that one particularly appreciated activity was for me to provide a translated presentation on the differences between Western and Asian education at a PTA meeting, with discussion following. While they are aware of many of these differences, seeing it in visual form and explained to them in their own language was (from the feedback I received) very much appreciated. Hopefully this book will provide to Western educators the other side of that same equation. In this way both parents and educators can avoid a lot of cultural frustration.

11. Lack of physical presence in school does not indicate a lack of interest by parents in their children or their education. Parents in any culture are or course very proud of their children — and in Asian cultures they are very much valued as the future of the extended family. However, parental roles can be quite different among cultures, even Asian cultures. Fathers tend not to be involved in children's education as much as moms do, but may have a much better command of English. In a Western school this thrusts the dads into a new role — that of the school contact — in which they might feel quite uncomfortable and may see as somehow "below" them. Mothers, on the other hand, who traditionally are responsible for educational decisions, as well as children's academic success (or failure) may be embarrassed by their lack of English language ability, be hesitant to admit that they are having difficulties with their children, lack understanding about what their role is in the school, or simply fear the unknown of a new educational environment. Actually, their English is often much better than they believe it to be, but a natural humility often prevents them from admitting it. If they seem hesitant to attend parent conferences, invite them to bring along a friend to interpret. Teachers should not be afraid to make contact and invite both parents to school. It may be necessary to insist on the father's attendance at conferences if you suspect that the child's mother isn't handling a difficult situation effectively. Because the mother is held responsible for the behavior and success of the children, she can sometimes "get in trouble" from her husband and even in-laws if the children are having difficulties. Therefore, she may not let dad in on a situation until it gets serious. If you suspect that mom is not able to handle the situation for whatever reasons, insist on dad's involvement in discussions before things reach a critical stage either academically or socially. This situation is more frequent among Korean families than Chinese, in my experience. Because of the highly defined Confucian roles imposed on mothers and fathers in Korea, like many characteristics mentioned in this book, they are magnified in Korea. For the most part, Korean moms still do not work outside the home, and their "job" is raising the children, providing for her husband, and fulfilling extended family responsibilities (particularly if her husband is an oldest son).

In Mainland China, male/female roles are much more fluid due to the last 70 years of Communist rule, particularly since the Cultural Revolution in the Sixties and Seventies. Both parents may work outside the home, and due to the one-child policy, until recently once a child started school there was little for mom to do at home. In many Chinese homes, the husband is the cook, something that would be very unusual in Korea. Furthermore, in China one set of grandparents often live with their adult children and one grandchild, and have the primary childcare and child-rearing responsibilities. A stop by the gate of a school in any Chinese city at afternoon dismissal time will find hundreds of grandparents crowding the sidewalks, waiting for their little one to get out. When he or she appears, the grandparent will whisk away the backpack lest the little one tire him or herself out before afternoon academy classes. I have observed ethnic Chinese high school girls getting off in international school bus, met at the bus stop by elderly grandmothers who immediately take the full backpack and trudge off behind the girls who are already on their cell phones talking to friends, leaving grandmas trailing behind. Confucius would not have been happy, and neither was I!

In Mainland China, it is not uncommon for dads to spend most of their working week living someplace other than at home with his wife and children. Due to the size of the rapidly developing interior of China, and the fact that most international schools are located along the coast (with the exception of Beijing), many dads (and some moms) of students in international schools are "on the road" a good deal of the time (this is true of expatriate dads as well). If both mom and dad are working outside of their home city, it could well be that the only contact to the school is a non English-speaking grandparent who understands Western education even less than the parents presumably do. At least mobile phones make it possible to contact the parents wherever they may be. I have more than once called a parent, expecting that they were working right there in Shanghai, only to find that I woke them up in Paris or LA! Many schools have enrollment regulations requiring at least one parent to be in the city at all times, and if they cannot be to temporarily designate an English-speaking guardian. However, parents, who see the grandparents as perfectly capable guardians often ignore these regulations, the grandparents having in many cases raised the children from birth. However capable, too often kids don't keep grandparents informed of problems, or grandparents don't sense when things are going wrong with their Westernized grandchild and can't communicate when the school has to call home for some reason.

In Korea, unless dad or mom has a very high powered job that takes them out of the country, for the most part Korea is small enough that at least one parent returns home at night, although Korean obligatory business/drinking culture often results in dads coming home in the wee hours after an evening of drinking with co-workers. This is slowly changing in Korea, with younger men insisting on more family time than their own fathers could afford. However, there is a high degree of social pressure for men to perform in traditional roles, few of which put them in daily contact with their children.

Once again, we see that the phenomenon of parental roles in both China and Korea are heavily influenced by Confucianism, but just less so, and differently. Of course, this varies among families as well. I refer you again to the article in the Appendix All the Korean mothers were valiant.

12. Help parents network with each other. While Korea or Chinese or Japanese parent groups often develop spontaneously through their own expat grapevine without any involvement from the school, a newly arrived family often needs the security of interacting with others who have had the same experience before them. Once a Korean or Chinese mom is connected with others from her homeland, they will usually take it from there, much as any expat new to a city will be tutored on local survival skills. If this network can be brought to work for instead of against the school, all the better. If possible, administrators should maintain contact with some of the leaders (both fathers and mothers) in the school's Korean and Chinese communities. Once connected, other families will look to them for advice and leadership. It is advantageous for these leaders to understand your school, your priorities and your programs rather than for the community to react to the latest rumor or tidbit of news on WeChat or KakaoTalk. Otherwise, you may find that some of your work is being unwittingly sabotaged from outside without your knowledge, due only to a lack of understanding and misinformation. One natural outcome of this is for language-based organizations to form, which may work at odds with each other, with the Western group and various Asian groups working at cross purposes. Try to encourage those parents who can effectively work within both groups to be the bridges. It's important to hit a balance between language-based splinter groups and those with limited English skills simply opting out of school activities. For example, the more separate language-specific meetings you have, less the groups will work together. However, it may be helpful at times to host specific programs in Korean or Chinese, with visuals in those languages and a bi-lingual and bi-cultural presenter (or standing next to the school official as translator). Once again, often the PTA or similar organization can take on this challenge.

Some schools have employed a bi-lingual and bi-cultural "Korean/Chinese Community Liaison" to be an on-call translator of both language and culture, and to organize activities that enhance the relationship between the Korean, Chinese and Western communities. While this type of position may seem like a good answer to ongoing communication and cultural difficulties, it is crucially important that the right person be hired who will be accepted and trusted by the community. If the individual is younger than most of the parents, he or she may not be respected due to their age. If they are too involved in the community already, they may not be trusted to keep confidences, particularly if they are involved in difficult child/family discussions. (The issue of keeping professional confidences can be a challenging one in Confucian cultures, where the maintenance of relationships often conflicts with the necessity to keep confidences – and relationships often win. I was hiring a Singaporean Mandarin/English secretary for our counseling department in Shanghai who would be handling sensitive student information. She was also the parent of a current high school student. I had every confidence in her professionalism would prevail, but there was some pushback from the community who questioned whether or not she would share confidential student information with others. I hired her anyway, and she quickly put all concerns to rest with her strict sense of professionalism.) It is important, however, that the liaison not be seen as a stand by translator and message carrier ("please find Lei-Lei and make sure she asks her math teacher about her recent test") for parents who would simply rather call the office themselves, but would rather text the liaison. Again – this is a good reason to not have a much younger liaison who might be seen as a go-fer. A young male liaison would probably also not be abused in this way.

13. Develop a school policy on gift acceptance. Before I say too much about gifts, I must admit that many educators have had very different gift-receiving experiences in Korea and in China. In Korea, gifts can be very generous and frequent, in line with the local Korean culture. When I moved to Shanghai from Seoul, this immediately changed, even among our Korean parents (in Shanghai). I thought that this was a difference between Korean and Chinese culture, until I read the excellent book "Little Soldiers" (see bibliography) and learned how demanding Chinese teachers could be even to the point of specifying particular gifts, and how anxious Chinese parents were to fulfill their wishes so that their child would not be "forgotten." With the same motive Korean parents were very generous to teachers and administrators. While Western parents may send in a plate of Christmas cookies and a card to a favorite teacher (or principal!), a Korean parent may send in expensive celadon, neckties or scarves, or even cash. Perhaps the most egregious situation I experienced in Seoul was when a longtime parent at the school made the rounds at parent conference day, leaving behind with each teacher an envelope with $500 in crisp new bills as a token of "thanks." While the "thanks" may have been appropriate in this case, it obviously put teachers in a difficult spot, and I soon had teachers coming in and dropping the envelopes on my desk like they were toxic waste.

Periodically, governments in both countries have campaigns against gift giving, as tokens of appreciation can quickly grow into large "donations" with strings and expectations attached. In Confucian cultures, generous gifts have long been used as vehicles to cement and maintain relationships — political, business, social, or otherwise, and the parent-teacher relationship is no exception. While not exactly bribes for good grades, they are a not-so-subtle way of saying "I appreciate the care you have shown my child. Please keep it up." While this may seem understandable in a classroom of 50, it doesn't make much sense when there are 15 in the class and the parents is already paying a hefty tuition.

Once a gift is accepted, reciprocity (be good to my child) is expected. This is not to be confused with an outright bribe for good grades (which I have never seen happen; Asian culture is seldom quite so direct). Bribes are certainly not unknown in Korean and Chinese society, however, and one would be wise to be conscious not only of the possibly that the real intent of a gift is not so harmless, but also of the outward appearance of accepting something less than a token of simple thanks. This is especially important to keep in mind for those with admissions responsibilities or those who write college recommendations.

How can Western educators, who probably lack understanding of the nuances of gift receiving, protect themselves from the charge of accepting bribes while also building and maintaining relationships with parents? Most gifts are just that — gifts. If they are excessive in value, however, a teacher or administrator may feel obliged to return them. This can not only be uncomfortable for the educator but is truly horrifying and humiliating for the parent, as returning a gift is a slap in the face to the giver and a real cultural faux pas. To help teachers (and administrators) the school should develop a school "Gift Limit Policy" which is publicized widely among teachers and parents, and closely adhered to. This will take administrative involvement, and will inevitably cause some embarrassment for both parents and school. One school handles this by requiring that teachers give all gifts over a certain value (US$50???) to their administrator, who will accept the gift with thanks in writing to the parent "in the name of the school." Cash might be put into a student activity fund (as I did with the multiple $500 gifts mentioned earlier) and "real" gifts held for the annual faculty party door prizes. If a gift policy is widely known and followed, the word will soon get out that while a meal out, a massage ticket, or a box of Korean rice cakes is appreciated and acceptable, an expensive watch or an envelope of cash puts the teacher in a truly awkward spot and is against school policy. Another way to approach this is to let it be known that only gifts collectively given by the "parents" in the class will be accepted ("Room moms" can organize this.) As can be imagined, this can be a sticky problem requiring tact and courage on everyone's part. Leave it to the administrator to make the decision, in line with Policy, as to whether or not the gift is of such value that a letter of thanks needs to come from "the school" or whether the teacher can keep it.

If you receive a gift, whatever the value, correct etiquette is to act slightly embarrassed and protest, and then take the gift gently with both hands and quietly put it aside unless asked to open it, and thank the giver. Normally, in Korea gifts are not opened in the presence of the giver, lest the giver be embarrassed at the "small size and worthlessness of such a gift." Chinese seem to have no such qualms; I always asked, but normally the Chinese parent wanted to see me open the gift.

Attempted bribes for admission are not unknown. I was once asked whether the school needed a swimming pool during an admissions interview with parents, and have been told that it was common knowledge that one year's tuition was the standard "bribe" for acceptance of an unqualified student. (Thankfully, the school was squeaky clean in this regard; I'm sure there are schools not so scrupulous.) Interestingly, this sort of gift acceptance is common practice among many independent boarding schools and colleges in North America. How many libraries, auditoriums, and science buildings are named after a particular family with a long history of "support" for the school, and how many unqualified students from some of those same families might have gotten acceptance letters as a result? "Thank you for your past support of generations of children from our family, and thanks for the acceptance of future generations, as well" seems to be a common income source for some private schools (and certainly colleges) in the U.S.

Well publicized articles in the U. S. in recent years involve bribing coaches to recommend a specific child be admitted on a full ride sports scholarship, in effect purchasing admission whether or not the student had any talent in said sport. These cases have thankfully ended up in the courts. One wonders how many public figures, prominent in politics or business, had their college acceptance purchased for them due to their own lack of talent?

14. Learn something about Korean and Chinese cultures and histories and help others in your school do the same. Hopefully, you have already done this; if not this book can be a start. Knowing about the culture from which many of your students come each morning will greatly strengthen relationships between the school and the home. However, as stressed repeatedly, never assume that Mr. Kim or Ms. Zhang are stereotypical Korean or Chinese parents. Even more so, don't assume that all "Asian parents" are the same. While Korean and Japanese parents, coming from mono-cultural societies, may be more alike, don't associate a Chinese last name with any particular culture. Mainland Chinese, Taiwanese, Hong Kong Chinese, and Singaporean Chinese can be very different culturally, although to your ear they may speak the same language. Although there are many Confucian similarities from our limited Western perspective, there are some real and important differences, as well. Asians who have lived in the West for an extended period of time also will be quite different. There is also a good deal of prejudice between and among these groups, including Japanese. There exists superiority by many Japanese towards their "uncultured" Korean neighbors across the sea to the west, whom they traditionally disparage as "garlic eaters." Koreans tend to look down on their own Chinese neighbors to their west as "dirty." Mainland Chinese look down on non-mainland Chinese as people who have somehow abandoned the motherland and are no longer "purely" Chinese. Conversely, Taiwanese and Hong Kong Chinese often look down on mainlanders as uncultured bumpkins and political threats to their own existence. Further separating Taiwanese and Hong Kong Chinese is the fact that most also speak native Taiwanese and Cantonese respectively. Singaporean families often emigrated hundreds of years ago from China, and have a generous mix of British and Malay cultures in their backgrounds. I have heard Chinese say that "Korea once was a part of China," which doesn't make them any friends with Koreans who overheard them (While it is true that much of Korea was once under Chinese control, a good chunk of China was also once ruled by Korea. Everyone seems to write history and geography in ways that serve their own nationalistic interests.) Korea and Japan continue to fight over whether the large body of water between the two nations is correctly called the "East Sea" (which makes perfect sense from the Korean perspective, but not so much from the Japanese perspective) or the Sea of Japan (which upsets Koreans greatly.) Understanding that you may be aiming at a number of cultural targets as you work to first differentiate and then understand these various groups, take the time to learn a few useful phrases of Korean/Mandarin. You will find that while Korean is easier to pronounce for Westerners, the grammar is very challenging, as is the terror of using the wrong level of verbs with a "superior." Conversely, modern Korean is sprinkled with English cognates, so it is easier to try to "fake it" using accented English words, which most educated Koreans would understand. However, Koreans are also not particularly forgiving of poorly spoken Korean, and not at all forgiving of mistakes in verb level (speaking "up" or "down" depending on the relative status of you and the person you are speaking to). Written Korean, while difficult to master, at least can be learned to a degree that a foreigner can sound it out, which may or may not help with communication or following location signs. Mandarin grammar is much easier than Korean, but pronunciation can be challenging, with four different tones (nine in Cantonese). However, Chinese are quite forgiving of poorly spoken Mandarin, perhaps because with 52 dialects in the country, Mandarin is a second language to millions upon millions, and uneducated people may speak Mandarin poorly. Unfortunately, learning to read and write Chinese is a lifelong process, a challenge that few working foreigners have the time or inclination to take on seriously, and even in spoken Mandarin there are very few English cognates. Making some initial steps and survival language, starting with greetings, will go a long way towards establishing positive working relationships with parents. Learn about Korea and China and their amazing histories and cultures by going beyond Wikipedia and Korean "war stories" of former soldiers (see the annotated bibliography at the back of this book). Both nations have rich, long, and fascinating histories and cultures of which they are justly proud. Resist the urge to head to the beaches of Thailand at the first opportunity, and travel within your host country. Eat locally (but not foolishly). Despite their ancient histories, in the cities at least these are modern, vibrant, cultured, and exciting nations, both of which have leapfrogged over many Western nations technologically and in transportation. Both nations have amazingly widespread mobile phone coverage, and Korea has some of the fastest Internet speeds on the planet. China is fast catching up, although the "Great Firewall of China" is always a consideration that I'll not discuss here. There is ample information of various levels about any nation and it's culture; beware of Hollywood's version. If you are invited into a Korean or Chinese home, gladly accept, as this is very unusual; in 14 years in Shanghai I was invited to a Chinese home only once. You will have a terrific meal and will be treated like royalty. In Korea, don't be surprised if mom spends most of the time in the kitchen, though, and remember to take your shoes off at the door! Taking a bouquet of flowers (not chrysanthemums) as a gift is appropriate, if you wish, as is any homemade baked good. If you are invited out, be sure to clarify whether or not your spouse is also included, as often in Asia they are not. You'll probably never be considered a member of the family, but take advantage of any opportunity you have to learn more about your host nations and the families you serve. In reality, you are much more likely to be invited out for a restaurant meal than invited to a student's home.

Beyond the book you have in your hands, read about today's Chinese and Korean child-rearing practices and education. Judge for yourself how the various children in your classroom seem "Korean" or "Chinese" and how they don't. For an in-depth look at the stereotypical (?) role of many Asian mothers, read some of their own words. The unapologetic and controversial Battle Hymn of the Tiger Mother by Amy Chua (2011) is well-known; for a different perspective read Little Soldiers: An American Boy, a Chinese School, and the Global Race to Achieve by Lenora Chu (2017). I like Little Soldiers, as it is the autobiographical journey of a Chinese-American journalist who moved to Shanghai and puts her son in a "top" preschool. In it she not only describes the inner world of Shanghai schools and the role of mothers, but also describes how the experience changed her son as she herself journeyed through cultural clash to a greater understanding and appreciation of the Chinese system.

Looking Back, Looking Ahead

What difficult situations have you experienced with Korean/ Chinese parents that now make more sense? Knowing what you have learned, how might you have handled the situation differently?

What might your school do to better serve Korean and Chinese parents? How is your school communicating with them? What's working? What isn't?

How can your school accommodate the needs and demands of Korean and Chinese parents while remaining true to the goals and philosophy of the school? How might you better communicate these goals to parents?

Where and how can you learn more about the native cultures of your students? How could you share that with your co-workers? How might your school develop a professional library about these cultures?

If a sizeable portion of your student body if from a particular ethnic group, what is your school doing to enhance understanding of these students and parents by your teachers?

CHAPTER XVII: WORKING WITH KOREAN AND CHINESE STUDENTS

As mentioned above, there is a huge range of "Korean-ness" or "Chinese-ness" among individuals, and the students we find in our schools are no exception. Some come to us directly from local schools or from schools in their "home" country. For example, at international schools in Shanghai there are Koreans who come directly from Korea, with little or no English or background in Western education. Others have grown up in Shanghai, speak fluent Mandarin and even local Shanghainese, but attended the "foreign" section of a local Chinese school in Shanghai before knocking on the door of an international school. Still others went to Korean school in Shanghai. Others have spent most of their educational lives in international schools, acquiring varying degrees of English ability depending on the length of time they have experienced English-language education, as well as the degree to which they integrated themselves into the Western international school culture. A few have grown up in North America and are culturally "American" and are Korean in ethnicity only. Given this wide range of experiences and acculturation, the comments in the section below should be approached with a good deal of care.

Each individual is different in background, needs, language, and culture. They need to be treated as individuals. Below we will discuss some ways that you can address their cultural backgrounds as well as their individual characteristics.

As we did above in Chapter XVI, "Working with Korean and Chinese Parents." much of what is discussed below reflects the more theoretical concepts about Confucian thought and education. Here is where we operationalize the theory and put it into practice.

1. For students coming new to an international school environment with limited English, pay particular attention to class placement, specifically teaching practice and practice, when possible. As anyone who has worked in school administration knows, class placement of any particular student is influenced by all kinds of variables – class size, scheduling restrictions, gender balance, class makeup, and teaching style, among others. Most of these variables are somewhat generic and quantitative, but one is not: that of the classroom environment and teaching style. In today's world, for good reason often the teachers who are considered the "best" are those whose classrooms are filled with solo and collaborative activities focused on 21st Century teaching and learning, that encourage and require creativity and foster independent learning. Students in these classrooms are interacting with one another, embracing choices as to what and how they learn in an environment that displays a good deal of ambiguity and lack of visible organization. For most students, this provides an environment in which they can stretch their mental and creative wings and really learn to fly. These teachers are the ones that administrators compete over at hiring fairs. However, for a student new to learning English, whatever their educational or cultural background, I believe that this type of exciting, creative environment can actually hinder initial language development. For those without any prior experience in Western-style education this type of active environment, full of choices and sensory input, can be confusing and disorienting. Learning to survive in a new language alone is a huge task, as most of us know. Yes, students can pick up social language quickly in a more social environment. They will get their formal English language training (hopefully) in an E.S. L. class, supported by classroom teachers. However, in the regular classroom, they (all E.S.L. students, but particularly those coming from Asian schools) need more structure as well – in fact, the kind found in more traditional classrooms. They need to know what is expected, and what the boundaries are. They need specific directions and detailed assignments. Directions such as "Let your imagination soar and come up with a unique idea on how to demonstrate this scientific principal – a skit, a song, a poem, a presentation . . ." leave them completely at sea. They have no idea what is expected, or what the boundaries are. They have never been given this range of choices, and it may simply frighten them into simply copying someone else's work. They have never been expected, or taught, to let their innate creativity show itself and to trust their imagination. Given a "compare and contrast" or "thought" question on an exam that requires pulling together old information in new ways, they may simply freeze and not know how to respond, having been trained to prepare by memorizing lists of terms and pages of facts (remember Charlie from the introduction of this book?) How can we address these children's need for structure and direction while slowly introducing them to more interactive and less "fact based" instruction? I would suggest that the easiest way is to place a student in a class with a teacher who uses a more traditional approach, one whose assignments are clearly stated and unambiguous, with firm deadlines announced far in advance. Expectations should be clear. Study sheets and examples of test questions should be provided ahead of assessments. Exemplars of projects should be provided. Activity in the classroom should be orderly and structured. When students work together, all should be expected to contribute, but within understood guidelines. In any event, such a "traditional" teacher will almost certainly have a more creative, less "fact based" classroom than whatever Asian-style school the child came from. Thus, if a choice is available when a new second language Asian student is scheduled, this type of more traditional classroom is preferable. The newer the student is to Western education, the more important such placement is. The younger the student, the more crucial it is that he or she receives clear instructions (although they will catch on to new expectations perhaps more quickly than their older siblings). Note that this is true for two reasons – one is simply that a student with little English language ability doesn't need a lot of extraneous input to complete the work while simultaneously acquiring English. The other reason is simply to somehow lessen the educational culture shock that the student is facing as he or she moves from a rigid, formal, teacher-centered educational style to one that is much more flexible, informal, and student-centered.

2. On the other hand, as students become acclimatized to Western education, their natural inclination may be (and quite possibly parental expectations will include) to continue to focus on memorization and facts. Teachers need to intentionally de-emphasize memorization and encourage thinking and understanding. As mentioned above, an assignment demanding thoughtful, creative answers at higher levels of thinking can often create something close to panic in students when confronted with this for the first time. Students who have been in Asian schools have been trained to find the one right answer coming from some higher authority, usually either the book or the teacher. If faced suddenly with a "What do you think, and why?" question, the student may be genuinely confused. They need to be taught to expect such questions, and must learn how to develop and express their own opinions without fear of reprisal. Students may not naturally know how to deal with thought-provoking essay questions for which there is no "right" answer, discussions in class which demand individual expression of opinions, or assignments requiring higher thinking skills. Gradually adjusting to an atmosphere in which it is safe to take intellectual risks without fear of being "wrong" are crucial. Teachers need to be sure to grade in such a way that such attempts to go beyond fact regurgitation are rewarded. This may require alternate assessments for a while.

While language learning is very important in Korean and Chinese education, writing thoughtful essays requiring anything more than a paragraph or two while regurgitating ideas already presented is uncommon in Asian schools. Learning to write extended written assignments and developing formal oral skills is simply not part of the curriculum. Where Western schools would lean towards the clear expression of novel ideas (as opposed to focusing on the intricacies of perfect grammar), Asian schools would more likely focus on the mechanics of the writing. The teaching of research skills is notably lacking in Asian education. These need to be taught intentionally, with special focus on the evaluation of source materials and the necessity of proper citation (more on that below).

While little project style education is done in the classroom, in Korean elementary schools "summer vacation projects" are often assigned. Unfortunately, in a competitive system where a good deal of public comparison takes place among students and mothers, adult "input" may be somewhat higher than is acceptable in Western education to ensure that the project doesn't cause embarrassment. Note: If a project looks too good to be true, it might be smart to ask some questions about how, who, and when the project was done, or require it to be done during class time.

3. Understand cultural differences in writing styles. We've all suffered reading through anything more than a few lines that have been mangled by Google translator. I don't fault Google; languages simply do not translate word for word. Not only are sentence structures different, but some ideas and words are simply non-translatable, resulting in some awkward constructions and imprecise communication. Additionally, the structure of composing is different among cultures and languages. In English, we teach structures such as the proverbial five paragraph essay: introduction, three main points with supporting information, conclusion. It is all very Western and linear. Using deduction, we introduce what we are going to say and state our thesis, we provide information to support that thesis, and then we re-state and review what we said, hopefully arriving at some logical conclusion. The intent is to logically prove a thesis, point by point and hopefully, as we say, "real nail it." It seems natural and very straightforward to a Western thinker and writer. However, to an Asian individual, raised and educated to be less direct and obvious in expression, it can seem too direct and even blunt. Rather, their writing style is more inductive, in the style of story telling. The reader is responsible for coming to the conclusion – sort of in the style of an Aesop fable without the final tag line "slow and steady wins the race." The story conveys the message; there is no need to point out the obvious to the reader. It's up to him or her to figure it out. You may have students who write in this style; who may begin with seemingly little reference to the topic, followed by any number of statements related to the message, and suddenly end without any apparent summative wrap up. The student may begin without an introduction, wander around (seemingly) aimlessly and circuitously, and then abruptly end, without stating their point or coming to any kind of conclusion. To the Western reader, we may cry, "What are you trying to say? Just SAY it!" To the Asian writer, they did say it. They may be thinking, "Why is this teacher such a dunce that she didn't get my message?"

I learned this lesson in an interesting way. Some years ago, before I was introduced to the concept of differing cultural writing styles, I was asked to help a Korean graduate student complete her application to dental school in the US. As the student was the child of a school employee whom I had worked with for many years, I agreed, although I did so with some trepidation. First, she wanted help with her "letter of introduction." As much as I could, I could not find any request in the application materials for such a letter. I told her it was not necessary, and she should not waste time writing it. It would be a superfluous piece of paper in an already voluminous application. However, the young woman insisted that she had to introduce herself to the admissions officer, thus establishing a relationship (remember the importance of relationships?) After a few go-arounds I reluctantly agreed, and she quickly pulled out her draft that she wanted me to edit and clean up. It began "In the springtime, the leaves sprout anew from the branches, while last year's crumpled brown leaves scatter across the pond . . ." I thought she was showing me the wrong piece, so I asked her "What are you trying to say here?" She looked at me quizzically, and then said, "Well, I want to start by tell about the springtime leaves sprouting anew . . .". I was completely taken aback. Further questioning revealed (to this dunce) that she was trying to express how she was like a new leaf, ready to sprout and thrive in a new (dental school) environment. It took a couple of weeks, but I finally got her to write the three most important points he wanted the admissions officer to know about her and we worked from there. My linear mind (and I thought, that of the admissions officer, if he or she ever took the time to read this Letter of Introduction) was at war with this young woman's more gentle, indirect approach and need to develop a relationship. In the end, she included it with the application. Eventually, she was denied acceptance to that dental school, and she never asked me for

help again! If you have found yourself in a similar situation with a student, you can help them by asking them to reduce their thoughts to three or four important bullet points – not paragraphs, and go from there. Using mind-maps can really help as they don't allow for sentences, but force the writer to boil down ideas in a few words, and then branch out from there.

Compounding the challenge of this writing style issue is students' use of word processing when composing, before any planning takes place. I'm a huge fan of word processing; without it this book would never have been written. However, students of all backgrounds can easily get caught up in thinking, editing, and writing all at the same time, which makes for poorly constructed composition, and very inefficient use of time. Enforced pre-planning without the laptop – again, I think mind-mapping works well – can force them to think before they write. I have had students ask if they can mind map on their laptop, and I tell them "no," because almost immediately they begin to write sentences, and while doing so edit the sentences for grammar, word choice, spelling, and even font and color. I have had to forbid some students from using the Delete key until they had finished writing – in the midst of editing, they forget what they are trying to say. Before a word is written, close the laptop covers, pass out blank paper, and tell the students that you want to see the visual plan of their composition before they ever take out their laptop.

While this tendency to think/compose/edit/polish in one operation is common among students of all backgrounds, for Asian students whose minds work in "story telling" mode it simply exacerbates the problem. Mind-mapping forces linear thinking; in contrast readily editable paragraph writing encourages story telling.

It's helpful to know about various culturally based writing styles up front, before you wonder why a student is such an unorganized writer. You may have to go back to teaching basic writing styles, and lead the student through it until he or she gets the idea. They may find it uncomfortable, but part of your job is to ensure that they learn the skills that will make them successful in their future Western education (and lives). Just like other areas of culture and language, they need to learn to be "bilingual" in their writing styles. When writing for an Asian audience, a more Asian style is certainly appropriate.

4. Acknowledge the possibility of language-based or ethnic cliques in your school, particularly among middle and high school students. The natural tendency of any group of children (or adults) of any nationality or language when there are more than four or five individuals is to begin to segregate themselves socially. Adults do it; kids do it. It provides a level of safety and cultural and linguistic comfort. If your school is like any I have been involved with, just look at the faculty lunchroom seating arrangement. Chances are that the local teachers are seated together by choice. I suspect that at a local school a group of foreign teachers will do the same thing. In my experience, and in my informal research with other international school administrators, students also follow this pattern. Once a group is large enough to have it's own "area" of the cafeteria, it quickly lays claim to that area. It may be intentional (at one school I visited the Korean students had occupied one of the many outdoor pavilions on the campus and made it known that it was "Koreans Only" territory. Unfortunately, while some of these characteristics are common to any ethnic group, Koreans are unfortunately particularly well known for being cliquish. I have heard this from very Korea-friendly (and bi-cultural) educators who have experience on North American college campuses, as well as at international schools across the globe. Coming from a nation that prides itself on its "racial purity" and has a long tradition of feeling victimized, perhaps it is natural for Koreans to do this. It is imperative upon counselors, teachers, and administrators to actively watch out for this self-imposed isolationism and talk to kids about the necessity of integration. There are some specific ways in which the school can structure the educational experience to encourage mixing, which I'll discuss below.

When does this issue normally emerge? Experienced teachers see it begin to take hold in Grade 6 and come to full flower in Grades 8 and 9, when egos can be fragile and students are struggling with their own identity issues. Parents, who might be afraid that their children, particularly in social situations, might be negatively affected by more liberal Western ideas, sometimes actively promote this growing separation. As students reach puberty (when many middle and high schools in Korea become segregated by gender) parents fear that "loose" Western morals will infect their children. Most Korean parents will protest when they find out that their son or daughter has any kind of romantic attachment to a friend of any ethnicity other than Korean; if that person is Japanese or Chinese it is bad enough, but if they are Caucasian or south Asian, things get really serious. In reality, many Asian parents actively teach their children that romantic involvement with anyone is not appropriate up until college, when all restrictions are off. Unfortunately, due to some long-standing bias and fear against people from any kind of African background, it is a very rare Korean parent who will not simply forbid their child to date such an individual. At whatever age, this type of isolation and discrimination against non-Koreans can be destructive to a school climate. Particularly in international schools in Korea, it is nearly impossible for a non-Korean to be elected to a class office or reach any position of leadership, however talented they may be. Their Korean classmates simply will only elect other Koreans. As a person who spent much of his adult life in Korea, and who is deeply invested personally in the country and its culture, I have to admit that the Korean tendency and need to stick together against a perceived unfriendly outside world is one of the least endearing aspects of the Korean character. Koreans are generally generous, friendly, outgoing – but unfortunately quite exclusive.

What can the school do about this tendency towards self-imposed ethnic segregation? There is little that can be done to ensure ethnic mixing in the lunchroom or at a dance where students have freedom to choose their tablemates or dance partners, but attempts should be made in the classroom to consciously mix students as much as possible in work groups. Activities that encourage ethnic mixing, particularly sports, should be encouraged. Two of the greatest integrative forces among students of different ethnic backgrounds are the basketball court and soccer field. Teachers of classes in any subjects should be aware of groups of students, of whatever language, who isolate themselves to the extent that they are learning from each other in their own language rather than in the identified school language (most often English), and teachers need to take deliberate action to be sure students work in mixed language groups in which they will be forced to use their common English – which after all is very often the academic language in the school. (I would say the same thing in a Korean school in which a group of Caucasian, English-speaking students are isolating themselves and not using the common language of Korean.) Why is this important? Because any external assessments will be in English, and while students may learn the content in another language (English certainly does not have a monopoly on academic learning) they will be at a disadvantage in externally administered exams such as IB and AP exams. Further, if they plan on pursuing further study in that subject area in English, they need to be sure they have the requisite vocabulary to succeed. Generally, students who are enrolled in a school in order to learn English should be, as much as possible, learning in English, not through translation from their same-language friends. Teachers should be aware of this and quietly assign students to mixed groups – by gender, ability, language, personality, etc. – rather than let students self-assign. There are seldom educationally valid reasons to allow students to self-assign themselves to work groups, and many reasons that dictate against it. One exception to this would be for students at the middle or high school level who are also very new to English. Pairing them with a very bi-lingual student for a month or two might help them get their academic feet under them. However, I would mentor the bi-lingual student in how to support a new student without becoming an enabler who is depended upon.

Another negative result of such a strong group identity is that students may cover up for each other in times of trouble. As we have noted earlier, in a Confucian-based culture relationships very often outrank honesty when put to the test. This trait is not unique to Koreans, obviously, but the solidarity with which they may refuse to "tell on" a Korean friend is often surprising to the Westerner. Often, one older student may "take responsibility" for the misdeeds of other younger students in the group, but refuse to identify them. This is similar to what happens in Korea when some calamity occurs. As long as a high-level officer (often a government minister) resigns in shame, his taking "moral" responsibility (even if it was clearly not his personal fault) satisfies the community that the matter has been dealt with and punishment meted out - someone has been blamed and shamed. Korean students may expect you to treat their transgressions in the same way.

5. Beware of culturally based of issues of hierarchy, "face," and "respect." This is especially apparent between older and younger students of the same gender. These can become major issues among Korean children in international schools, just as they are in Korean schools, and should be dealt with head-on by the school. As discussed earlier, Confucianism is a two-way street: respect and obedience by younger towards older should be reciprocated by protection and care by older students of younger ones. Unfortunately, too often only the first half of this equation is practiced. Among both boys and girls, there is a strong hierarchy, mostly based on grade in school and age. Students younger by even one year address their older compatriots as their "seniors" and use the common Korean words for older brother ("hyung" or "o-pa") and for older sister ("noo-na" or "uhn- yi.") They look up to them, they do their bidding, and they are all too often abused by them. Most older students genuinely care about their younger "brothers and sisters," as long as the younger ones treat them with outward respect. This can take the form of expecting from a younger student a simple nod of the head in the hallway (the common informal Korean greeting), or it can escalate to a forced purchase of lunch, demands to run errands, or orders to do other even more menial tasks. Students should know that "Confucius was not a bully!" Of course, the more confident, secure, and mature an older student is, the less demeaning his or her expectations are. However, to the insecure young person (or to the garden variety bully) it is a socially acceptable system too good to be true. The price a younger student pays for not going along with this system is all too often physical abuse, threats, and intimidation. In Korean (and Japanese) society, this often results in serious psychological or physical harm, and results even in suicide. Although this type of bullying is decried in Korean society, it is also accepted as "the way things are," for Korea is a nation steeped in hierarchy and special respect towards those higher up the social or political ladder. Parents tell their children that they should respect their "elders," and that if it gets too rough they should just go along with it. It is a rite of passage and an unfortunate aspect of acculturation. This type of adolescent bullying morphs into more physical abuse in the Korean military, and in a more polite form is endemic to the business world. The famous Korean Air "nut rage incident" discussed earlier by an executive (and daughter of owner) of Korean Air when she publically abused a lead flight attendant on board a departing flight, even demanding that the plane return to the gate to toss the offending flight attendant off, is a prime example of this type of bullying and hierarchy as experienced by adults.

Particularly vulnerable to this type of abuse is an ethnic Korean child who was not brought up in Korea or in a Korean community and who is not aware of the rules of this game in his or her new school. It is all too easy for them to look at or speak to an older student too casually, to not bow deeply enough, or to offend the wrong person. Such newcomers will be "educated" as to their errant behavior, and if they don't get the message quickly they may be more forcefully indoctrinated into the realities of Korean social norms. This is seldom pretty.

Confucian-style intimidation may go on right in front of unsuspecting Western eyes, and unless the school has built a strong culture among students of not tolerating bullying, it will seldom be reported by either students or parents. As parents are often at the root of this behavior by encouraging what Westerners might consider excess "respect," parent groups must be involved in the solution if this becomes a widespread problem. A Westerner trying to step in, unless he or she truly understands the nature of the structure and has the trust of the Korean community, will only be seen as a meddling foreigner who just "doesn't respect our culture." Don't fall for this reasoning. Bullying is bullying! Make your institutional values clear in this area, apart from your own cultural values, and expect compliance. Fortunately, this type of hierarchical behavior is seldom expected of younger non-Koreans. My own experience is that this behavior is rampant in international schools in Korea, given the influence of the host culture. However, in my experience in Shanghai this wasn't observed among Korean students, and certainly not among ethnic Chinese students. As high school principal I periodically checked with younger Korean students (grade 9 boys, specifically) to see if there was any bullying going on, and was pleased to hear that it wasn't happening. Hopefully they were being honest with me. One reason for this may have been that only about 15% of the students in the school were of Korean background, and most of them had grown up in China. Other international schools with higher proportions of Korean students, however, report this type of bullying, although not to the extent that is experienced in international schools in Korea.

Remember that whenever there are more than a few Korean students in a school, particularly if they are in different grades, it is not a question of whether a hierarchy exists — it does exist – but whether it is a negative force. The real questions we need to ask ourselves are these: "In our school, has this behavior become negative? Is it dangerous? Are some children afraid to come to school because of it? Is our school really the physically and emotionally safe place we think it is for all our students? Are we ignoring real danger to students because of our fear of stepping on sensitive cultural toes?" We need to be willing to "call a bully a bully" in any language and in any culture. This is an example of where our desire to be culturally sensitive must be overcome by our more deeply held values of having a school that is safe and free of harassment.

Interestingly, this sense of hierarchy also exists in the parent community, with adult-level signs of respect and subservience expected as part of the way things are. In a small expatriate Korean community overseas made up of employees from the same company, it may follow the ranking in that organization. Not unlike a military community, where a general is clearly superior to a colonel and so on down the line, a company has the same strict hierarchy. Also not unlike the military, the spouses (normally the wives) have a parallel hierarchy, with the company manager's wife enjoying a higher position than that of the chief engineer's wife, etc. When such a built-in structure is not already in place, a hierarchy will quickly form, often according to age, university attended, or year of graduation from university. This parental hierarchy can be of real help to the school when the school is trying to get the community to buy into a program or carry out some change. If the top of the social structure - the Alpha Mom - is identified and is won over, half the battle is won. It would be very difficult for those of lower social standing to assume a leadership position or speak out against a social "superior."

One might wonder how and why this hierarchy follows Koreans wherever they go. Part of it is just the way people have been brought up. Just as a culture of social equality follows Westerners half way around the world, so does a culture of social inequality follow those from more hierarchical cultures. One outward sign that supports the hierarchy is the structure of the Korean language, something not found in Chinese. It is impossible to speak even one sentence in Korean without revealing the relative social positions of the speaker to the addressee. Verb endings vary according to who is considered the higher of two in the conversation, who is the speaker, and who is being spoken to. There are very specific verb forms to used when speaking to (and among) children, to those of equal age and status, to those of higher rank (or age), and so on up the line. The more social distance between the two, the higher honorifics are used in speech. Even prayer has its own honorifics used when addressing God. In English, we often use careful vocabulary choices and sentence structures to be polite to those "above us" in organizational or social structures, and a level of informality can even connote respect. In Korean, it is much less subtle. Chinese does not have verb structures that denote relative status.

6. Encourage students to be involved in extracurricular activities. As was mentioned in the previous chapter, while Korean and Chinese schools do have clubs and activities, there is no culture of competitive sports among high schools (unless they are specialty "sports" high schools), and after elementary or middle school, classes in areas such as music and art, and extracurricular special interest clubs take very much a second row seat to academics. The student is simply too busy with Korean/Chinese academics and after school academies. Therefore, students (and parents) will not necessarily lean towards involvement in extracurriculars upon enrolling in an international school, and may see these as distractions to the "real" work of school rather than an integral part of any academic program. Students should be strongly encouraged to join clubs, play sports, get involved in music, and attend dances and other activities, if for no other reason than to have greater exposure to English out of the classroom. Parents also need to understand that a student headed to a Western university with a 4.0, but with no activities on their resume, stands little chance of admission. There is ample opportunity for parent education in this area. Work to get parents involved in supporting extracurriculars through your parent-teacher group.

Unfortunately, the greatest enemy of involvement in extracurricular activities, especially those that take place after school or on weekends, is attendance at academies, which we have discussed earlier. Parents need to understand that while academies may help in the short term, they probably do much damage to long-term academic and personal development.

7. Teachers should intentionally encourage students to ask questions – and then reward it. Generally, students in Korean and Chinese school are not encouraged to ask questions in class. There are a number of reasons for this. One is that with large class sizes, it is simply too disruptive to have individuals ask questions. Another reason is rooted in the Confucian-based concept that the teacher is the font of all knowledge, and therefore to challenge that academic authority by questioning the teacher is very difficult and is in fact disrespectful. In addition, even by asking a question, the student may feel that he or she is implying that the teacher didn't do a very good job of explaining (lecturing) in the first place, which would be rude or disrespectful. You may remember from our discussion of writing that the responsibility for effective communications lies with the recipient, not the writer or speaker; we'll address this further below. An English language learner may be unsure of his or her English ability, and not want to make a grammatical mistake in front of classmates. Finally, the student might be afraid to let the teacher know that he or she doesn't understand something and rather than admit it, just stays quiet and hopes that somehow they can get it from a classmate later on. Therefore, teachers need to be sure that students are encouraged (even required) not only to ask questions in class, but to see the teacher after school for extra help, if that is appropriate (something that is also not encouraged in Korean and Chinese schools). For particularly hesitant students, the teacher can work with the student before class to "plant" a question so that the student can rehearse it and get over any fear of speaking out. Be sure your students' parents know that extra help is available at school, (for free) and when. Parents need to be trained to send their child to the teacher for help first, rather than default to hiring a tutor. Some teachers require students who seem hesitant to be involved verbally in class to ask at least one question each class period and lets them know that their grade will depend on it. While using grades as a motivation may rub some of us the wrong way, it might be that focusing on grades may be the most effective motivation you have with both students and parents to get them over a cultural hurdle as they adjust to Western education. Moreover, both students and parents need to understand that grades depend on more than just memorizing facts, listening to the teacher lecture, and spewing information back on an exam. Students need permission and encouragement to ask questions, to challenge the teacher, and to take an active and contributing role in the class rather than simply sit in the class and expect themselves to absorb everything just by listening. This is a skill that is learned, but may not come naturally to some students.

Related to this is an interesting comparison between Asian and Western communication styles, discussed earlier. In Asian cultures, the onus of communicating effectively is on the listener (student), rather than on the speaker or writer (teacher). In Western societies, teachers (and writers) work hard to be sure that they are communicating effectively; the responsibility is on them to get it right. Applied to a school situation, this supports the reality that in Asian schools the responsibility for understanding what the teacher is saying is on the student. The teacher bears less responsibility to make their "lecture" understandable, or to create learning activities that will engage and motivate students. It is the student's responsibility to read, listen, and learn, regardless of the pedagogical talents of the teacher.

As discussed earlier, there is a strong tendency among Korean and Chinese parents to rely on paid, after school tutors rather than on the child's regular teachers to provide extra support in a particular subject. Unfortunately, despite parents' efforts to get the best tutors available (who often charge exorbitant hourly fees), sometimes these tutors have little or no qualifications save being a "former Harvard student." The fact that this person might not be a native English speaker, may have few teaching skills, or may have no interest in young people may be mitigated by the professed Ivy League pedigree. Additionally, seldom do tutors collaborate with the international school teachers to support students with school assignments, depending instead on other non-school related resources. Thus, while hiring a personal tutor may be done with good intentions and at considerable cost, it may be of limited value to the student's success at school. This can be avoided by teachers making it clear that they are available to help, and by providing regularly scheduled hours when this can happen.

8. Ensure that girls who are new to the international school system are encouraged to use their "voice" and be heard. In a Confucian society such as Korea's females are taught, either overtly or by example, to defer to males, at least outside of the home. This is much less true among Mainland Chinese students, where equality of the sexes is much closer to the Western ideal than is found in Korea, even in the second decade of the Twenty-first Century. Socially, and (until the last generation) legally as well, Korean males have been very definitely the dominant sex. Generally, women have worked in low-status jobs (bank teller, office worker, waitress) or just stay at home until they get married. Even today married women do not normally work unless they are teachers, nurses, or doctors. The legal profession, the business world, the clergy, and the medical profession (except nurses) are overwhelmingly male, although not at all closed to women, and there are of course exceptions to this – women dentists, pharmacists, and doctors are not uncommon. Particularly when a woman becomes pregnant, she is expected (by society, by the family, and by the company) to resign her position. Staying home, raising children and being a good wife, mother, and daughter-in-law are still very strong expectations for women in Korean society. Girls thus learn to defer to males and develop the role of being quiet and subservient, particularly in public.

In addition, many girls coming directly from Korean middle or high schools may have been in single-gender schools, which are still very common. Being with boys in a school environment may be initially uncomfortable for them. Thus, in the classroom some Korean girls may tend to "disappear, " compounding the tendency for English language learners to prefer to remain in the background. Certainly this phenomenon is not limited to Korean girls, but they tend to exhibit this behavior to a greater extent than more Westernized girls might. Therefore, it is imperative that the teacher intentionally directs questions to girls, to actively engage the girls in class discussion, and to praise their involvement. Given practice and time, they will become many of your very strongest student leaders.

9. Address issues of academic integrity head on. Simply, be clear with students what constitutes cheating, both generally and for a particular assignment, and make it a part of your curriculum. Additionally, provide them with tools such as *turnitin.com* to help them avoid unintentionally making costly mistakes that can damage both their reputation and their GPA. This is a delicate topic, open to a good deal of debate and discussion within the international school community. Certainly, Asian students do not have a monopoly on cheating or dishonesty. However, there are some cultural issues that may make it more common among Asian students, often catching them unawares, particularly if they are new to Western education. These issues are at least five: a) extreme academic pressure, b) the societal pressure of group loyalty and relationships, c) historic respect for writers, the "sages of the distant and recent past," d) societal disregard for copyright laws (and thus no particular stigma against copying the work of others), and e) lack of previous instruction in the rules and culture of academic integrity, and thus a sincere lack of understanding of the nuances and specifics of what constitutes plagiarism. This is a complicated issue that cannot be explained away by just crowing "These kids cheat!" Let's look at these one by one.

a. Extreme Academic pressure. Extreme academic pressure from home, friends, or one's self can become all consuming. Students speak of being under so much pressure to be at the top of the class that they are "forced" to cheat – for some there are few other ways to succeed, and after all, there can only be one #1! Quite simply, academic success, when push comes to shove, sometimes takes on a higher value than honesty; "the end justifies the means" to a greater extent than we are usually comfortable with in the West. In a highly pressured situation how the work gets done is not always as important as getting it done. When schedules get tight, you may even find parents or tutors helping out by doing homework, as homework is not considered by parents to be practice work but rather a performance that must be correct. Unfortunately, in some widely publicized scandals parents have gotten involved in actually arranging standardized testing scams in Korea. Fortunately, these are the exception, but they to show how results can sometimes trump honesty.

b. The societal pressure of group loyalty and relationships. Intense loyalty to friends and "the group" can often be the cause of dishonesty among students. Not letting a friend copy homework or not telling what was on last period's test is even harder for a Korean child than for many Western children, and if a social "superior" asks for this information, it is nearly impossible for a student to not provide it. This is complicated by the fact that while the school may classify copying homework or glancing over a neighbor's test paper as dishonesty, in the Asian context it may be considered to be cooperation, helping a friend, or just doing what is necessary to succeed in what is perceived as a highly competitive environment. (remember the emphasis on groups and relationships) Teachers need to make very clear to both parents and students what the expectations are regarding homework — how, when, and by whom it should be done. The difference between "getting help" and copying work needs to be explained unambiguously. Teachers should be clear and distinguish expectations among various assignments: "This project should be done by working in pairs," or "This is not a group exercise. Everyone should be working on their own. I want to see what you can do, not what you and your neighbor can do together," or conversely "I expect that over the next week you will work collaboratively with others in the class to reach these stated goals." Be specific, and don't take it for granted that students will just "know" that they are supposed to work alone. The school would do well to develop a statement on academic integrity, defining what is cheating and what it is not, and developing clear and appropriate guidelines for discipline for various infractions. These guidelines should be published in both student and parent handbooks, be discussed in detail with students each year (as expectations change as students advance in grades), and be frankly discussed with parents.

One reason teachers are often so shocked by (or blind to) dishonest behavior is that often the students who cheat are the same ones we would trust completely in other situations. They are sincere, respectful, hard-working, high-achieving, and otherwise totally honorable kids. However, the academic pressure is often so strong, and the consequences for poor (by their standard or that of their parents) performance so high, that they give in to the pressure. While they understand that it is wrong, academic success and grades may take precedence. Honesty is certainly an important Asian value, but in the hierarchy of values solidarity with one's group, educational success, and the fear of embarrassing one's family with poor grades may temporarily become a higher priority. You can "hate the sin and love the sinner" in these cases. Be vigilant! Many parents would agree with this assessment of values, but may blame the teacher or the school for being lax by making it easy for kids to cheat. I have seen too many situations in which they are right. With Asian students and parents, teachers may be operating with a different set of values and ethics than they are used to. Of course, it should also go without saying that many, if not most, Asian children and parents abhor cheating in any form — they may just define it differently in different situations.

c. Historic respect for writers, the "sages of the distant and recent past" can actually lead to sloppy citation. The culture of "one right answer" and societal respect for those older, wiser, and more educated (and quite likely, dead) creates a level of infallibility that is not compatible with an inquisitive and questioning mind. The thinking goes something like this – this individual was so well known, and what he or she wrote is so infallible, that for me to cite this source in a paper assigned by a teacher is actually somewhat of an insult to the teacher – of course the teacher knows where the information or quote comes from! In an American context, it would be as if a quote was taken from the Gettysburg Address, and the student didn't cite it. Of course, the student thinks, the teachtell her? In the West, academic writing is generally not directed to a certain individual (although in most cases, the only reader will be the teacher) but to an amorphous, invisible audience. In a relationship-based society, however, a paper submitted to a teacher is written *to* that teacher – which makes the idea of telling a teacher something that they already know (in this case, the non-cited source) redundant.

d. Societal disregard for copyright laws. A related issue is plagiarism that goes beyond sloppy citation. In Korea and China, despite repeated and ongoing international discussions to the contrary, plagiarism and copyright violation are so widespread that even university professors routinely tell students where they can buy pirated copies of foreign texts for a fraction of the cost of the original text. (This author was told by a professor at Yonsei University, one of the big three universities in Seoul, that she would like to use my earlier book *Confucius Meets Piaget* as a text for a course that she was teaching on culture and education. When I asked how many copies she would like, her answer was, "Oh, don't worry, I only need one. I'll just have them copied for the students." That was true for almost all college level texts in Seoul.) Outside the gates of every university one can find "print shops" where professors leave original copies of required texts to be reproduced and printed. Along the streets of any Chinese city sit carts filled with DVD knockoff copies of the latest movies and TV shows from the West. The quality isn't consistently great, but they are available for about 10RMB – about $1.50. Incidences of Chinese patent infringement and stealing of intellectual property are legendary; Western companies are in constant fights over technological and intellectual transfer. Whether it is copying Mickey Mouse paraphernalia or stealing trade secrets from Lockheed, China's penchant for skipping the "imagine and creative" steps and jumping right into production are well documented, and reportedly often government sponsored. Every expatriate who lives in Beijing or Shanghai is familiar with the "fake markets" that sell cheap brand name knockoffs (in fairness, I should mention that these markets are very popular among foreigners, including struggling authors.) This is clearly a case of different West/East cultural norms. Certainly a high school student brought up in such an environment of blatant (and acceptable) disregard for intellectual property rights cannot be expected to understand the finer points of what constitutes plagiarism. When organizations like respected universities and governments don't seem to have respect for intellectual property rights, the fifteen-year-old EAL student in your social studies class can hardly be expected to develop such a respect without intentional and specific instruction.

e. Lack of previous instruction in the rules and culture of academic integrity, and thus a sincere lack of understanding of the nuances and specifics of what constitutes plagiarism, including rules of citation. Previous lack of practice in original thinking or creativity encourages lots of cutting and pasting from web sites during research. While this is certainly a problem in other countries as well, in Korea and China it is quite openly tolerated within academia. Well-educated Asian adults who study in the United States are very surprised at the rules governing citations and copying, and even more so at the consequences for breaking those rules. As noted above, both the respect placed on the wisdom of the past, as well as lack of respect for intellectual property, work against the standards of proper citation. International school teachers should be expected to carefully and intentionally, assuming little prior knowledge, instruct their students as to what is acceptable and proper and then follow up, expecting (as with any other new concept) some stumbles along the way. Never assume that just because a Western student would have some idea of what constitutes plagiarism by a certain grade level (even if they don't follow the rules) that an Asian student would have the same background or level of understanding. Almost certainly your school will be their introduction to these practices and concepts. International schools have a unique opportunity to help bring Asia up to international standards in this important area through the education of at least some of its young people.

Gradually introduce various citation styles. It's hard enough for a student to learn the rules of citation using one style sheet (MLA, APA, etc.) if they have never been exposed to this concept before. However, in many international schools various academic departments or even individual teachers require the use of different citation styles – but don't have any organized way of introducing them to students. While it is valuable for any student graduating from high school to understand that there are various style sheets, it is also very confusing when a student who is still learning the nuances and rules of citation to be presented (and required to follow) a number of different stule sheets at the same (or even different) times. Schools can help in this area by selecting on one relatively simple citation style to be used across subject areas, at least through Grade 10. By Grade 11, the concept of multiple style sheets should be introduced, and perhaps departments could collaborate in introducing a second style be introduced simultaneously. Grade 12 teachers could coordinate, but maybe have science departments use one style, and humanities another – and the differences and similarities be intentionally taught to students. Which styles are chosen is not important, but what is important is that this sometimes confusing and conflicting array of styles be introduced step by step, so that students are not frustrated, wondering what styles four or five different teachers expect They should graduate from your high school with a healthy respect for the ideals of proper citation, understanding that there are a multitude of styles that they may be expected to use in university. They should be able to navigate and learn any new style with a quality style sheet wherever they go with graduated introduction to them by your school. Note – This is NOT solely the job of the English department. If different styles are used in different subjects, the responsibility for teaching their use falls on the teachers in a given subject area. If you are going to be the one assessing the work, then you should be the one to teach it.

10. Understand the difference between counseling and advising students – and don't be afraid to advise. Cultures that place a very high value on strong family solidarity, often against "outsiders," tend not to react well to Western style counseling (see Sue and Sue), which looks at underlying causes of a problem rather than surface symptoms and practical solutions. If a parent or student from such a culture (some Hispanic groups share this characteristic with many East Asians, including Koreans) approaches a teacher or counselor for help, they are most likely not coming to work through some deep personal or family dysfunction such as divorce, suicide, alcoholism, or abuse that may be causing academic distress. Those serious problems are secrets that are kept safely guarded behind the wall that surrounds the traditional Korean and Chinese home. Rather than coming for counseling, a role that is often handled by older relatives, they are probably coming for advice within your international school environment, with which they willingly admit they are not totally familiar. Unfortunately for many of our students overseas, they are not living near older relatives to give them advice, and because many of the problems they face are cultural ones between parents and children, the children have no one to go to except friends or adults at school. It may take some very direct questioning by teachers or counselors to even begin to get to the root of a problem that is first manifested in school – dropping grades, sleeping in class, aggression, anxiety, depression, eating disorders, etc. Don't be surprised if you never seem to be able to get to the bottom of a situation—it may be a family difficulty the child just can't and won't discuss. Compounding this problem is that often such difficulties are not discussed at home, either, and the first person to whom a child has really talked about it after suffering for months or even years may be a teacher or counselor. Parents may resent "the school" prying into family matters, but a professional decision must sometimes be made as to what is best for the child, and the parents brought on board as soon as possible. If parents understand that a personal or family problem might be having academic repercussions, they may be more open to your counseling their child. Unfortunately, older kids often won't be open with parents. I was fortunate over my decades as principal to be able to hopefully guide some students through some pretty difficult situations involving their families. Sometimes, once a level of trust had been established, the student would start to stare at the floor, not responding to my encouragement to talk about whatever is going on. I would just wait. Eventually, the tears would drop and a tissue quickly grabbed. That's when a student would open up. Quite often, after the student had shared their pain, I would ask whom else they had talked to about this. All too often the answer was "Nobody." Here are a few true scenarios (with some details changed to protect the students):

Chinese 8th grader Peter quite suddenly experienced a drop in grades. Work stopped coming in; test grades plummeted. Peter told his counselor he had no idea what the problem was, he was just having trouble concentrating. We called in the mom, who was also concerned about his grades, and who also said that she had no idea as to the cause. I asked about any changes in the family – moves, impending moves, deaths or sicknesses, etc. She said that apart from the fact that she and her husband were in the midst of a messy divorce, she couldn't think of anything that would affect Peter's grades! I assured her that a divorce would very likely be a cause of concern for Peter and could well affect his grades. Her response was that he was only a boy, and therefore would not be bothered by his parents' adult problems. In fact, she had asked him if he was upset about the divorce, and he had said not to worry about it. Mom obviously had little understanding of 14-year-old emotions and psychology. Knowing that I wasn't getting anywhere with mom, I thanked her and assured her we would continue to support Peter. When I spoke with Peter again that afternoon, he acknowledged that the divorce bothered him a little, but couldn't see any connection between his parents' breakup and his schoolwork. When I pressed him to describe his feelings about the divorce, however, his lower lip started to quiver, and the flood quickly followed. He was much more surprised at his tears than I was – he hadn't realized that he was holding in his fear and anger. At that point I enlisted the counselor to help him, and once he was able to talk it out, identify some coping mechanisms, and most importantly be assured that he was not the cause of the divorce (a very common assumption that kids will make), a huge load was off his shoulders. He was able to understand that in fact his anxiety regarding these family issues was the root of his academic problems, and he was able to pull things together academically reasonably well for the rest of the year. I don't think that mom ever fully understood that the problems between her and her husband were affecting their son in school. I can only hope that one day he was able to let both parents know how their adult conflict affected him as a young teenager.

Korean 11th Grader Sam was suddenly a mess academically

and socially. A popular, athletic kid with good grades, he was falling apart academically. I had met his parents, and they both impressed me as being supportive and understanding people who understood and loved their son. I asked him to come in to talk about his grades, which he readily did. Initially, he had no particular explanation about his deteriorating grades until I asked him about how things were going at home; how was his relationship with his parents. At that point, he suddenly got very quiet and stared at the floor. I let the minutes tick by, and soon the expected tears began. After accepting more than a few tissues that I offered, he looked up and blurted out between sobs "Dr. B, I don't know what do to. I found out that my dad is cheating on my mom with his secretary. My dad knows that I know, but we haven't talked about it. It's really awkward. Now I feel that I should tell my mom, but I know they would break up if I did. But if I don't tell my mom, then I feel like an accomplice. What should I do?" Wow. That's a problem that no sixteen year old should have to face. I had no helpful answer for him, but he was very relieved to be able to talk about it and share his burden. Mom eventually found out about Dad's dalliance on her own, and Sam was off the hook after a few months. Over the next couple of years we developed a pretty decent principal/student relationship, to the point that when I was handing him his diploma on stage two years later he suddenly gave me a hug. That got a reaction from the audience, but I'm guessing that no one imagined what that hug was all about, least of all his parents. I am still in touch with him from time to time, and I believe his parents are still together.

Chinese 6th grader Sue came to an international school in China mid year from Los Angeles. She was not doing her work, was showing aggression, and frequently was defiant. We knew that recently her father had died, but not how. The mom did not want to discuss it. Discussions with the girl *revealed that the dad had been murdered in his grocery store, but that no one had told her what had happened; she read about it in the Los Angeles Times. When we realized that Sue was going to need some serious time with a counselor or therapist to work through some of this, we tried to approach the mom about it. Mom was adamant that we not be involved, and that she did not want to discuss it. Sue left our school at the end of the year, and I have often wondered how she is doing.*

In these three cases, the important point is that it is crucially important for school adults – whether a trusted teacher, a counselor, a coach, or even (in these cases) an administrator take the time to recognize some change in a student, often academic, and not just tell a kid to study harder (whatever that means). Taking time, asking questions, pushing and sometimes probing a little, and being ready with a compassionate heart and a box of Kleenex is crucial to sorting out these situations. Some would say that it is not the school's role to be involved in this type of situation; I disagree. If it affects relationships in school or more often academics, it seems to me that it is the business of the school to gently and professionally find out what is the root of the problem. Ideally, the parents are involved in the solution. Sometimes – as in these cases – the "school" and the student need to sort it out themselves, as the parents were a major part of the problem. We can't always "solve" the problem, but we can be a listening ear and a shoulder to cry on, and hopefully a thoughtful voice, to help the student through a rough patch in life.

Schools can play a vital role in providing access to help for kids who are experiencing family issues and have no one else to go to. Often, the issues are cultural – between a much more traditional set of parents and a more Westernized child. These cultural differences compound the normal generational culture clashes that occur between teen and parents in most cultures. Therefore, while psychological counseling may be difficult to dispense, be free with advice. If you are not as a teacher comfortable speaking with a child who has come to you about a family or personal issue, offer to go with the child to the counselor, who can take it from there. Most often, the student just needs to talk to someone to "lighten the load." As a teacher, counselor, or administrator the student will respect your opinion.

Be open with students and parents about discussing local social ills such as the availability of drugs, places to avoid "hanging out," on-line gaming, pornography, or any other potentially sensitive areas. Both kids and parents need to know that confidential and non-judgmental help is available at school. These topics might be off limits for "good boys and girls" in traditional homes, and the teacher or counselor might be the only adult who can give a young person a Western perspective. If the student is coming directly from Korea or China, where discussion of these social ills is more taboo, he or she might be simply naive. Conversely, smoking and excessive drinking is a regular rite of passage for young Asian males upon (and now even before) high school graduation. The health hazards of smoking and drunkenness are understood but widely ignored in East Asia. Junior may possibly be just following dad's example in these areas.

11. Learn something about language acquisition. Just as every student is a language learner, constantly honing language skills at some level, every teacher is a language teacher. Every and every teacher in an international school comes into contact with students who are still learning a second language – in the case of Western-style international schools, that language is often English. Although there may be ESL or EAL (or whatever acronym is chosen) teachers, every teacher is an English teacher to some extent if their class is taught in English. Learn some basics of language acquisition such as the following (a qualified EAL teacher can give you much more detailed guidance):

a) Students should continue to advance in their native language (L1) age-appropriately as they learn a new language (L2). This not only enhances their L2 acquisition, but also ensures that they will become a bilingual adult.

b) Recognize and understand the "silent period" of language acquisition. Often, for the first few months, students are silent in English, but are learning English just the same. Suddenly, they may begin to speak in complete sentences. It doesn't mean that they were holding out on you, just that they were gaining confidence before they make their newly developed ability public.

During the period in which they are still not able to communicate their needs and feelings verbally (often this coincides with the silent period) the student may act out, and get angry or aggressive. These emotions are normally just a reaction to the frustration of not being able to communicate. I remember one fifth grade Israeli girl who was making herself very unpopular among her classmates and teachers, pushing, shouting out, grabbing materials, etc. However, once she found her voice and could communicate her needs, she quickly became what was apparently her real self – a polite, friendly, socially appropriate young lady. It just took a few months for her to get to that point. Interestingly, adults suddenly immersed in another language and culture may also act out in frustration until their language skills allow them to more appropriately express themselves.

c) Students should be encouraged, and even required, to get involved in extracurricular activities that allow them to practice and use their newly acquired English. Being on stage, for example, allows them to use English, but with the advantage of having to learn lines. Sports require communication, but often only with limited "on court/field" vocabulary. I would encourage involvement in team sports (which can also give the child some social status) instead of individual sports such as cross country or swimming (how much conversation takes place under water?) Clubs encourage conversation in areas of the student's interest where they may already have some vocabulary. The opportunities inherent in extracurricular activities for learning vocabulary, engaging in conversation, and gaining confidence in language will be time well spent – perhaps better spent than another hour after school studying SAT vocabulary.

d) Watch for the child who stalls in language acquisition when their English becomes "good enough." Many are the students who gain a level of social vocabulary and decide that their work is over. Related to this is confusion on the part of parents to assume that verbal, social fluency equals academic fluency in reading and writing.

Related to this is the problem of students who are assigned to EAL classes perennially. Watch out for students who get too comfortable being classified as EAL students and being enrolled in EAL classes. I have seen instances in which capable students are enrolled, year after year, in EAL classes, even up to five or six years. While research shows that fluency takes about seven years in a new language, sometimes schools (and EAL teachers) enable students enough so that they become linguistically lazy; special instruction is seldom necessary for that long, especially for students who began to learn English as younger elementary children. At a certain point, they need to stand on their own, perhaps with mentoring support as necessary.

e) If you are at all involved in the enrollment process in which language proficiency (EAL) diagnostic tests are given, be sure to vary the exam, particularly the writing sample, from time to time. Unfortunately, some parents are quite adept at getting samples of your school's admission test from other parents (think about the previous discussion about copying and relationships), and prepare their children accordingly. Your language ability entrance test should measure all four realms of language – speaking, listening, reading, and writing. One I would recommend is WIDA (World-Class Instructional Design and Assessment). Simply taking an average of those scores and using that as a screening tool doesn't tell the story at all. Is the writing score high, but the reading score low? Maybe they got ahold of the writing prompt and practiced. Is their spoken level high, but reading level low? Find out what that might be - this might be OK in 3d grade, but a disaster in 10th. It is crucial that the admissions office and the administrators work together in the acceptance and placement process, particularly in cases that may be questionable.

f) Be empathetic of new EAL students. Understand that they find themselves in a very stressful social and academic environment every day they come to school. They may develop physical symptoms from the stress, and may even have emotional outbursts in school or at home. Try to get them involved in class at least a little each day, even if you need to prep them ahead of time. Understand that by the end of the day, they will be exhausted. Constantly paying attention to everything in a new environment while also trying to understand what others are saying, and worrying about making some social faux pas that will stick to them for months, is very stressful. Think of how quickly you get tired when traveling in a country where you don't know the language or culture! It's *hard* being outside our cultural comfort zone!

g) Except for very new language learners, don't allow them to self-group in your classroom (as discussed earlier). Insist on English in your classroom, a goal that is often helped by assigning mixed-language groups, regardless of your subject. If a student needs some quick explanation by a peer in his or her native language to understand a concept, that's fine, but it should not become the rule, nor should constant translation (either spoken or written). Students should not be allowed to depend solely on native language web sites, which is not conducive to language acquisition, unless they are completely fluent in English, nor should they become too dependent on their electronic dictionary.

h) Allow native language use at lunchtime. While it is ideal for students to be in a completely immersion environment, realistically after four or five hours in English, they need a mental break. Constantly processing a language in which you are not fluent is hard work, especially when you are constantly being observed and evaluated (either socially by peers, or academically by teachers). Give them an hour to "go home linguistically" if possible to recharge and refresh. They still have the afternoon and a pile of homework in English ahead of them!

At the same time, be aware of the development of exclusive, same language cliques, as discussed earlier. Students who are proficient in their new language should be socializing outside their cultural group.

i) Always make assignments both orally and in writing. Missing or misunderstanding oral instructions, particularly for homework, is much more common when the teacher shouts out the assignment as students are collecting their books at the end of class. Whether on a web site, or on the board (left for later checking), be sure the assignments can be found in writing for later reference.

This list of how best to support EAL students could go on for pages. Do your own reading in the area of language acquisition; take some courses. See if your EAL teacher can provide some group professional development - "Ten tips for teaching EAL students" or something similarly manageable. Use your EAL teacher as a resource to help you work with some of your students. You will find that good EAL teaching techniques apply to your other students as well.

12. Be alert to issues of physical, emotional, or sexual abuse and neglect, and encourage the development of a school board adopted Child Abuse and Neglect Policy at your school. Of course, as we well know, these sensitive areas are not limited to Asian parents and students. However, they often play out a little differently in different cultural contexts as one might expect, and in ways that are not easily recognized by Western educators.

It is crucial, in order to protect children and school personnel, that a well-crafted set of policies be developed that identify what constitutes abuse and neglect (in the eyes of the school) and what the consequences are for parents who continue to abuse their children. Acceptance of these policies should be part of annual re-enrollment agreement requirements to keep them fresh in the minds of parents and personnel, and counselors and teachers should work with administrators to protect children through the use of these policies. Such a Policy should be carefully translated into the major parent languages and made readily available to parents and students for referral. Let's look at these various areas and see how issues of abuse or neglect may play out in an Asian/Confucian context.

Physical abuse. The possibility of what many Westerners would consider physical abuse is very real. Spanking, hitting, otherwise physically disciplining children is very common in Asian society, and even in Asian schools. Although physical abuse is now illegal in most public school systems in Asia, a generation ago it was not at all unusual for a teacher to line students up in front of class and give them a crack with a bamboo stick over outstretched palms for not doing their homework. I have personally witnessed a teacher demand that a student kneel on the floor in front of him, and smack the student across the face with the sole of a sneaker. (the boy, who could not afford sports shoes for P.E of his own, "borrowed" another student's pair for the class). Another common punishment 25 years ago was for a teacher to demand that students bend over and hit them repeatedly on the back of their calf with a piece of wood. Fortunately, these punishments are no longer allowed in school. However, at home parents have a great deal of leeway as to what kind of punishment to mete out to their errant children, and like much else in parenting, we tend to follow in the footsteps of those who we knew as children. The legal systems and the courts will generally not interfere in family discipline except in the most egregious cases (which make the evening news); in fact were a complaint to be made the police by the school they would shrug it off as effective parenting techniques. This leaves the school with little backup by police or even social services (which are seldom available in cases such as this in non-Western societies). Therefore, the school needs to develop a comprehensive plan of response that will get the attention of parents without outside intervention. One common consequence that a Policy might list is that the parent's behavior will be reported to the their employer. Of course, if it is a local company, this is an empty threat. If the parent works for a Western company, however, it can be a very real concern for parents who don't want reports of child abuse from the school to reach their Western boss. Usually it is sufficient for the school to suggest some alternative methods of discipline at home. Parents who were raised receiving physical punishment from their parents may simply not have many disciplinary strategies in their parental toolbox. Parent workshops in this area, delivered in Chinese or Korean, may be helpful. Parents want to do the right thing, but they might not yet have the disciplinary skills to satisfy Western standards. One strategy that I have used to some effect is to ask the parent if they want their child to some day hit their grandchild. The answer is almost always negative. I have suggested that most people discipline their children the way they were disciplined (parents will usually admit that yes, they were hit as children by their own parents), so it stands to reason that unless they "break the chain" of generational physical punishment, their grandchildren will suffer just as they did.

Of course, be on the lookout for bruises, particularly on the legs or face. If you suspect that a bruise comes from home, send the student to the school nurse to examine the bruise, photograph it, and record it in the logbook. The nurse should be on the lookout for students who seem to suffer frequent bruises. Students will often not admit that their parents are responsible, and will beg school personnel to not contact parents for fear of retribution for embarrassing the family. This is where the Policy comes in handy for all - it takes the onus off the individual counselor or principal and puts it on the Board adopted Policy. In regards to that, it would also be smart to be sure that the Board understands the policy as well, and that they understand that they should stand ready to back up the school employee who is facing a resistant parent.

Emotional abuse. Emotional abuse is more common than physical abuse, and is also more difficult to identify or even define. Mentioned earlier is the strategy of exclusion or isolation from the group as a means of shame and discipline. Parents may punish a child by saying things such as "Fool!" or "You are not my daughter!" The silent treatment by parents, even lasting a few days, is not unheard of (and is a variation on isolation). Threats of I'll send you back to Chinese school!" or I'll pull you out of that internaitonal school!" can be some parents' first line of defense when confronted with a child who they feel may be taking advantage of the "easier" international school. As Western educators, we have been trained to be very concerned about a child's self-esteem and self-confidence, which are certainly not supported by shaming. However, this is less of a concern to many Asian parents.

Asian discipline can often seem harsh and demeaning to the Western mind. This reflects a basic cultural difference in childrearing. The Western, Piagetian theory of child rearing focuses more on encouraging a child to develop his or her own talents, to develop their interests, and to "follow their dreams." This is commendable, but to the Asian mind it seems like too much is being left to an uneducated and inexperienced child to figure out for themselves. As Western parents, we train children to make their own decisions (and hopefully live with the consequences). We tend to offer a great deal of positive reinforcement, even when things are clearly not going in the right direction. Think back to when you asked a student a question, and she gave what was obviously an incorrect response. Did you reply "Sorry, Karen, that isn't correct" or did you reply with something like "That's an interesting response, Karen. Let's continue to give this more thought"? An Asian teacher would clearly tell the student where they erred, and correct them on the spot. Many Western teachers would consider a negative response stifling to the child's development and sense of inquiry. To an Asian teacher, a direct response is simply setting the child on the correct course.

Western child rearing (and educational) theory takes the position that if we encourage a child enough, he or she will be inspired to do better and better, eventually reaching their goals. Positive feedback is always more valuable than negative feedback, we are trained to believe; we "catch more flies with honey than with vinegar." We talk a lot about intrinsic motivation, but ironically we apply extrinsic motivation through positive feedback. We downplay failures, calling them "learning opportunities." We offer lots of carrots. Asian child rearing theory is more based on negative feedback. Because the child is thought to be intrinsically motivated to do well, they need to be molded, through negative feedback, into the kind of person they want to be. Adults (teachers, etc.) in true Confucian style know better than a mere child, and should make the decisions for them lest they waste valuable time making mistakes. A child will only grow through discipline, criticism, and high expectations.

An interesting illustration of this is in artwork. For example, a class of twenty Western children is told to draw a house after talking about houses and what they mean to us. Of course, we would expect to get twenty different house drawings, each representing the child's background and creative urges, and of course, each one would be "beautiful in its own way." During the process, the Western teacher wanders around the room, commenting on the variations in the drawings and encouraging each student. She may look at technique, but in the end, she celebrates how each house is different and dispays them all on the bulletin board, "celebrating diversity and creativity." Eventual grading (if there is any) is based on aspects such as creativity, neatness, and following whatever basic artistic skill the teacher was focusing on for that lesson. The emphasis is on the process and skills of artistic expression and the range of acceptable outcomes is wide. The Asian art teacher, on the other hand, introduces the idea of a house, and displays a sample house drawing. The students' role is to create identical houses – to conform to the "correct" house drawing done by the teacher. Even if the teacher doesn't explicitly say so, students will feel that copying the teacher's example is the safest path forward. The Asian teacher wanders around the room, correcting the students, maybe choosing one that is perfect and holding it up to other students as the goal to which they should strive. Grading would be based on how closely the house reflects the teacher's original one (much as Chinese calligraphy is evaluated based on how closely it mimics a sample by a famous calligrapher). The focus is on the product of the house drawing, not on the creative process.

Experience tells us that constant positive reinforcement doesn't always work for some kids. Some will take the easy way out, and fall into a cycle of laziness. These are the students that Western education just isn't serving very well. Many Asian educators and parents see this as a weakness of Western education, and perhaps it is. Repeated worldwide testing (yes, primarily in math and science, which lend themselves to "correct" responses rather than creative ones) shows how much higher Asian students, particularly in large cities with high quality public schools such as Shanghai, consistently outperform American students. This data is often held up by those critical of Western education to demonstrate the superiority of Asian education.

Experience also tells us that an environment of constant correction and discipline doesn't work for some Asian students, either. They may become withdrawn and negative – in fact, these are often the "failures" of the local systems that we sometimes see in our international school admissions offices. Certainly, ministries of education throughout Asia decry the fact-based, exam based educational practices that stifle creativity and independence in Asian schools, but little really changes. It is ironic that Asian educational experts are encouraging more Western methods and philosophies, while Western educational experts decry the lack of discipline and focus in Western education, and hold up Asian educational models to follow. I used to joke that perhaps the best of all educations was in Hawaii – half way between North America and Asia. Rather, I think that perhaps some of the best possible learning environments in the world are in international schools located in Asia, where liberal Western education fosters creativity and free thinking, disciplined by Asian habits of hard work and academic focus. What an unbeatable combination when Confucius meets Piaget, and they actually get along with each other!

The important point to remember and reflect upon in all this is that as Western educators we maybe need to control a knee-jerk reaction to more strict Asian child-rearing practices. What looks unquestionably as emotional abuse to the Western eye might simply be good parenting to the Asian eye. I am certainly not excusing constant demeaning of young people or bringing kids up in an environment of negativism and criticism, but I am suggesting that perhaps the opposite can be just as debilitating and growth inhibiting for some kids. We need to help parents to understand that yes, firm guidelines and expectations are necessary, and kids do need to learn to work hard. However, that needs to be tempered with encouragement and compliments as appropriate. A student dissolving into tears because she earned an A- in English in fear of her parents' reaction simply should not happen. Being less than #1 in everything should not be cause for personal disgrace and shame.

Sexual abuse. In over 40 years of working in Seoul and Shanghai, I only rarely had to personally deal with instances of sexual abuse of a child by a family member. I do know of instances of it occurring, however, and unfortunately international schools have not been immune to allegations and instances of actual abuse by school personnel. In a highly hierarchical society, where questioning elders is not socially acceptable, the opportunities for older individuals to take sexual advantage of children are certainly common enough, particularly if the adult is an older relative or teacher. Certainly keeping embarrassing family issues within the family is a factor in the seeming rarity of reports of sexual abuse; when there is some type of sexual or sex abuse scandal in Korea, it is front page news. On-line abuse, as well as peer sexual abuse at the college level or by higher ranking soldiers in the military is well documented, and harassment (even by superiors) of openly gay individuals is common in the military.

However, you may overhear comments that make you think that sexual abuse is occurring, particularly involving boys up through puberty, that in reality is not abusive within the cultural context, and probably seldom leaves any lasting scars because it is so common and accepted.

As modest as Koreans are, and shy about talking about things that would be considered sexual, they don't consider all things that are genital to be also sexual. Korean bathhouses (now most are called "saunas") are completely legal and socially acceptable places to go with same-sex friends or family members. Everyone is completely naked once you pay your money and use the locker/changing rooms. People wander about, scrub friends' backs, lie on their backs, get massages, and soak in various communal tubs of various temperatures, from ice cold to scalding hot. There are herbal rain rooms, and hot slabs of marble to fall asleep on. Sometimes there is an enclosed open-air roof area with its own tubs. Anyone who might try to go beyond the locker rooms wearing underwear (which never happens) would be told to take it off, or worse, stared at. You will see fathers and sons, mothers and daughters, same-sex co-workers or groups of friends, just sitting around naked and chatting away. It's a social occasion. It can be very touching to watch a teenage boy scrub his elderly grandfather's back in a way that is very intimate, yet not at all sexual. Customers can pay extra for full body scrubs, lying on their back on a table, completely open to the other bathers. Same sex Fathers, mothers, sons and daughters, grandparents, friends, co-workers, classmates, and complete strangers are very used to seeing each other naked in this healthy and steamy environment. So if you overhear Tae-woo telling his friends that he went to the bathhouse with his dad last night, don't be alarmed. They are very common in Korean cities; most neighborhoods will have one. It's a very relaxing and enjoyable cultural experience, and the sense of nakedness soon disappears as soon as you realize that everyone else is naked, too! There is very strict bathhouse etiquette in Korea and Japan that keeps dirty bodies out of clean water, which unfortunately has yet to be fully understood in China. It's always best to go with a local friend the first time to be sure you don't do something culturally inappropriate. If a same sex friend invites you to go to the sauna with him (or her), swallow your modesty and agree. A relatively new addition to traditional bathhouses, which normally include a sauna room, is the "jinjilbang" – an upscale bathhouse with a variety of small rooms or "caves", often each with a theme and varying from hot to unbearable. These are separate from the single gender bath areas, and are co-ed (and require a supplied bathrobe). This kind of bathhouse is relatively new to China, but is catching on quickly as a place to relax and socialize. Again, any mention of this by students is not sexual in any way; a group of middle or high school Korean boys or girls going to the bath-house together would be very socially acceptable. One word of caution - reportedly the one person a student does NOT want to see in the neighborhood bathhouse is their teacher!

Another example of behavior that looks sexual, but isn't meant to be, is rooted in the Confucian desire for male off-spring. Traditionally, when a baby was born in a Korean home, the family hung a string of red chili peppers on the doorframe (the Korean child's word for "penis" is the same as the word for chili pepper; "goh-chu" due to the obvious simi-larity in shape to an uncircumcised penis.) Conversely, when a girl was born, instead of a chili pepper a string of coal chunks was hung (sort of like getting coal in your stocking at Christ-mas). There was traditionally a great celebration when a baby boy was born and a sigh of resignation when a girl was born. This preference for males has decreased greatly in recent years among younger parents, but it is still very much alive in many parts of Asia, as evidenced by the 10% imbalance of males over females in today's China. But the celebration doesn't end with birth of a boy; he is reminded that he is a boy re-peatedly, and physically, for the next few years. Adults (par-ticularly everyone's grandmother, it would seem) feel free to celebrate the masculinity of the little tyke by gently touching the child's appendage through his pants, asking "Do you have a goh-chu?" or "Let's see that little goh-chu!" or something similarly endearing. This is not at all sexual in anyone's mind, just celebratory. There is an urban legend Los Angeles was sitting on a park bench when a little Caucasian boy walked by with his mother. The old gent started to talk to the boy, and suddenly reached out and fondled him, just as he would have done in Korea with the complete understanding and ap-proval of the boy's mother. The Caucasian mom was not quite so receptive, and rightly so! Of course the police were called, accusations were made, translators called in, abject and em-barrassed apologies made by the old gentleman's daughter, and quick plane reservations made to whisk him back to safer territory. Such is the nature of culture clash when something considered innocent – even endearing – in one culture would likely send you to jail in another.

In sum, I would just say that we should always keep our eyes and ears open to signs of sexual abuse. However, before taking action we would be well served to quietly investigate a little bit and see if this "abuse" is intentional within the child's culture. If not, then be all means we need to rely on our adopted Child Abuse and Neglect Policy and move forward as outlined in the policy.

13. Learn to interpret Korean or Chinese body language and manners. As anyone who has lived or worked internationally knows, body language and manners are almost as different between cultures as is spoken language. Here are some common examples pertaining to Korean culture. Most are not found to the degree described among culturally Chinese children.

Respect towards superiors in Korea is demonstrated by having downcast eyes and a slightly bowed head. For an adult to say "Look me in the eye when I talk to you!" will put a child in a real dilemma — it's like telling an American child to look the other way when spoken to. Looking someone directly in the eyes in Korea is considered aggressive and confrontational. The bowed head is a way of showing respect, subservience, shame, and ensures that there will be no eye contact. This behavior is particularly apparent when a child is being scolded. It can be very frustrating to the uninformed Westerner when a child simply will stare at the floor between their feet, not look up, and refuse to say anything. Take a deep breath and ask the child calmly to look up (but not look you in the eye.)

When being scolded, children will usually remain quiet. Asking questions like "Why did you hit Susie?" will more often result in silence and the accompanying bowed head than in any kind of meaningful answer. This, like the bowed head, is a sign of submission and shame, not defiance. If a teacher really wants to know why Tae-jin hit Susie, she should sit down with the child later and ask quietly. An answer still might not be immediately forthcoming, but the chances of eventually finding out what happened are at least greater.

Giggles or laughter often accompany embarrassment, especially in girls. This is one of the most frustrating behaviors for Westerners living in Korea to get used to — it's pretty irritating to ask a question, fall down, drop your books, or do something embarrassing and be answered with giggles and laughter! Understanding that this is a learned cultural response may help — but it will take a real effort. Adolescent Korean girls are particularly adept at giggling behind a demurely held handkerchief or fingers.

It's better for a child to sniffle through a class than blow their nose. In Korea, it's acceptable (for an older person) to belch loudly, to hungrily slurp one's noodles, and to sniffle forever — but really honking the nose is unacceptable! (If you honk, plan on hearing some of those embarrassed giggles!) Even a discreet and quiet blowing of the nose gets attention, easpecially during a meal. Keeping a box of tissuex handy in the classroom is always a good idea, and students should be sure they know that they're expected to use it without your telling them to. If you start to hear serial sniffling from a child, just quietly put a box of tissues on his or her desk and ask them to step out in the hallway to take care of it. Westerners who visit a Korean home or Korean restaurant would be advised to go to the lavatory before blowing their nose — and then do it quietly. Sneezes are likewise not responded to with a "Bless you!" The thinking goes "Of course you are embarrassed to sneeze. Why embarrass you further by calling attention to it? Why, too, should I apologize after sneezing and thus further disrupt the class?" It's best just to just ignore the sneeze (or maybe circulate that box of tissues).

Be prepared to have a door swung closed in your face. (this one does apply to China.) Everyone who has ever lived in Korea or China has approached the swinging supermarket door, arms full of bundles, and have a person breeze through the door ahead of them and let it swing shut in their face. Holding a door open for a stranger simply has not yet become part of the manner set in much of Asia. This is related to the importance of relationships; a person would never think of not holding a door (and even carrying the bags of groceries) for someone they knew personally and with whom they had a relationship. However, there is a certain level of invisibility towards people who don't share a relationship of some kind. This is starting to change; when you hold open a door for someone following you, they will often acknowledge your effort - but just as often not! This irritating behavior may also have something to do with the fact that except recently, and in large cities, buildings are not centrally heated in the winter, and doors in public places are often left propped open – thus, no need to hold them open for anyone.

"Thank you," "I'm sorry," and "You're welcome" may not be used as often as you may expect. There are perfectly good words for these expressions in Korean and Chinese, but they are just not used very often. Korea, like China, is a "high context" culture — lots of what is communicated is not spoken directly, but understood from the context of the situation. Of course a person is thankful to you or feels regret, but it simply is often not verbalized. You are expected to understand that they feel this way, and there is no need for them to point it out verbally.

Should the school try to understand these behaviors? Of course. It is always good to understand that other cultures have different manners and codes of behavior, and apply them appropriately. But should they be accepted as normal in a Western-style school? I don't think so. Part of any unwritten curriculum in a school is teaching culturally appropriate manners and behaviors. As students attending a Western style school, students should learn (and use appropriately) Western manners, just as we would expect a Western child to adopt Asian manners were they to attend Korean or Chinese school. We should teach Western manners as we would anything else — tools that work in another culture and are the oil that lubricates human relationships. Just as we teach appropriate language for use in Western settings, we should teach appropriate Western etiquette. Your learning to use some Korean or Chinese manners with them will encourage them to learn to use Western manners with you and other Westerners, and will send the message to students that you do not consider Asian manners to be "bad," but just inappropriate in a Western setting. The key here is that students need to learn to use situationally appropriate behaviors, as long as they don't conflict with deeper moral or ethical codes.

14. Remember that adjusting to a new school and language does not happen in days – or even weeks. While in the process of learning English and acculturating to the Third Culture of an international school, children will not fit in totally with the new school environment and may feel left out. If there are enough same-language children in the school they may seek out soul mates, those who understand what they are going through and who know what together they will face when they return to their native country. Culturally based cliquishness also works against rapid acculturation to the new school environment. They may also think that teachers don't understand them — and they may be right. Try to empathize with your students as they adjust; international teachers sometimes find that their own transitions to new schools and countries do not always go without some bumps and tears. Hopefully books like this will help teachers better understand their students who are going through these difficult transitions.

15. Celebrate and honor multiculturalism. Young people of middle or high school age struggle with their emerging identities in the best of situations. Finding themselves in a mixed cultural environment in which they may be getting conflicting messages about who they are from their friends, from the school, from parents, from family back home, and from their own fragile egos, identity confusion can become quite apparent. It is natural that in the process of adjusting from a secure cultural identity (back home) to one of some cultural ambiguity (an international school) young people and adults may swing from one extreme to another. Korean children who have just moved overseas (or a Korean-American who has just moved to Korea) may try to fit into their new youth culture as quickly as possible in order to be accepted. They may quickly adopt extremes in dress, language, or habits in the new culture to overcompensate for their own lack of security. Later on, if this doesn't seem comfortable to sustain long term, or when they feel a sense of disloyalty to their home culture, they can swing back to the other extreme, identifying themselves, for example, as "super-Americans" or "super-Koreans" depending on their circumstance. Neither of these extremes is very attractive. Students need to know that their ability to "code change" from one culture to another depending on whom they are talking to or whose home they find themselves in is not being disloyal to anyone or any nation; it is a gift that will give them greater flexibility in life later on, and may even bring them real financial and career advantages. Just as people learn to switch languages depending on the situation, kids need to be given psychological permission, and encouragement, to embrace multiculturalism in behavior. Support this in every day interactions in your school as appropriate; appreciate, but the move beyond the annual "Korea Day" or "Chinese New Year Celebration" when moms descend on the school loaded down with kimpap and other goodies. Culture goes beyond our taste buds!

16. Work with your school to provide re-entry counseling for students returning "home," whether at graduation or at earl-

ier ages. Whether a child is returning to Korea or China from abroad or leaving Asia after a temporary stay, the re-entry adjustment can be difficult. They will most likely experience reverse culture shock, and find themselves hidden immigrants (as discussed earlier). Hosting lunches or seminars for students returning "home" on the challenges they may fact can be helpful. Pollock and Van Reken (see reference list) give tremendous insight into the challenges of such a move.

Finally, again remember that all of these suggestions are general to a population but maybe not always to an individual. This cannot be stressed enough. Each parent, family, and child is unique in background, in history, in values, and in plans for the future. Use the information in this book as a guide, understanding that no family or child will display all these characteristics completely. Don't make any assumptions about an individual. It is just as dangerous to assume that a Korean or Chinese child or parent will exhibit all of these characteristics as it is to assume that they are totally Westernized. because their English is fluent. Take time to get to know each student and family. Give each young person a chance to be an individual — one whose uniqueness is a developing mosaic of both Asian and Western experiences. That is a gift that can never be taken away from them. It is also their special gift to you!

Looking Back, Looking Ahead

Is your school using any of the strategies suggested in this book to help new students coming from Asian-style schools adjust to the new demands of your international school? If not, what might you be doing to ease their transition?

Is there a hidden bullying problem in your school? Do fights seem to erupt for reasons that seem silly to you - often related to matters of "respect"?

Are your ethnic Korean students or other ethnic groups forming exclusive cliques? If so, how might cliques be detrimental to your school culture? What might you be able to do to alleviate some of this behavior?

Have you ever thought, "MY students are so nice they would never cheat in my class!" Have you ever been disappointed when "nice kids do bad stuff under pressure?"

Is your policy on plagiarism intentionally and repeatedly taught to your students, and enforced? Has you school adopted a sensible progression of style sheets, imbedded in the curriculum in all subject areas?

What are you doing to encourage reluctant students to ask questions in class? What questioning strategies are you using to ensure that all students are involved in class discussion?

What are you doing to help English language learners feel comfortable asking questions in class? Do all teachers understand their role as EAL teachers?

How do school personnel make themselves available for kids who need to talk about personal problems? What protocols do you have in place to ensure that if things get serious the student is referred to a qualified counselor?

Does your school have a published Child Abuse and Neglect Policy? If not, find some from other schools and adapt them to your school.

Do your admission and administrative staffs share a common understanding of admissions standards? Do they work together to make decisions on questionable applications?

What is your school doing to help students prepare for reentry to their home nation and culture?

CHAPTER XVIII: WORKING WITH LOCAL STAFF

This section is directed particularly to administrators who supervise or work with local staff. Similarly to working with parents or students, all interactions are filtered through cultural lenses. In most cases, the staff will adapt their own behaviors to match those of the Western institution if that is the dominant culture. The closer the local staff member works with Westerners, the greater the chances of their learning to work in Western ways. However, certain cultural habits, especially those deep under the water in our cultural iceberg, can remain strong, and should be expected in your local employees. It would behoove the Western administrator to have a develop a trusting relationship with a "cultural interpreter" on whom they can depend for advice, understanding that they also may have their own cultural lenses. Below are found some examples of the types of culturally nuanced situations that you might run into and suggestions as to how to handle (or avoid) them:

1. Expect local staff members' to be hesitant to speak as "representatives," or voice opinions in group situations. I remember well the frustration of heading accreditation self-study teams, when "stakeholder" voices from the entire school community were required. Representative committees were created, including local staff, parents, teachers, and administrators. As each committee grappled with various areas of school operation, the representatives were to contribute their opinions, reflecting the general perspectives of their constituencies. This worked fine, until we solicited input from our local Korean staff committee members. The representatives were very hesitant to voice their individual opinions without first going back and checking with their groups.; their sense of collectiveness wouldn't allow them to offer their individual opinions. One possible way we found around this was to be sure that all representatives had written lists of questions and items for discussion a few days before the meeting. This allowed the local representatives time to solicit opinions from their group and to be able to represent their constituencies with a good deal more confidence.

2. Expect for decisions be made differently by Asian and Western staff. Western culture prizes individuality, as we have discussed at length. Therefore, when Western staff make decisions, they often weigh such variables as being expected to disagree with management and speak the truth (but not too loudly); weigh the variables of future success and achievement (but not too obviously); consider their own sense of individuality and personal freedom (while respecting the organization); and financial repercussions of the decision (short term or long, good or bad, for themselves or the institution). Asian employees, however, use quite different measures when making decisions. Brought up to understand that their own value as a human is critically tied to the organizations to which they belong, they will seriously consider how their decision will affect the group rather than how it will affect them personally. They will defer to formal authority, and have a very difficult time directly saying "No" to any request. They will take the long view (in career advancement or pay); and see standing out or standing up as negative behaviors. If they do push back, it will be as a group. One way I have seen this done in Korea is to express disapproval to the administration by refusing to accept their pay while continuing to work with a smile, rather than refusing to work while expecting to be paid. That strategy is amazingly effective!

3. Understand that local staff are often hesitant to criticize, even constructively, the organization in front of leadership. Additionally, leaders may find it difficult to get their Korean and Chinese committee members to offer constructive criticism, so necessary in any organization, and doubly so during an accreditation or certification process of some kind. They may fear expressing their concerns, or simply feel that they are being disloyal to their organization by being critical, particularly to outsiders and especially in any kind of group activity. You may find that you can get more helpful feedback in private, but in general, individuals are not willing to stand alone and speak out. The lower they are in the local staff hierarchy (for example, the youngest custodian or school guard or driver). Normally, if criticism is going to be made, it will be done in unison as a local staff group, even to the extent of wearing armbands, wearing the same colors to work, or staging a peaceful demonstration.

4. Adjust, as quickly as possible, to the challenges of working within formal hierarchical structures as would be found in local organizations. In Korea, this is called the Ho-bong system. The informal cultural hierarchy already in place is formalized with pay brackets, titles, and responsibilities. While this structure offers a high level of transparency, and ensures that employees of equal rank are paid equally, it is fraught with conflict and resentment by individuals who not only think that their assigned title and level is too low, but are dissatisfied with the pay grade attached to that level. Particularly if this system is imposed on a formerly less formal pay structure (with pay being worked out individually upon hiring) it can result in real dissatisfaction, but after it is firmly in place you can enjoy a clear hierarchical structure and trans-

362

parent pay scale as you work with your local staff – and as they work with each other. Also note that the title and formal level is often more important to the individual than actual pay, especially among older, more traditional workers.

5. Before accepting a job offer, be sure to know what your roles and responsibilities are in relation to others above you in the hierarchy. The hierarchical structure of Asian organizations defines a very real difference in formal and informal status to the head of that institution. Leaders in Asian organizations are usually in their positions due to age, longevity in the organization, or relationship to the institution's owning family. They are seen as being far above the level of employee – in the case of schools, the teachers. They have the titles (used exclusively), the perks (large black car), fancy office, and secretaries who bring them tea and snacks. Their office may be down the paneled hall where people speak in hushed tones. Western leaders, on the other hand, value their ability to share lunch with teachers, drop into classrooms, tell jokes, expect to be challenged, and dress down occasionally. They see themselves as "leaders among equals." If this is the first time an organization has had a Western (or Asian) leader, it can be initially disconcerting to all. I have observed in a number of schools where the local head of the school (sometimes the owner) has a large and fancy office front and center, and the actual operational principal of the school – the Westerner - is relegated to a small office down the hall and around the corner. The message of who is in charge is obvious, but it also opens the door literally to parents who want something and go right to the top, bypassing the actual Western principal. Before taking a job in a locally owned school, particularly if the owning family has an office in the building, it would behoove the new Western head to establish firm lines of responsibility to avoid later misunderstandings and distrust. Find out who the "Chairman" and "President" are and what their roles are in the day to day operations. Specifically, ask questions about finances, where your level of discretion falls in spending (and whether everything needs to be approved by someone up the food chain), and who is responsible for student discipline in cases where the principal and parents may be in conflict. Ensure that you will have backing for your decisions, and that a simple phone call to the "Chairman" by someone who graduated from the same high school a hear ahead of him or her doesn't overturn your considered decisions. Having written and published documents and handbooks can go a long way to supporting you if things get difficult.

6. Seek out a "cultural translator" and encourage that individual to speak freely to you about cultural matters. Remember that both culture and language never translate 100% perfectly. There are always nuances of meaning that are unspoken, and perhaps non-translatable. Not withstanding, Western leaders should make every effort to be culturally sensitive by really trying to understand the local culture. Particularly when new to a culture, we all make faux pas. These are understood, unless we neglect to correct them as we acculturate ourselves. Whether or not we agree with all these "new" ways of doing things or not we should do our best to accommodate ourselves to them. A trusted cultural translator can help you immensely to navigate these cultural waters. Choose carefully and thoughtfully, taking the advice of those who have been there longer. Keep your "translator" close. However, if you suspect that you are being led to simply ignore things that really need to be addressed, it's time for a serious discussion with your "translator." While we should be open to learning how things are done locally, and not insist on doing it "the way we did it in my last school," it is far too easy to fall into the "Well, in China we . . . (Korea/Japan/Thailand ...)" trap of making excuses for things being done in inefficient or even illegal ways – sometimes the foreigner DOES have a better idea; in some ways that is why you are there, and not a local, in your position. This can get very sticky; I have been in situations where I realized that things were being done in an unethical way, and was told, "Well, here in Country X that's the way it has to be done." Whether it is a bribe to government officials, or avoiding taxes in illegal ways, or using school supplies for personal purposes, some practices are simply wrong. Speak to your supervisor and follow up in writing. Keep your correspondence. If you realize that you are being implicated in something that may get you in legal trouble, and it continues, distance yourself as far as possible from the practice. Choose your battles - remember our discussion of "I like it, I can live with it, NO WAY" at the beginning of this book? Decide what is worth a fight, and try to determine what it will cost you in the end.

7. **Ensure that your cultural translator/assistant is representing you, not the local culture.** If it is not possible, be sure that your chosen translator (normally your secretary or office assistant) understands that he or she is there to translate and help you understand, not to represent the local parent's position, which is often difficult for them to do. Learning enough of the local language so that you can follow a conversation and correct misunderstandings is very helpful, although in touchy or sensitive matters I would always suggest using a translator unless you are very fluent in the local language. It is too easy to choose the wrong word with the wrong nuance. Again, choosing the correct assistant is crucial to your success as an administrator. Many experienced administrators who have "been around" various schools have stories of the assistant who, either intentionally or not, nearly sunk their careers at that school because they simply were not loyal to the administrator.

8. **Form positive working relationships with the local staff.** In China and Korea, the employer/employee social distance is wide, so there is little chance of your getting too friendly with your local maintenance staff. However, greeting them each

day, learning about their families and children, taking them out as a group to eat from time to time, or stepping up to help with the heavy box or holding that hammer for them will ensure that when crunch time comes, they will be at your side. The old saying about the secretary and janitor actually being the ones who run the school is not far from the truth. They are usually the ones who have been there long before you appeared on the scene, and will be there long after you leave the school. They know where the skeletons are buried and can save you from becoming one of them.

9. **Enjoy your exhalted position (while being humble)!** Being a school administrator in Asia can get rather heady. Not only are educators honored and respected, in good Confucian tradition, but your position in the organization will create much more social distance than would normally be found in a Western setting. So enjoy, while staying humble. In the end, we in international education are well paid migrant workers. We come, and we go. The local staff will be there much longer than we will be, most likely, and it is they who provide the stability and continuity to the school and its reputation.

Looking Back, Looking Ahead...

As an administrator in an international school, you most likely work more closely with local staff than most teachers. You are a guest in their culture, just as they are guests in your Western school culture. Are you meeting them half way? Are you attempting to understand their working style?

Have you figured out your place in the school organization, particularly if it is operated as a family owned business? Do you know who really makes the decisions?

How can you better get to know, and support, your local staff?

Do you have a trusted "cultural translator" who can keep you from making embarrassing or costly mistakes?

CHAPTER IX: CONCLUSION

I trust that through reading this book you have gained a deeper understanding of why so many East Asian students and parents behave in ways that sometimes seem to be at odds with Western padagogy and child raising strategies. We have examined the long histories, both ancient and more recent, of two great cultures, Korean and Chinese, and examined how Confucianism has affected the cultures of both. We have seen how traditional educational philosophy and practice reflect that bedrock Confucianism even today. We have also throughout the book compared and contrasted how the influence of Confucianism plays out somewhat differently in modern day Chinese and Korean contexts. In general, we have seen repeatedly how similar these two educational cultures are, yet how, although Korean education is based historically on Chinese roots, today's Korean education and culture are more traditional than Chinese. Simply, Korean education and culture are much like those found in China - just more so.

Hopefully you have found Chapters VI and VII, which apply theory to practice, helpful in your day to day interactions with your East Asian students and their parents. And finally, I cannot emphasize enough that my opinions suggestions, and insights only provide a background to working with these groups - a baseline from which to build an personal understanding and working relationship with each unique individual, understanding his or her own unique family and personal experiences and how these have affected the people they are today.

* * *

I'd like to end this book as I began – with Charlie. Every international teacher has a Charlie – or pieces of him – in their classrooms. Whether it is dealing with a parent with unreasonable expectations, teaching a child who is learning English, struggling with helping students and parents understand what a Western education is all about, or just sitting with a child who is temporarily overwhelmed with cultural overload, you find Charlie and his sisters are sitting in your classroom every morning. He, or she, is a wonderful package of potential. Unwrap that package with care, and enjoy the wonderful gift that you discover inside.

APPENDIX

Below I'll share a newspaper column in a series entitled "Cultural Kaleidoscope," written by a Korean professor some years ago. He somewhat lyrically describes and extols the role of mothers in Korea. Granted, this is one Korean man's perspective, but many of his words do ring true to my experience working with Korean families. I take no responsibility for the rather awkward title.

All the Korean Mothers were Valient

Dr. Kim Seong-kon, Seoul National University

Professor of English

Executive director of the Language Education Institute of Seoul National University

Korea Herald, August 13, 2003

Is it true that most Korean mothers act like managers for their children. Of course, it is. Believe it or not, a Korean mother's role as a manager for her child begins as early as the child reaches the ate of four; she begins to teacher her child the basic survival skills by sending her child to English classes, swimming lessons, and piano lessons. When a child enters elementary school, the fateful 12-year battle for college entrance exam begins, and the mother practically becomes a road manager for her little warrior.

Korean mothers, for example, arrange study groups, hire private tutors, set up study plans, and organize scheduled for their children. They drive their children to school in the morning and also to various private English or math academies after school. "My mom drives me crazy" complain many Korean students who are suffering from the formidable petticoat government that controls their lives. Yes, knowing their future success depends entirely on their mothers' management skills, they choose to remain docile.

In that sense, the college entrance exam is not so much a survival game for stressed students as it is a war among aggressive mothers. Indeed, few college students in Korea would deny the fact that they owe their mother greatly for what they are today, without whose skillful management they would not possibly have entered college.

Korean mothers continue to manage their children through college and even after graduation. They choose their children's majors and courses, and carefully monitor their grades and GPA. Often they advise their sons and daughters of which company to apply to for a job, and what kind of boyfriend or girlfriend they should choose. Eventually, Korean mothers arrange their child's wedding and interfere in their married life. Under the circumstances, the conflicts between a bride and her mother-in-law seem inevitable.

Throughout Korean's turbulent history, Korean mothers

have sacrificed themselves for their children and husbands, while miraculously enduring and overcoming hardship. In a male-dominant Confucian society where priority is given to men and emphasis to head of the house, Korean mothers have always been submissive and marginalized. The image of Korean mother is, therefore, a highly unselfish, enduring, and virtuous woman whose life is devoted thoroughly to the welfare of her family.

Perhaps that is why the Korean word, "eomoeni" (mother), entails such a special meaning to Koreans, it evokes a tremendous amount of affection and a strong sense of nostalgia long after Koreans have grown up and started their own families. When a Korean goes abroad, he immediately misses his mother, to whom he feels permanently attached. Missing one's sweet, tender mother, therefore, has always been one of the favorite motifs of hundreds of Korean poems and pop songs. It seems that Koreans, regardless of age, easily become sentimental whenever they are far away from their mother. . . .

SUGGESTED READINGS

In recent years there has been a plethora of books dealing with Korean and Chinese history and education. Reading some of these will help you understand the culture "below the waterline of the iceberg." The list below is by no means exhaustive; it simply includes some of my personal favorites that you might find helpful in deepening your understanding of Korean and Chinese cultures. While some of these are not new to the genre, I think they still provide valuable insights into these fascinating cultures.

Korean History and Culture:

Still Life with Rice (1996, be Helie Lee) is an historical novel tracing the actual life of the author's Korean grandmother during the Japanese occupation and the Korean War

A quick primer in Korean social customs, especially those that often cause comment among non-Koreans (particularly Americans), is *Ugly Koreans, Ugly Americans* (2014) by Min, Byoung-chul (Seoul: BCM Publishers). While the cartoons in this book are somewhat stereotypical of Asians and Westerners to the extent that some might find them offensive, the reader can learn a good deal about how not to offend (and how not to be offended by) Koreans who may not have spent much time in the West (A similar book, *Ugly Japanese, Ugly Americans*, is published by the same author).

For a broad, unbiased, and enjoyable trip through Korean history and culture from prehistoric times to the early 2000's read *Korea's Place in the Sun* (2005), by Bruce Cumings (New York: W. W. Norton & Co.)

An excellent history of both North and South Korea is found in *The Two Koreas: A Contemporary History* (2014), by Don Oberdorfer (Reading, MA: Addison-Wesley).

Another valuable resource for understanding Korean culture is from the Culture Shock! series; *Culture Shock! Korea* (2018, by John Brocskay) provides valuable insights into Korean culture both for the tourist and resident.

There are any number of "I was there" genre Korean War books on the market, but certainly one of classics of the war is *In Mortal Combat: Korea, 1950-1953* (1991) by John Toland (New York: William Morrow and Company). For a Korean perspective on the war, *From Pusan to Panmunjom* (1992), by General Paik Sun Yup is very readable (Dulles, Virginia: Brassey's). For a true tale of the horrors of being a North Korean prisoner during the war, read Larry Zeller's first-hand account of three years in captivity, *In Enemy Hands* (The University Press of Kentucky, 1991).

An Amazon search will introduce you to many other titles about Korean history and culture, and the internet has many scholarly articles and government publications in English. For up-to-date information on Korea contact the Korean embassy or consulate in your city.

China/Cultural Revolution:

There are many histories of China available for the reader. One area of particular interest is the Cultural Revolution (1966-1976), because it was during this era that many of the grandparents of our current students grew up, as well as many staff members at international schools. Generally, Chinese are not anxious to talk about this horrific period of their history, although some will provide their fascinating personal stories. Some cultural revolution classics are listed below:

Life and Death in Shanghai (2010) by Nien Cheng (Grove Press) is a classic, first person story of a Westernized Chinese woman who became a target of the Red Guards during this period. It is a tragic, fascinating account.

Wild Swans: Three Daughters of China (2003) by Jung Chang (Simon Schuster) is the true story of three generations of women in the author's Chinese family throughout the 20th Century.

Mao's Last Dancer (2005) by Li Cunxin (Berkley Books) is the memoir of a Chinese peasant boy who was chosen from his village to spend his life as a government sponsored dancer.

Red Scarf Girl (1999) by Ji-li Jiang (HarperTrophy) is the true story of a middle school girls' journey through the Cultural Revolution.

China's Son: Growing up in the Cultural Revolution (2001) by Da Chen (Delacourt Press) is the autobiographical story of the author's journey as a young boy through the Cultural Revolution.

Asian Education/Parenting:

For an in-depth look at the stereotypical (?) role of many Asian mothers, read some of their own words. The unapologetic and controversial *Battle Hymn of the Tiger Mother* by Amy Chua (2011) is well known; many of the parenting behaviors she described are described in this book.

For a different perspective read *Little Soldiers: An American Boy, a Chinese School, and the Global Race to Achieve* by Lenora Chu (2017). Little Soldiers is the autobiographical journey of a Chinese-American journalist who moved to Shanghai and put her son in a "top" Chinese preschool. She not only describes the inner world of Shanghai schools and the role of mothers, but also describes how the experience changed her and her son as they journeyed together through this cultural clash to a greater understanding and appreciation of the Chinese system.

For a more academic look at Chinese education, investigate the works of author **Young Zhao,** who has published a number of books on the subject. Having grown up in China but educated in the United States, Dr. Zhao (who is also a well known speaker) provides a fascinating perspective on the differences between Chinese and Western educational systems and cultures.

Cultural thought and theory:

An excellent resource for those who counsel or work with people across cultures is *Counseling the Culturally Diverse: Theory and Practice* (6th ed.), (2013) by Derald and David Sue (New York: John Wiley & Sons).

The classic work on children growing up outside their own culture is *Third Culture Kids: Growing Up Among Worlds* (3rd Edition, 2017) by Michael V. Pollock and Ruth E. Van Reken (Nicholas Brealey Publishing) This book is one of a kind, and is "a must" for any former, present, or future Third Culture Kid or their parents or spouse, as well as for educators working with TCK's.

For a more theoretical, but highly readable and brief investigation of the origins of Western and Eastern thought is *The Geography of Thought: How Asians and Westerners Think Differently – and Why* (2011) by Richard E. Nesbitt (Nicholas Brealey Publishing)

RESOURCES

Below are some of the various resources that have been referenced in the text:

Diamond, Anna. *South Korea's Testing Fixation.* The Atlantic, Nov 17, 2016.

Gladwell, Malcolm. (2011) *Outliers: The Story of Success*; particularly the chapter entitled "Rice Paddies and Math Tests." (Little, Brown and Company)

Hofstede, Geert. (2001) *Culture's Consequences: Comparing Values, Behaviors, Institutions, and Organizations Across Nations. Second Edition.* (Sage Publications).

Hultberg, Patrik and David Santandreu Calonge, Seong-Hee Kim & Sergio Rossi (2017) *Education policy in South Korea: A con*temporary model of human capital accumulation? Cogent Economics & Finance, 5:1, DOI: 10.1080/23322039.2017.1389804. This source is a research-based, scholarly discussion of the after-school academy dilemma in Korea.

Kim, Seong-kon. *All the Korean Mothers were Valiant.* Korea Herald. August 13, 2003

Kirk, Donald. Forbes Asia, December 14, 2014 *"Korean Air 'Nut*

Rage' Exposes Risk To Safety Of Hereditary Family Rule" Kohl, L. Robert. *Survival Kit for Overseas Living,* (4th ed.) 2001, Nicholas Brealey

Nesbitt, Richard E. (2011) T*he Geography of Thought: How Asians and Westerners Think Differently – and Why* (Nicholas Brealey Publishing)

Sue, David and D. Sue. (1990). *Counseling the Culturally Different: Theory and Practice* (2nd ed.). (New York: John Wiley & Sons)

https://www.theatlantic.com/education/archive/2016/11/south-korean-seniors-have-been-preparing-for-today-since-kindergarten/508031/

Cultural Iceberg image adapted from Gary Weaver in R.M. Paige, ed. *Cross-Cultural Orientation: New Conceptualizations and Applications* (Rowman & Littlefield, (1986)

Remembering Dave Pollock

One of my "heroes" in the area of cross cultural education and child adjustment was David Pollock, who I knew personally as he ministered and presented at international schools around the world. The international community suffered an irretrievable loss with the untimely and sudden death of Dave in April 2004. Dave was co-author of *The Third Culture Kid Experience*, as well as a speaker and workshop leader in international schools and communities around the world on the topic of the TCK experience. He was, appropriately, "on the road" in Europe when he died. Much more than a gifted writer and speaker, though, Dave is missed for his empathy, his listening ear, his caring heart, and his real love for TCK's wherever found them, and of any age. Many of us lost a dear friend with Dave's passing. The world is a better place, and we are better people, because Dave served among us.

ABOUT THE AUTHOR

Jonathan Borden

Dr. Jonathan Borden lived and worked in Korea from 1975 to 2005. After a brief stint as a missionary volunteer on the southern island of Kojedo, he worked at Seoul Foreign School, an international school serving expatriate children from across the globe living in Seoul. While at Seoul Foreign School he taught elementary, middle, and high school grades, and served as secondary and middle school principal. From 2005 to 2019 Dr. Borden served as high school principal at Shanghai American School in China. His Korean born wife, Soon-ok, taught Pre-Kindergarten in both schools. Dr. and Ms. Borden have two adult sons; TCK's born in Korea and graduates of Seoul Foreign School. They and their friends were much of the inspiration for this book. Dr. Borden received his doctorate from Walden University, where he concentrated on early adolescent and intercultural (particularly Korean/American) education. Dr. and Mrs. Borden have lead workshops on the subject of Asian children and their parents at international schools and at international educational conferences. During his career in East Asia Dr. Borden worked with thousands of ethnic and native Korean and Chinese students and parents from all types of backgrounds. It has been a labor of love, and it is to them that this book is dedicated.

BOOKS BY THIS AUTHOR

Confucius Meets Piaget

Made in the USA
Monee, IL
14 April 2021